Indigenous Tourism

Cases from Australia and New Zealand

Michelle Whitford, Lisa Ruhanen and Anna Carr

 Goodfellow Publishers Ltd

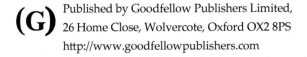

Published by Goodfellow Publishers Limited,
26 Home Close, Wolvercote, Oxford OX2 8PS
http://www.goodfellowpublishers.com

British Library Cataloguing in Publication Data: a catalogue record for this title is available from the British Library.

Library of Congress Catalog Card Number: on file.

ISBN: 978-1-911396-40-6

 Design and typesetting by P.K. McBride, www.macbride.org.uk

Cover design by Cylinder

Printed by Baker & Taylor, www.baker-taylor.com

Contents

Biographies

Maria Amoamo is a Research Fellow in the Department of Management at the University of Otago. Her research specialization is in the area of cultural and Indigenous tourism development with particular focus on the value of identity in relation to iwi development. Current research projects examine elements of Maori social and economic development with the intention of understanding the modes of economy within which Maori enterprise operate. Her publications have also explored the interface of post-colonialism and hybridity theory in relation to the transformation, production and mobility of cultures.

Hamish Bremner is a senior lecturer in Tourism Management and an Associate Director of the New Zealand Tourism Research Institute at the Auckland University of Technology, New Zealand. His research interests include the intersection of history, sociology and tourism development with particular regard to Indigenous societies.

Andrew Cardow is a Senior Lecturer with Massey University at Albany Auckland. Since 2000 he has made several visits to the Chatham Islands and written academic articles and consultant reports on tourism on the Islands. His research interests include tourism, entrepreneurship and popular culture often within the context of management history.

Anna Carr has been a researcher at the Department of Tourism, University of Otago, New Zealand, since 1999. Her research on ecotourism, visitor interpretation, cultural landscape management in protected areas and Indigenous tourism development has been published in various academic publications. She has Pākehā and Māori ancestry (Ngapuhi, Ngati Ruanui). Anna is the cofounder of the Centre for Recreation Research and has led consultancies and externally funded research contracts. She recently co-edited the books *Mountaineering Tourism* and *Political Ecology of Tourism: Communities, Power and the Environment.*

Tania (Tahn) Donovan is a Wardandi Yok from Busselton and has a deep understanding of the Western Australian bio diversity values and wide variety of landscapes, people and experiences. She started work in the hospitality industry at the age of 12, helping at CWA wedding catering events in Busselton. Diversity is a key characteristic of Tahn's career path, where she has gathered a wide range of skills and experiences in the farming, transport, environmental, disability employment, and hospitality/tourism industries. Project and management roles in employment and training have nurtured Tahn's interest in developing future leaders. She is currently involved in Leadership and Governance training to the Noongar community in the development and delivery of programs. "The young people I meet continually inspire me to do more and to do it better and more effectively".

Tahn is also the creator of Max's Black Sauce, an Australian bush herb infused sauce that captures the flavours of Australia, and established the label Deadly Divas Clothing. She says "Deadly Divas Clothing is seeking to make change in how Aboriginal and Torres Strait Islander women are respected. It captures the beauty and grace of our culture and community through the garments we create, and the way in which we demonstrate respect and professionalism through our business".

"Tourism offers Aboriginal and Torres Strait Islander peoples the opportunity to tell our stories, care for our country and culture and build economic independence for our families and communities".

Ross Dowling OAM is Foundation Professor of Tourism in the School of Business & Law, Edith Cowan University, Australia. He conducts international research on ecotourism, geotourism and cruise ship tourism. In Western Australia he has worked with a number of Indigenous communities to develop sustainable tourism in regional and remote areas. He is a Member, World Commission on Protected Areas (Switzerland); Co-founder, International Cruise Research Society (Germany); and Advisor, UNESCO Global Geoparks (France). In Western Australia he is Chair of Cruise Western Australia; Vice President, Royal Automobile Club; Member, Conservation & Parks Commission; and a WA Parks Ambassador. He has authored or edited many books including *Natural Area Tourism, Geotourism* and *Cruise Ship Tourism.*

Johnny Edmonds is the Director for the World Indigenous Tourism Alliance (WINTA), a role that has enabled him to support the development of an international network of Indigenous tourism organisations, as well as partnerships with international institutions that support the development of tourism as a vehicle for the empowerment of Indigenous peoples. Johnny has held executive management positions for various Indigenous organisations for over 20 years in NZ and Australia. He has served on various tourism industry Boards in NZ and Australia and the Tourism Management

Advisory Group for the Victoria University of Wellington, New Zealand.

Stuart Gifford has been a restaurateur for more than 35 years and is co-founder and co-owner of Sarah's Sister's Sustainable Café in Adelaide, Australia. An urban activist, he holds a special interest in Education for Sustainability, and is active in promoting further collaboration between local schools, businesses and the community, encouraging locals to use the Cafe as an informal 'Go to' Hub/ Third Place. He has worked with researchers with the School of Management of the University of South Australia since 2011 on a variety of research, teaching and industry engagement projects.

Rob Hales is the director of the Griffith Centre for Sustainable Enterprise in the Griffith Business School. Rob currently teaches in the Griffith Business School's MBA program where he convenes the course sustainability and systems thinking. His research interests include climate change policy, sustainable business, sustainable tourism, Indigenous studies. His published works related to Indigenous studies include climate change adaptation and world heritage consent processes. His background in running a small business in tourism and environmental education informs his research and teaching.

Freya Higgins-Desbiolles is a non-Indigenous academic that has researched and taught on the subject of Indigenous engagement with tourism for nearly two decades. Her approach as a critical scholar is to seek the emancipatory capacities of collaborative research to co-create change for better futures.

Sharleen Howison is a Māori academic working at Otago Polytechnic in Dunedin and her main areas of research include cultural tourism, sustainable tourism management and destination management. She has worked in the tertiary education sector over the past 20 years and has maintained strong links with local tourism and business community participants. She is also involved in developing and delivering undergraduate qualifications in tourism and events and supervising student internships with various industry participants.

Gabrielle Russell-Mundine is the Academic Leader-Cultural Change in the National Centre for Cultural Competence (NCCC) at the University of Sydney. Her PhD, *From Pumpkins to Property Management: Developing the Organisational Capacity of the Jubal Aboriginal Corporation* (2011) looked at Aboriginal community enterprise development and capacity building in a Northern NSW context. Gabrielle's current research focus is on service learning in Aboriginal Communities as well as creating online courses on cultural competence and addressing cultural change at the individual and systemic levels. She is particularly interested in facilitating transformative ways to learn and work together.

Helen Murphy completed her PhD at James Cook University, Cairns, Australia. Her thesis investigated the relationship between educational tourism and Aboriginal development aspirations. Her research has focused on exploring Australian Aboriginal approaches to social and economic development including social enterprise development in remote regions, educational tourism and Aboriginal participation in Payment for Ecosystem Services markets.

Lisa Ruhanen is an Associate Professor in Tourism and Deputy Director of Education with the UQ Business School, The University of Queensland, Australia. Her research areas include Indigenous tourism, sustainable tourism destination policy and planning, knowledge management, and climate change. She has been involved in over 30 academic and consultancy research projects in Australia and overseas. Lisa has worked extensively as a consultant, external collaborator and executive committee member with a variety of divisions of the United Nations World Tourism Organization.

Lori-Ann Shibish operates a small tourism consultancy (Sustainable Tourism Solutions) in Western Australia. This book chapter is drawn from her Masters of Tourism Management research which explored the overlapping relationships between, tourism development, national and marine parks and Aboriginal joint management. Her dedication to excellence in academic pursuits and volunteerism has been recognised with a Zonta Jane M. Klausman Women in Business Award, Tourism Industry Assoc. of BC Pat Corbett Leadership Award and the Forum Advocating Cultural and Ecotourism (FACET) Student Award. She is passionate about parks and nature-based tourism and generously volunteers her skills to the Western Australia (WA) Parks Foundation.

Chellie Spiller, (Māori and Pākehā), is an Associate Professor at the University of Auckland Business School. Chellie is a passionate and committed advocate for Māori Business development. Her vision is to create relational wellbeing and wealth across spiritual, environmental, social, cultural and economic dimensions. She has extensive experience in tourism, finance and marketing, holding senior executive positions in New Zealand and abroad, and brings this experience to her leadership within academic work within leadership and management development programs. She has created and led tour programs into countries as culturally diverse as Bhutan, North Korea, Myanmar, Indonesia, Vietnam and India.

Zexuan Sun (Suzanne) is a PhD candidate in the Department of English and the Department of Languages and Cultures at University of Otago, New Zealand. With previous training in tourism, literature, translation and interpreting, she is interested in a variety of research fields including culture tourism, garden tourism, comparative studies and modern poetry. More specifically, her current doctoral project examines literary utopias in New Zealand.

Tricia Vilkinas is an Adjunct Professor of Management at the University of South Australia. Her main research area is leadership and it application in various settings such as academia, public and private sectors, and in remote enterprises in desert Australia. She has been leader of several OLT projects focussed on academic leadership. Her most recent project is investigating the role of Academic Boards. Professor Vilkinas has also published many journal articles on leadership including academic leadership for heads of university departments and program directors, on the supervision of PhD students, on using 360-degree feedback and on the success factors of businesses in desert Australia.

Michelle Whitford is an Associate Professor and the Deputy Dean Learning and Teaching of the Griffith Business School. She has worked in both academic and commercial consultancy roles for more than 15 years co-ordinating projects in Indigenous tourism and events with a focus on the supply and demand, capacity development, entrepreneurship, authenticity, commodification and management. She has co-coordinated research projects for various organisations including the Australian Institute of Aboriginal and Torres Strait Island Studies and Indigenous Business Australia and she is the recipient of the 2016 Getz Biennial Award for Outstanding Research in Planned Events.

Gayathri (Gee) Wijesinghe is a lecturer in the School of Management teaching and researching in the areas of Tourism, Events and Hospitality Management. Prior to joining academia Dr Wijesinghe worked in the hospitality industry. Drawing on her experiences and knowledge of the hospitality industry she researches into hospitality employee experiences and service management issues tourism sustainability concerns, and how to educate students to be creative thinkers.

Keri-Anne Wikitera is a lecturer/researcher working in the School of Hospitality and Tourism at AUT University. Her Māori tribal affiliations are Tūhourangi, Ngāti Wahaio and Ngāti Whakaue of Te Arawa. This tribe is from the Rotorua region and are recognised as one of the nation's principle drivers of Māori tourism. As such her personal and academic interests are specifically positioned within promoting and enhancing Māori cultural identity, intercultural exchange, the tourism industry, Indigenous history and knowledge systems.

Greg Wilson is a lecturer in tourism and marketing in the School of Business & Law at Edith Cowan University, Perth, Western Australia. His interests are in spiritual and life-impacting travel, volunteer, heritage and environment based tourism. He has published widely in these areas. He also has an extensive background volunteering, with organisations including Make a Wish Foundation and the Waikato Cancer Society.

Peter Wiltshier's role as senior lecturer and program leader for tourism management at the University of Derby is to ensure that the public and private sector work together to develop resources and skills for communities to take charge of their own destinies. It is the pursuit of bottom-up planning and policy development that is sought and is to be enabled through my work and teaching. Peter is currently researching small business and lifestyles in the Peak District. He is also working with the Diocese of Derby to identify how tourism can benefit churches and through local government offices evaluating the impact of tourism on host communities. Peter supports the county, the district and parishes within Derbyshire and the Peak District in their endeavours to create a better environment for all through purposeful leisure and recreation.

1 Introduction to Indigenous Tourism in Australia and New Zealand

Michelle Whitford, Lisa Ruhanen and Anna Carr

Our shared global history has been shaped by travel for a range of reasons, including trade, migration and/or the desire to explore. It was in the 19th century when the trend for adventure and to experience the 'exotic other' (Beteille, 1998; McLaren 1999; Meadows, 2001) gained momentum and was taken up by the European elite, writers, artists, anthropologists and scientists (MacCannell, 1984) who sought, among other things, opportunities to visit distant lands and see their 'exotic' inhabitants. These novel Indigenous tourism experiences could be found around the globe and ranged from Māori cultural performances in New Zealand, observing Sami cultural traditions in Scandinavia, and visiting reservations of the First Nations peoples of the USA and Canada, to experiencing Aboriginal cultural ceremonies in Australia (Whitford & Ruhanen, 2016).

Curiosity, exploring the unknown and a craving for new knowledge and experiences still resonates in the 21st century with the demand for unique cultural experiences tending to be more prevalent amongst those tourists who are increasingly well travelled and well educated (Hinkson, 2003; Ruhanen et al., 2015a; 2015b). Thus as Indigenous tourism continues to be a drawcard for a niche sector of the tourism market in this second decade of the 2000s, contemporary Indigenous tourism operations around the world provide these tourists with opportunities to participate in a myriad of Indigenous tourism experiences which include visiting a Sami reindeer farm in Northern Finland, participating in dog sledding near the north pole with the Nunavummiut of Canada, attending Austronesian and Formosa

Indigenous cultural festival in Taiwan or visiting a Mapuche handicrafts production and sales center at nature parks in Misione, Argentina. These and other authentic Indigenous experiences continue to emerge onto the global tourism market as Indigenous peoples around the world increasingly seek the economic and socio-cultural benefits that can be derived from developing a sustainable tourism enterprise.

While the potential economic benefits of tourism enterprises are attractive to Indigenous peoples and communities, in many instances it is the potential socio-cultural benefits of tourism (i.e. cultural pride, preservation and maintenance) that often provide a stronger drawcard as to why an individual or community might embark on developing a tourism business. In fact, according to Johnny Edmonds, Director of the World Indigenous Tourism Alliance, there are "scary similarities between Indigenous peoples in all parts of the world as they work to reclaim their cultures after the effects of colonization" (cited Tancock, 2015).

Thus as more and more Indigenous cultures around the globe actively engage in the maintenance and/or preservation of cultural traditions, history and heritage, we are witnessing a steady increase in the development of intangible cultural heritage which is representative of a community's cultural authenticity and identity and includes oral traditions, performing arts, festive events or traditional craftsmanship which have been inherited over generations (UNESCO, 2003).

In Australia, Aboriginal and Torres Strait Islander culture has long been an important, albeit niche, part of the country's tourism experience. Much of the Indigenous tourism product in the country is cultur e and/or nature based, for example: guided bushwalks, Indigenous food (bush tucker experiences), and dance performances. Australia has a number of very successful Indigenous tourism businesses, nevertheless a key challenge facing Indigenous tourism in Australia is to increase visitor demand. In spite of the marketing efforts of the national tourism body, Tourism Australia, market awareness is generally low and the products and experiences on offer appear to have limited appeal to the broader international and domestic market. Addressing the underlying reasons for this declining demand is arguably key if tourism is to deliver the much anticipated improved socio-economic opportunities for Indigenous peoples in Australia.

In New Zealand, Māori cultural experiences have long been an important component of the country's tourism offering and marketing messages.

Tourism New Zealand actively promotes Māori culture as a 'must see' component of the New Zealand experience, and cultural imagery forms a large component of these marketing messages. In the past three decades, Māori have increasingly engaged in the sector through the management, development and promotion of cultural and non-cultural tourism experiences. Importantly, tourism ventures have demonstrated sustained success and there are many examples throughout the country where businesses have used sound business principles to leverage intergenerational wealth and wellbeing for the Māori of New Zealand.

This volume focuses on Indigenous tourism developed by Aboriginal and Torres Strait Islander peoples of Australia and Māori of New Zealand. The volume covers a wide range of topics with chapters focusing on issues pertaining to Indigenous tourism and education, national parks and eco-tourism, native foods, policy, economics of identity, inclusion, empowerment, self determination, cross-cultural understanding and respect, and Indigenous business management models, authenticity, sustainability value chains and the tourism network.

Indigenous tourism in Australia

The first section of this volume focuses on Indigenous tourism in Australia. Ruhanen and Whitford provide the opening chapter in this section, presenting an overview of Indigenous tourism in Australia charting major evolutions in the development of Australia's Indigenous tourism sector, and key demand and supply issues. The future of Indigenous tourism in the country is also discussed.

Chapter 2, by Helen Murphy, presents a case study on a family operated tourism enterprise in northern Queensland, Australia, which provides learning experiences about country and culture to visiting educational tourist groups. The chapter discusses what motivated the Aboriginal family to become involved in tourism, and the opportunities and challenges the family encounter as they work towards fulfilling their aspirations, which include the creation of jobs, fostering knowledge exchange and increasing community wellbeing.

Chapter 4 is a case study of an Aboriginal-led tourism initiative in Yawuru Nagulagun Roebuck Bay Marine Park in Broome, Western Australia. The authors, Lori-Ann Shibish, Ross Dowling and Greg Wilson, examine the creation and development of the tourism business, and also the key stakeholders who have worked collaboratively through a joint management framework to enable its success. Scaffolding the case study is an examination of tourism, ecotourism and the development of, and relationship between Indigenous tourism and national parks in Western Australia. The case study illustrates the interplay between ecotourism, Indigenous peoples, national parks and the joint management of natural and cultural heritage and discusses the barriers, opportunities and challenges that arise in this environment.

Chapter 5 from Gabrielle Russell-Mundine presents a critical case study of the Jubal Aboriginal Corporation (Jubal) located near the township of Tabulam in Northern New South Wales, Australia. The aim of the case study was to identify the needs of Aboriginal communities in developing a tourism business, and what capabilities are required to develop a sustainable tourism business. The chapter discusses the difficulties Indigenous organisations encounter when developing viable tourism businesses, and the reasons why Jubal decided that tourism was not the right pathway to development for them at the time. Additionally, the chapter highlights factors that enable and empower Indigenous communities to develop enterprises, and explores some of the external factors that can make the difference between a measured approach to tourism development and a business that fails because of a rush to develop something without first addressing the foundations of the organisation.

Freya Higgins-Desbiolles, Tricia Vilkinas, Gayathri Wijesinghe and Stuart Gifford's case study of Koomal Dreaming in Western Australia, focuses on native foods in Australian restaurants. The chapter adopts an Indigenist philosophy to analyse the native food industry in Australia and the capacity of Indigenous Australians to supply native foods to the restaurant sector. Ensuring Indigenous Australians benefit from the economic and cultural opportunities led the authors to pose the question of, 'who owns native foods?', cautioning that much more must be done to protect the rights of Indigenous Australians and ensure they benefit from this emerging sector.

The final chapter in the Australian section, from Rob Hales and Freya Higgins-Desboilles, provides a thought-provoking discussion pertaining to the negotiation of neoliberal forces with a goal of 'addressing the gap' in Australian society. The chapter is theoretically underpinned by Fraser's (1999, 2009) justice framework (i.e. recognition, redistribution and representation) and presents a series of short cases to demonstrate how attention to each element of the justice frame is important in maintaining tradition and livelihoods in ways determined by Indigenous people. The chapter concludes that Fraser's framework is a useful lens to ascertain the extent to which tourism promotes positive contributions to the self-determined futures and livelihoods of Indigenous peoples.

As a transition from the Australian to New Zealand cases, Freya Higgins-Desbiolles, Sharleen Howison and Zexuan Sun's chapter explores the values that could reshape our understanding of tourism and its cultural interface. They suggest that operationalizing Indigenous tourism according to Indigenous cultural values will lead to cultural encounters that make a difference in terms of cross-cultural understanding and respect. The chapter discusses Indigenous peoples' engagement with tourism in New Zealand and Australia, and suggests that Indigenous values may shape a form of tourism quite different from the current and predominant western paradigm of tourism. The authors note that an Indigenous led business practice is essential for Indigenous peoples, such as the Māori and Aboriginal and Torres Strait Islander peoples, to be able to successfully engage with tourism on their terms. The chapter suggests that a value driven form of tourism, which embeds Indigenous values, will facilitate a meaningful cross-cultural engagement and learning experience for tourists by accentuating the social and human values over and above the economic values of tourism.

Indigenous tourism in New Zealand

Chapter 9, by Anna Carr, is the first chapter focusing specifically on Indigenous tourism in New Zealand. This chapter presents an introduction and overview of the development of Indigenous tourism in New Zealand and highlights the sustainable development of Māori tourism ventures that have the capacity to endure over time. The chapter discusses ongoing issues around authentic experiences, professional delivery, economic efficiencies and the marketing of New Zealand Māori tourism (among other issues). The chapter concludes that the continued potential of tourism as a socio-economic development tool for Māori people is dependent upon the active participation and engagement of Māori in all facets of the tourism industry.

Maria Amoamo's chapter is a case study of Māori tourism development in Otepoti Dunedin, that examines the economics of identity in relation to (re)thinking Māori tourism in New Zealand. The chapter challenges tourism academia to move towards a more flexible form of understanding and interpreting identifications and aspirations of contemporary Indigenous populations, and suggests that tribal differences are key elements in the development and sustainability of Māori tourism product. The case study integrates social theories of identity with Māori epistemology and analyses Māori tourism with an approach that is space- and subject-centred, and facilitates Indigenous Māori to develop an economics of identity.

Chapter 11, by Peter Wiltshier and Andrew Cardow, is a case study of the Chatham Islands of New Zealand, a small community some 700 kilometres from mainland New Zealand. This chapter reviews tourism development on the Chatham Islands and suggests that development is largely driven by the needs of the community and the socio-cultural expectations, values, beliefs and goals of the Indigenous peoples. The chapter also charts the contemporary political structure and policy implications impacting tourism development, and explores the extent to which local identity is reinforced by new tourism strategies. The chapter concludes that there are a number of positive aspects to tourism on the Islands, such as identity, a sense of place and ownership. However, the authors conclude that there is a need to ensure tourism opportunities are community-owned and that there is a shared understanding of the nature of both the product and the market.

Keri-Anne Wikitera and Hamish Bremner provide a case study focusing on the perspectives, history and experiences of Whakarewarewa Village Tours located in Rotorua, New Zealand. Rotorua is famous for providing Māori cultural tourism experiences and the chapter examines the tourism development undertaken by the Whakarewarewa Thermal Village and uses the views of Indigenous tribal members to discuss the construction of the culture of a tourism organisation. The chapter highlights the importance of locally-driven tourism development, and this case study provides an example of the relationships that exist between local, regional and national tourism objectives.

Chapter 13, by Chellie Spiller, takes a different approach. This chapter examines value chain innovation through the networks of a Māori tourism company, but uses a case-based story to share these insights. This chapter discusses Navigator Tours, which has created a new business model that attempts to maximise value creation, while minimising costs. The case is an example of innovation at work in a cultural context. The case study discusses various value chains and identifies how they are held together, and raises issues pertaining to tourism business ethics, values and loyalty in a constantly changing competitive environment. Discussion questions are provided for those that may choose to use this chapter as a teaching case study of Indigenous tourism innovation.

The final chapter in this volume contains messages from two influential industry players in Indigenous tourism in the southern hemisphere. From Australia, we have a message from the Chairperson of the Board of the Western Australian Indigenous Tourism Operators Council (WAITOC): Tania (Than) Donovan has provided us with her thoughts about, and vision for, Indigenous tourism in Australia. WAITOC is the peak not for profit association representing over 50 Aboriginal tourism operators in Western Australia. "WAITOC believe that Aboriginal tourism is a unique industry in that it allows Aboriginal people to participate at a real and meaningful level while still maintaining and valuing their cultural heritage" (WAITOC, 2017).

From New Zealand, Mr Johnny Edmonds, Director of the World Indigenous Tourism Alliance (WINTA) discusses the history and context in which Indigenous tourism in New Zealand has developed, before considering the future of Indigenous tourism in New Zealand over the next two decades. "WINTA is the World Indigenous Tourism Alliance and is an Indigenous-led global network of Indigenous and non-Indigenous peoples and organizations who seek to give practical expression to the United Nations Declaration on the Rights of Indigenous Peoples, through tourism" (WINTA, 2017).

Overall, the chapters in this volume discuss a varied range of issues pertaining to Indigenous tourism in Australia and New Zealand. A range of perspectives are provided and the use of case studies gives detailed insights into Indigenous tourism in practice. There are however, a number of common threads to the papers. First, Indigenous tourism is an increasingly important part of the tourism product for these two countries. While in Australia it may be a much smaller part of the overall tourism offering, it is no less significant than in New Zealand, where Māori culture has a strong presence in the country's brand and destination image. Second, there is a growing expectation that Indigenous tourism research must be underpinned with an Indigenist paradigm. This message emerges clearly in a number of papers in the volume and provides a useful platform and call to action for researchers concerned with Indigenous tourism in Australia, New Zealand and beyond.

References

Beteille, A. (1998). The idea of Indigenous people. *Current Anthropology,* **39**(2), 187-192.

Fraser, N. (1999). Social justice in the age of identity politics: Redistribution, recognition, and participation, In Ray, L and Sayer, (eds.), *Culture and Economy after the Cultural Turn*, London: Sage.

Fraser, N. (2009). Social justice in the age of identity politics. In G. Henderson and M. Waterstone (eds.), *Geographic Thought: A Praxis Perspective*, London: Routledge.

Hinkson, M. (2003). Encounters with Aboriginal Sites in Metropolitan Sydney: A broadening horizon for cultural tourism? *Journal of Sustainable Tourism,* **11**(4), 295-306.

MacCannell, D. (1976). Reconstructed ethnicity: Tourism and cultural identify in third world communities. *Annals of Tourism Research,* **11**, 361-377.

McLaren, D.R. (1999). The history of Indigenous peoples and tourism. *Cultural Survival Quarterly,* **23**(2), 27.

Meadows, M. (2001). *Voices in the wilderness: Images of Aboriginal people in the Australian media.* Westport: Greenwood Publishing Group.

Ruhanen, L., Whitford, M. & McLennan, C. L. (2015a). Exploring Chinese visitor demand for Australia's Indigenous tourism experiences. *Journal of Hospitality and Tourism Management,* **24**, 25-34.

Ruhanen, L., Whitford, M. & McLennan, C. L. (2015b). Indigenous tourism in Australia: Time for a reality check. *Tourism Management,* **48**, 73-83.

Tanock, K. (2015). Wendake, Que, Special to *The Globe and Mail,* Oct. 26, http://www.theglobeandmail.com/life/travel/activities-and-interests/canadas-aboriginal-tourism-gives-travellers-a-taste-of-history/article26976171/. Accessed 15/03/2017.

UNESCO. (2003). Convention for the safeguarding of the intangible cultural Heritage. Paris.

WAITOC, (2017). About WAITOC. http://www.waitoc.com/now/about-waitoc. Accessed 15/03/2017.

Whitford, M. & Ruhanen, L. (2016). Indigenous tourism research, past and present: Where to from here? *Journal of Sustainable Tourism,* **24**,(8&9) 1080-1099.

WINTA, (2017). Who is WINTA? http://www.winta.org/about/ Accessed 21/04/2017.

2 Indigenous Tourism in Australia: History, trends and future directions

Lisa Ruhanen and Michelle Whitford

Introduction

In Australia, Indigenous culture has long been thought to have the potential to provide the country's tourism industry with a key point of differentiation (Buultjens et al., 2005). Thus Indigenous experiences have consistently remained an integral part of Australia's tourism product offering since the early 2000s (Department of Communications Information Technology and the Arts, 2003) and are marketed as one of the seven key experiences that underpin the country's global tourism marketing activities (see Tourism Australia, 2017). Similar to other parts of the world, the tourism industry in Australia has also been portrayed as a sector that can create socio-economic opportunities for Indigenous peoples through the development of tourism- focused businesses and the generation of employment, especially in the regional and remote areas of the country (Buultjens & Gale, 2013; Coria & Calfucura, 2012; Fletcher et al., 2016). As a consequence of these potential benefits, consecutive Australian governments have consistently touted optimistic and favourable assessments of the opportunities tourism provides for Indigenous people (Ruhanen et al., 2015b).

Indeed to varying degrees, all three levels of Australian governments (i.e., federal, state and local) have gradually increased their attention on facilitating the growth and development of this niche sector of Australian tourism. Increased awareness of Indigenous culture has led to a growth in the supply of tourism activities and experiences which are owned and/ or managed by Australia's Aboriginal and Torres Strait Islander peoples (Ruhanen et al., 2015b); particularly in remote and regional areas where, according to Buultjens et al. (2010), between 50% and 70% of Indigenous tourism businesses are located. The growth in the sector can be attributed to, among other things, the range of socio-cultural and economic benefits that can and do flow from Indigenous tourism activity. Nevertheless, while governments' attention to date have proved beneficial to specific Indigenous tourism businesses across the country, there is still considerable scope for scaling up the growth and development of the sector as a whole (Ruhanen et al., 2015b), including capitalising on the positive approach adopted by Indigenous peoples involved in tourism who are confident their products can exceed consumer expectations (Jones Donald Strategy Partners, 2009). Concomitantly however, plans for growth need to identify any issues raised pertaining to the success (or otherwise) of Indigenous tourism in Australia (Buultjens & Gale, 2013; Buultjens et al., 2010; Higgins-Desbiolles et al., 2010; Tremblay & Wegner, 2009) and incorporate strategies that address a range of issues including demand and supply side challenges (e.g., access to start-up finance and capital, recruiting and retention of appropriately skilled labour, product development).

To date, it seems fair to suggest that Indigenous tourism in Australia has enjoyed a slow but steady rate of growth from the last quarter of the 20th century. The development of the sector has been punctuated by a range of opportunities and challenges. The purpose of this chapter is to first present an overview of the development of Indigenous tourism in Australia, before identifying and discussing demand and supply issues associated with the tourism sector and finally presenting future pathways for consideration.

The development of Indigenous tourism in Australia

Indigenous tourism has been defined as tourism activity in which Indigenous peoples are directly involved either through control and/or by having their culture serve as the essence of the attraction (Hinch & Butler, 2007). An

Indigenous tourist or Indigenous tourism 'visitor' in Australia is defined as a person who participates in at least one Indigenous tourism activity (e.g., experiencing an Indigenous art/craft or cultural display; attending an Indigenous performance) during their tourism experience. This participation may be a one-off activity or a component of other tourism activities (Tourism Research Australia, 2011). In Australia, such activities include: bushwalks, Indigenous food experiences, safaris, staying in Indigenous owned/operated accommodation, touring with an Indigenous guide, visiting an Indigenous site or community, attending live performances (e.g., dance, drama, music) and appreciating visual arts in State museums and galleries, or through commercial and craft enterprises (Tourism Research Australia, 2011).

Indigenous tourism as a distinct sector of the tourism industry had its global beginnings in the early 19th century when a curiosity and interest in 'exotic' destinations and their indigenous inhabitants was ignited in wealthy European adventurers (predominantly from former world empires), who travelled to ex-colonies to see, experience and document exotic and unknown cultures (Whitford & Ruhanen, 2016). By the mid-19th century more indigenous peoples around the world were involved in tourism (to varying degrees), and in Australia there was a small increase in the number of visitors being invited to experience Aboriginal cultural ceremonies, which are known as corroborees (Cahir & Clark, 2010). In the second half of the 20th century, the widespread growth of global tourism and increased visitor access to ex-colonies, where 'exotic' indigenous peoples lived with intriguing customs, artefacts, arts and crafts, lifestyles, heritage and histories, spurred on the development of indigenous tourism. This was also backed by the universal growth of television documentaries that provided information about Indigenous cultures from around the world, and travel programs that promoted travel to these unknown worlds (Whitford & Ruhanen, 2016).

In Australia from the 1980s onwards, the participation of Indigenous peoples in the tourism industry was increasingly mentioned in a range of government policy documents and reports (Whitford, 2009; Whitford et al., 2001). Reflecting government policies in many other parts of the world, Australian policies were also underpinned by a common objective of utilising tourism as a development tool to provide Indigenous Australians with a pathway to "much needed opportunities for employment, social stability and preservation of culture and traditions" (Department of Communications

Information Technology & the Arts, 2003:41). In 1997, Australia's amalgamation of tourism and Indigenous culture was formalised when the Australian Federal Government released the *National Aboriginal and Torres Strait Islander Tourism Strategy*. Since then, consecutive Australian governments (both State and Federal) have consistently touted the advantages that tourism can provide for Indigenous peoples and their communities, claiming that "tourism offers particular opportunities for Indigenous Australians: in many areas of regional and remote Australia it offers the prospect of a pathway to economic independence" (Department of Communications Information Technology & the Arts, 2003:31).

According to Fletcher et al. (2016), the catalyst for Indigenous tourism in Australia occurred during the lead up to the 2000 Sydney Olympics and for the ensuing five to six years. During this time tourism was seen to offer "....enormous potential to Indigenous communities, both to create sustainable jobs and employment and as a means to protect and nurture cultural and environmental heritage" (Commonwealth of Australia, 2009: 10); thus there were many initiatives developed that enabled Indigenous Australians to offer tourism products and experiences (Whitford, 2009).

Over the following years, Australian States and Territories worked towards "increasing Indigenous participation in tourism, particularly through employment, (to) help 'Close the Gap' of Indigenous disadvantage and help address labour shortages in the tourism sector, particularly in rural and regional Australia" (Department of Resources Energy & Tourism, 2009:10). For instance, Indigenous tourism experiences were promoted by Tourism Australia, State tourism organisations and Federal and State governments. Despite the high levels of interest in Australia's Indigenous culture that has been consistently portrayed by Australian government agencies, the demand for, and interest in Indigenous tourism in Australia has not translated into sustainable visitor flows for many Indigenous tourism businesses (Ruhanen et al., 2015b). In fact, between 2005 and 2010, rather than an increase in interest in Indigenous tourism, the opposite occurred with interest from both international tourists and the domestic market declining. Interestingly, since its 2011 report on Indigenous tourism in Australia, Tourism Research Australia (the leading research provider of tourism intelligence across both international and domestic markets and whose data underpin government tourism policy) has not published any research dedicated to Indigenous tourism demand in Australia. Therefore to date, a small number of Indigenous tourism operators in Australia have and continue to experience the positive impacts of tourism, however the extent to which we can claim tourism has enhanced the overall socio-economic circumstances of Indigenous peoples in Australia remains questionable (Whitford & Ruhanen, 2010; 2016). Arguably as a result of low demand, tourism has not yet performed to capacity and produced the benefits that have the capacity to reverse the impacts of socio-economic disadvantage felt by many Indigenous peoples who continue to bear the burden of the legacies of colonial history, coupled with out-dated and/or ineffective and/or inappropriate government policies (Whitford & Ruhanen, 2016).

Demand for Indigenous tourism: The reality

Thus the issue of demand for Indigenous tourism remains a significant challenge in the Australian tourism space. While government and academic research alike have attempted to measure the demand for Indigenous tourism in Australia, we argue that the data which records that demand, and the receptiveness of visitors engaging in Indigenous products is often inconsistent and/or incomplete. Moreover, we suggest there are problems in the reporting of the data caused by (among other things): methodological issues, such as the use of generic tourism surveys; variances in research methods and tools; inadequate sampling techniques that lead to data which is not representative of a population; inconsistencies in how data is reported; and/or inconsistent definitions of what constitutes Indigenous tourism (i.e., inclusion - or not - of museum, art galleries, theatres, etc.) (Ruhanen et al., 2015b; Tremblay & Wegner, 2009). Ruhanen et al. (2015b) argued that one of the main problems leading to the inconsistences between the reported optimistic demand levels and actual Indigenous tourism visitation is the methodology applied in TRA's national visitor studies (the NVS and IVS). This methodology defines an Indigenous tourism visitor as one who participates in at least one Indigenous tourism activity during their trip. The problem with this definition is that it includes those visitors for whom participation may be a one-off activity and/or an unplanned activity. Often in such cases, engagement with Indigenous tourism activity is not the focus of the trip. For example, if engagement occurs as part of a wider tour itinerary, this engagement may not be the intended activity but rather serendipitous and/or ancillary activity. The consequence of using such a broad definition is the inflation of visitation figures through the inclusion of visitors for whom engagement in an Indigenous tourism activity is not the focus of their trip. Similarly, visitor spending figures attributed to 'Indigenous tourism visitors' are also inflated for the same reason. Another problem with much Indigenous tourism research is the general belief of high interest or growing demand in Indigenous tourism without explicit or convincing evidence to affirm this high demand and interest (O'Rourke & Memmott, 2005; Ruhanen et al., 2015b; Tremblay & Wegner, 2009).

Consequently, researchers more recently have argued that rather than the high levels of interest that is often espoused by government, Indigenous tourism is instead a tourism activity that is not considered a top priority for either international or domestic tourists when travelling within Australia and, as a consequence, is a tourism activity that attracts much lower levels of participation than has been previously claimed (Abascal et al., 2016; Jones Donald Strategy Partners, 2009; Ruhanen et al., 2015a; 2015b). Indeed empiri- cal studies examining demand have shown that participation in Indigenous tourism is generally not a primary motivator to visit Australia (Jones Donald Strategy Partners, 2009; Nielsen et al., 2008; Ruhanen et al., 2013). For example, in a study conducted on behalf of Indigenous Business Australia, Ruhanen et al. (2013) found that less than 5% of international tourists cited Indigenous experiences as an activity they wanted to experience while in Australia. Using attrition curve theory to map awareness, preference and intention, Ruhanen et al. (2015b) also found that tourists not only have a low awareness of Indigenous tourism experiences (less than 25% of domestic respondents and less than 20% of international respondents showed an awareness), but when awareness was converted to preference to visit and then intention to visit, this number declined from 12% for preference to engage in an Indigenous tourism experience, and then to 2% for intention to participate in an Indigenous tourism experience. Similarly, in a study on the domestic market, Jones Donald Strategy Partners (2009) found that relative to other Australian experiences, Indigenous tourism had low demand due to its limited ability to satisfy key domestic holiday needs of relaxation and indulgence. A study by Nielsen et al. (2008) also concurred, finding that for the domestic market, Indigenous cultural experiences were too 'outside' of normal visitor expectations and that participation in Indigenous tourism tended to sit on the 'outer edge' (p.1) of tourism participation.

Arguably, problems caused through the inconsistent reporting of data perpetuate the tendency to overstate purported demand for, and levels of visitor interest in, Indigenous tourism products and experiences (Ruhanen et al., 2015b; Tremblay & Wegner, 2009). Subsequently, this leads to a situation where Indigenous tourism operators overestimate visitor demand for their products, because of the overoptimistic reporting of demand data and thus develop unrealistic expectations regarding the potential success of operating an Indigenous tourism business (Ruhanen et al., 2013). Not surprisingly then, several studies maintained that as a result of inflated figures, there is a general misunderstanding about the reality of tourist intentions to participate in Indigenous tourism experiences and the barriers that may impede participation (Abascal et al., 2016; Jones Donald Strategy Partners, 2009; Nielsen et al., 2008; Ruhanen et al., 2013). As a result, Indigenous tourism businesses find themselves in an unsustainable business situation in a relatively short timeframe from start-up due to, among other things, unsustainably small visitor flows (Ruhanen et al., 2015b). This has also led to the current situation where there are not as many examples of sustainable Indigenous tourism businesses in the marketplace as anticipated (Abascal et al., 2016; Buultjens & Gale, 2013; Whitford & Ruhanen, 2016). Nevertheless, our ongoing work in the field reveals that an increasing number of Indigenous individuals and/or communities have an interest in developing Indigenous tourism product around the country. The focus then is ensuring that these businesses are not set up for failure, but rather can embark on building and supplying a tourism product for the market, based on reliable business data and realistic market analysis.

Supply of Indigenous tourism experiences: Barriers hindering Indigenous participation

In addition to understanding and navigating conflicting claims pertaining to demand for Indigenous tourism in Australia, Indigenous peoples interested in developing and sustaining a successful tourism enterprise face a range of supply side c hallenges. These challenges are generally very similar to those faced by Indigenous enterprises in other sectors and industries (such as mining, agriculture, and arts and crafts) and might include a mixture of (among others): low skill base and lack of experience; fewer business and professional networks; limited or ineffective training and education opportunities; restricted access to capital and/or financing due to a lack of property rights over the key assets needed to support the development of products and opportunities; remoteness/isolation; and costs of operations or accessing basic factors of production (in particular labour and training) (Buultjens & White, 2008; Coria & Calfucura, 2012; Dodson & Smith, 2003; Fuller et al., 2005; Higgins-Desbiolles et al., 2010; Nielsen et al., 2008; Russell-Mundine, 2007; Whitford & Ruhanen, 2009). Further barriers include the continued outside interference by government in Aboriginal communities, as well as excessive control by government in some aspects of business on the one hand, combined with lack of government support services on the other. Government involvement in Indigenous tourism enterprises often favour employment over profits, thus business failure is not uncommon (Buultjens & White, 2008; Fuller et al., 2005; Russell-Mundine, 2007; Tsey et al., 2012).

More specifically from a tourism perspective, studies have found that compared to other tourism products, Indigenous tourism products are often relatively underdeveloped, with a mismatch between the experiences sought by tourists and the product offered by the operators (Buultjens & White, 2008; Jones Donald Strategy Partners, 2009). Consequently, as a result of perceived inconsistencies in the product delivered, some larger tourism organisations (such as tour operators) have in the past been reluctant to include Indigenous tourism activities in their packages (Jones Donald Strategy Partners, 2009; Ruhanen et al., 2013). Further hindering product development are the specific challenges with respect to Indigenous employment in the tourism industry, including requirements for a high level of literacy and communication skills to cope with direct and intensive social interaction with tourists. A lack of requisite skills means that employment opportunities for Indigenous peoples in tourism have often been limited to unskilled or semi-skilled positions (Altman & Finlayson, 1992).

Inherent racism towards Australia's Indigenous people is also an ongoing and consistent inhibitor to the sustainability of the Indigenous tourism sector in Australia (Nielsen et al., 2008; Ruhanen et al., 2015b). From the perspective of tourist demand for Indigenous experiences, due to negative perceptions (stereotypes) and negative media attention, many tourists show limited interest in, and often an open disregard for, Indigenous tourism experiences (Nielsen et al., 2008; Ruhanen et al., 2013). From an operational or supply perspective, Indigenous tourism entrepreneurs must contend with the challenges of participating in the 'white fella's business world' (Ruhanen & Whitford, 2016: 10) where notions of individualism, business control, firm accountability and regular financial reporting are very different to the Indigenous identity which is grounded in family and kinship obligations, land affiliation and clan languages (Pearson, 2014). In addition, while a wide range of federal, state and territory government policies and programs proffer support to Indigenous businesses, there continues to be poor understandings of what works and under what conditions (Carson & Koster, 2012). Policy assumptions about factors for success in Indigenous tourism enterprises are often drawn from overseas literature, and this is problematic because the Australian situation has its own set of issues in terms of culture, sovereignty, service delivery arrangements and funding (Whitford & Ruhanen, 2009). The implication is that policy designed to encourage the development of Indigenous tourism businesses draws on an inadequate information base and consequently is more often than not, poorly targeted (Morrison et al., 2014). The unsatisfactory consequence is the situation where those government schemes and policies designed to support Indigenous tourism business development instead end up limiting the chances such businesses have for achieving long-term sustainability.

The future for Indigenous tourism in Australia

Despite conflicting reports pertaining to the sustainability of Indigenous tourism in Australia, this sector of the tourism industry has arguably not been in a position to realise its full potential nor has it yet convincingly secured a sustainable presence in the increasingly competitive global marketplace (Ruhanen et al., 2013). We suggest that one remedy for this situation is the ongoing development of a two-way strategy that incorporates the education of both tourists and Indigenous tour operators. For instance, on the one hand there must be a concerted cooperative and committed effort, made by governments and operators alike, to develop educational strategies for tourists engaging in Indigenous tourism experiences. Such educational strategies will enhance cultural understanding and awareness and build much needed cultural competencies amongst tourists. On the other hand, Indigenous tourism operators must ensure that they understand the tourism system and are in sync with what the Australian inbound and domestic markets are looking for, and that they more effectively match experiences they offer with the experiences sought by tourists (Ruhanen et al., 2013). We shy away from espousing the virtues of adopting a 'build it and they will come' strategy as the statistics to date show 'they' don't. Therefore, to enable more market driven product development to occur, we need to better facilitate opportunities for Indigenous tourism operators to gain accurate knowledge and necessary understanding about their market(s) and potential markets. This reinforces the significance of developing and providing government-based programs that assist Indigenous tourism operators with identifying, interpreting and/or collecting relevant data sources. An integral component of these programs must be the development of more appropriate and effective communication channels between the range of Indigenous tourism stakeholders. Importantly, these communication channels should be designed to meet Indigenous tourism operators' knowledge needs, rather than be developed to promote Western ways of pursuing knowledge needs (Ruhanen et al., 2013).

A significant element of learning to interpret tourism data is acquiring the ability to identify key and growth markets and to subsequently identify the tourism motivations, needs and preferences of those markets. One growth market predicted to play a larger role in Australia's tourism industry in the future is the outbound travel market from China (Ruhanen et al., 2015a). While Tourism Australia is currently investing considerable efforts into strategically positioning the Australian tourism industry to be 'China-ready' through targeted marketing programs, formalised policy and planning and industry education and training, it is important that Indigenous tourism operators recognise and capitalise on the opportunities that both this market and Tourism Australia's marketing and planning efforts offer. Research into the China market's preferences have shown that Chinese visitors currently display little interest in participating in Indigenous tourism and this is largely due to a lack of awareness (Ruhanen et al., 2013). At the same time, research utilising scenario analysis has also found that there is a latent demand (albeit minimal at this stage) for Indigenous tourism product however pricing, location and safety are the main barriers preventing this market from pursing an Indigenous tourism experience (Ruhanen et al., 2015a). This therefore presents a range of opportunities for Indigenous tourism operators, including an opportunity to develop marketing campaigns that increase awareness of Australia's Indigenous tourism products (it is also recommended that such campaigns should target both visitors and tour operators given the prevalence of group tours in this market) to counteract the current lack of awareness of Indigenous tourism by the Chinese market. Additionally, while there are currently perceived barriers that prevent the Chinese market from participating in Indigenous tourism, there is an opportunity for Indigenous tourism operators to develop and/or redevelop products to minimise the effects of these perceived barriers and attract the interest of a targeted market from China.

There is little argument that the understanding and pursuit of a target market is a necessary priority for Indigenous tourism businesses. An equally important, if not more significant priority of these businesses is the development of opportunities and policies that ensure the autonomy of Indigenous peoples in tourism activities in order to promote empowerment and facilitate sustainable Indigenous tourism enterprises (Peters & Higgins-Desbiolles, 2012; Scherrer & Doohan, 2013; Strickland-Munro & Moore, 2013). Autonomy is a key ingredient for empowering individuals and communities (Aref & Redzuan, 2009; OECD, 2012). Empowerment is the capacity for individuals or groups to determine their own affairs, and as such, it is a process where people take control over the factors that influence their lives. Recent incentives such as the *Reconciliation Action Plan for the Gold Coast 2018 Commonwealth Games* can indeed be seen to heed the advice that future efforts designed to support sustainable Indigenous tourism enterprises need to ensure empowerment through autonomy. According to the Queensland government, the plan will have a specific focus on *enabling* Indigenous arts and cultural business to benefit from the games (Yugambeh Museum, 2015).

Thus as we continue to observe the developments of the Gold Coast 2018 Commonwealth Games in relation to Indigenous tourism, alongside other current Indigenous tourism initiatives developed by government and private enterprise (e.g., Bangarra Dance, Mossman Gorge Centre) we argue that as we near the end of the second decade of the 21st century, some twenty years on from the establishment of the first national Indigenous tourism policy (i.e., NATSISTIS), it is an opportune time to forge ahead on a revised, realistic and enlightened pathway for Indigenous tourism; a pathway that facilitates 'closing the gap' by listening to, appreciating and learning from Indigenous voices. A pathway that clearly and non-discriminately identifies both the barriers and opportunities of Indigenous tourism and a pathway that effectively and appropriately utilises Indigenous tourism in Australia to close the gap via (among other things), the on-going sustainable preservation and maintenance of the world's oldest living culture.

References

Abascal, T. E., Fluker, M. & Jiang, M. (2016). Domestic demand for Indigenous tourism in Australia: Understanding intention to participate. *Journal of Sustainable Tourism*, **24**(8-9), 1350-1368.

Altman, J. C. & Finlayson, J. (1992). *Aborigines, tourism and sustainable development*. Canberra: Centre for Aboriginal Economic Policy Research, Australian National University. https://www.jcu.edu.au/__data/assets/pdf_file/0011/122204/jcudev_012859.pdf.

Aref, F., & Redzuan, M. (2009). Community capacity development for tourism development. *Journal of Human Ecology*, **27**(1), 21-25.

Buultjens, J. & Gale, D. (2013). Facilitating the development of Australian Indigenous tourism enterprises: The business ready program for Indigenous tourism. *Tourism Management Perspectives*, **5**, 41-50.

Buultjens, J., Gale, D. & White, N. E. (2010). Synergies between Australian Indigenous tourism and ecotourism: Possibilities and problems for future development. *Journal of Sustainable Tourism*, **18**(4), 497-513.

Buultjens, J., Waller, I., Graham, S. & Carson, D. (2005). Public sector initiatives for Aboriginal small business development in tourism. In C. Ryan & M. Aicken (Eds.), *Indigenous Tourism: The commodification and management of culture*. Oxford, UK: Elsevier Ltd.

Buultjens, J. & White, N. (2008). *Indigenous Tourism: The possibilities into the future*. Paper presented at the Desert Knowledge Symposium 2008 - Developing Desert Directions: Rethinking the Future, Alice Springs. http://www.desertknowledgecrc.com.au/resource/DKCRC_Indigenous-Tourism_-The-Possibilities-into-the-Future.pdf

Cahir, D. A. & Clark, I. D. (2010). An edifying spectacle: A history of 'tourist corroborees' in Victoria, Australia, 1835-1870. *Tourism Management*, **31**(3), 412-420.

Carson, D. & Koster, R. (2012). Addressing the problem of indigenous disadvantage in remote areas of developed nations: A plea for more comparative research. *Journal of Rural and Community Development*, 7(1), 110-125.

Commonwealth of Australia. (2009). *The Jackson report on behalf of the steering committee. Informing the national long term tourism strategy.* Australian Government, Commonwealth of Australia. http://www.tourism.australia.com/documents/THE_JACKSON_REPORT_JUL2009.pdf.

Coria, J. & Calfucura, E. (2012). Ecotourism and the development of indigenous communities: The good, the bad and the ugly. *Ecological Economics, 73*, 47-55.

Department of Communications Information Technology & the Arts. (2003). *Tourism White Paper. A medium to long term strategy for tourism: The future view of Australian tourism.* Canberra, ACT: Australian Government, Commonwealth of Australia. http://pandora.nla.gov.au/pan/41331/20060329-0000/www.industry.gov.au/assets/documents/itrinternet/TourismWhitePaper20050209174539.pdf.

Department of Resources Energy & Tourism. (2009). *National long-term tourism strategy.* Canberra: Australian Government, Commonwealth of Australia. https://www.austrade.gov.au/ArticleDocuments/5499/DRET%20Tourism%20Strategy.pdf.aspx

Dodson, M., & Smith, D. (2003). *Governance for sustainable development: Strategic issues and principles for Indigenous Australian communities. Discussion Paper 250.* http://caepr.anu.edu.au/Publications/DP/2003DP250.php

Fletcher, C., Pforr, C. & Brueckner, M. (2016). Factors influencing indigenous engagement in tourism development: An international perspective. *Journal of Sustainable Tourism, 24*(8/9), 1100-1120.

Fuller, D., Buultjens, J. & Cummings, E. (2005). Ecotourism and Indigenous microenterprise formation in northern Australia opportunities and constraints. *Tourism Management, 26*(6), 891-904.

Higgins-Desbiolles, F., Schmiechen, J. & Trevorrow, G. (2010). *A case study in the development of an Aboriginal tourism enterprise: The Coorong Wilderness Lodge of South Australia - an emic perspective.* http://www.academia.edu/24756519/A_CASE_STUDY_IN_THE_DEVELOPMENT_OF_AN_ABORIGINAL_TOURISM_ENTERPRISE_The_Coorong_Wilderness_Lodge_of_South_Australia_an_emic_perspective

Hinch, T. & Butler, R. (2007). Introduction: revisiting common ground. In R. Butler & T. Hinch (Eds.), *Tourism and Indigenous Peoples: Issues and implications* (pp. 1-14). Amsterdam: Butterworth-Heinmann.

Jones Donald Strategy Partners. (2009). *Project Indigenous Tourism: a research based consultancy to assist TA/RET to provide marketing guidance to promoters and suppliers of Indigenous tourism experiences for the domestic market.* Sydney: Jones Donald Strategy Partners

Morrison, M., Collins, J., Basu, P. K. & Krivokapic-Skoko, B. (2014). *Determining the factors influencing the success of private and community-owned Indigenous businesses across remote, regional and urban Australia. Final report prepared for the Australian Research Council and Indigenous*

Business Australia, December 2014. Charles Stuart University & University of Technology Sydney. https://www.csu.edu.au/__data/assets/pdf_file/0015/1311504/Final-Report-to-IBA-and-ARC-Linkage-LP110100698-Morrison,-Collins,-Basu-and-Krivokapic-191214_Executive-Summary-Only.pdf.

Nielsen, N., Buultjens, J. & Gale, D. (2008). *Indigenous tourism involvement in Queensland.* Gold Coast: CRC for Sustainable Tourism.

O'Rourke, T. & Memmott, P. (2005). *Sustaining Indigenous cultural tourism: Aboriginal pathways, cultural centres and dwellings in the Queensland wet tropics.* Gold Coast: CRC for Sustainable Tourism.

OECD. (2012). *Poverty reduction and pro-poor growth: the role of empowerment.* http://www.oecd.org/dac/povertyreduction/povertyreductionandpro-poorgrowththeroleofempowerment.htm

Pearson, C. A. L. (2014). Female Indigenous entrepreneurship in remote communities in northern Australia. *Information Management and Business Review,* **6**(6), 329-344.

Peters, A. & Higgins-Desbiolles, F. (2012). De-marginalising tourism research: Indigenous Australians as tourists. *Journal of Hospitality and Tourism Management,* **19**, 1-9.

Ruhanen, L., Whitford, M. & McLennan, C. (2013). *Demand and supply issues in Indigenous tourism: A gap analysis.* Indigenous Business Australia (Australian Government) & Department of Resources, Energy and Tourism, Indigenous Tourism Working Group. www.iba.gov.au/wp-content/uploads/2013/03/20130304ResearchReport_Demand-and-Supply-Issues-in-Indigenous-Tourism-A-Gap-Analysis.pdf.

Ruhanen, L., Whitford, M., & McLennan, C. (2015a). Exploring Chinese visitor demand for Australia's Indigenous tourism experiences. *Journal of Hospitality and Tourism Management,* **24**, 25-34.

Ruhanen, L., Whitford, M., & McLennan, C. (2015b). Indigenous tourism in Australia: Time for a reality check. *Tourism Management,* **48**, 73-83.

Russell-Mundine, G. (2007). Key factors for the successful development of Australian Indigenous entrepreneurship. *Tourism,* **55**(4), 417-429.

Scherrer, P. & Doohan, K. (2013). It's not about believing': Exploring the transformative potential of cultural acknowledgement in an Indigenous tourism context. *Asia Pacific Viewpoint,* **54**(2), 158-170.

Strickland-Munro, J. & Moore, S. (2013). Indigenous involvement and benefits from tourism in protected areas: A study of Purnululu National Park and Warmun Community, Australia. *Journal of Sustainable Tourism,* **21**(1), 26-41.

Tourism Australia. (2017). There's nothing like Australia: campaign focus. http://www.tourism.australia.com/campaigns/TNLA.aspx

Tourism Research Australia. (2011). *Snapshots 2011: Indigenous tourism visitors in Australia*. Canberra: Department of Resources, Energy and Tourism. http://www.ret.gov.au/tourism/Documents/tra/Snapshots%20 and%20Factsheets/2011/Snapshots2011Indigenous.pdf.

Tremblay, P. & Wegner, A. (2009). *Indigenous/Aboriginal tourism research in Australia (2000-2008): Industry lessons and future research needs*. Gold Coast: CRC for Sustainable Tourism.

Tsey, K., McCalam, J., Bainbridge, R. & Brown, C. (2012). Strengthening organisational capacity to improve Indigenous Australian community governance: A two-way approach. *International Review of Social Sciences and Humanities, 2*(2), 162-175.

Whitford, M. (2009). Aboriginal and Torres Strait Islanders' tourism policy: The current state of play. *Journal of Tourism, 10*, 19-42.

Whitford, M., Bell, B. & Watkins, M. (2001). Indigenous tourism policy in Australia: 25 years of rhetoric and economic rationalism. *Current Issues in Tourism, 4*(2-4), 151-181.

Whitford, M. & Ruhanen, L. (2009). *Indigenous tourism businesses in Australia. Development, analysis and evaluation of a national diagnostic tool profiling SME Indigenous tourism product*. Gold Coast: CRC for Sustainable Tourism.

Whitford, M. & Ruhanen, L. (2010). Australian Indigenous tourism policy: Practical and sustainable policies? *Journal of Sustainable Tourism, 18*(4), 475-496.

Whitford, M. & Ruhanen, L. (2016). Indigenous tourism research, past and present: Where to from here? *Journal of Sustainable Tourism, 24*(8-9), 1080-1099.

Yugambeh Museum. (2015). Yugambeh News(July). http://www.yugambeh.com/news/gtcms/structured/strc__resource_769_101___Yugambeh%20News%20July.pdf

3 Achieving Aboriginal Development Aspirations through Educational Tourism:
Learning on country with Bana Yarralji Bubu

Helen Murphy

Introduction

Aboriginal entrepreneurial activity in tourism is often promoted as a strategy for economic development (Whitford & Ruhanen, 2010). However, despite government support, the fragile state of the Aboriginal tourism sector continues (Schmiechen & Boyle, 2007). This has been variously attributed to lack of assets, poor education outcomes, lack of business experience, business models at odds with Aboriginal community and cultural norms, and weak land rights (Buultjens et al., 2010; Pearson & Helms, 2013). Also important is the historical lack of Aboriginal choice and control over involvement in tourism (Pitcher et al., 1999). Nielsen (2010:2) argues there is a link between Aboriginal control of involvement in tourism and the ability of tourism to be "a sustainable and viable tool in the social and economic development of Indigenous people". This link between positive outcomes from Aboriginal tourism and Aboriginal-driven, self-determined approaches to tourism planning has been widely recognized in the literature (Notzke, 1999; Ryan & Huyton, 2002; Butler & Hinch, 2007). However, while these links have been explored on a regional or community level (Nielsen, 2010), studies of family or individual-run tourism planning processes are less common. More understanding of the planning processes applied by Aboriginal families and individuals for tourism development would be useful in understanding not only the motivations for involvement in tourism, but how these motivations affect the development and operation of the tourism enterprise.

This chapter presents a case study of Bana Yarralji Bubu, an educational tourism enterprise run by an Aboriginal family in northern Queensland, Australia. The Wallace family have developed a tourism business that reflects their multi-dimensional development aspirations. Their educational tourism enterprise provides learning experiences to visiting educational tourist groups about their country and culture, with the profits of the business used to fund projects benefiting their community. Through this case study, the opportunities and challenges facing Aboriginal tourism operators in fulfilling their development aspirations through involvement in educational tourism are examined. This research is important as it describes how an Aboriginal family identified a gap in the tourism market and are using this opportunity to create jobs, foster knowledge exchange and increase community wellbeing. The results from this research demonstrate that learning about Aboriginal culture and land can be achieved through a tourism enterprise, and that educational tourism offers scope for achievement of broader Aboriginal development aspirations. This chapter first reviews the literature on educational tourism and Aboriginal development, and this is followed by an outline of the methods used for this research. The case study is then presented, exploring the Wallace family's view of development, how they seek to fulfil these aspirations through Bana Yarralji Bubu and how tourists have reacted to the experience. The findings are then discussed before conclusions are drawn.

This chapter uses the term 'Aboriginal tourism' because it refers to mainland Australian Aboriginal tourism opportunities, recognising that this term is most appropriately used to refer to the specific identity of mainland Aboriginal peoples within Australia on a national level. I have been guided by my discussions with Bana Yarralji Bubu in deciding to use the term 'Aboriginal', and use this throughout for consistency. In this research, Butler and Hinch's (2007:5) definition of Aboriginal tourism is used, that is "tourism activities in which Indigenous people are directly involved either through control and/or by having their culture serve as the essence of the attraction". Nielsen (2010:8) points out that this definition has value because it "recognises Indigenous agency and control, rather than Indigenous people being merely the passive *producers* of tourism experiences".

Educational tourism and Aboriginal tourism

Educational tourism occurs when tourists travel to a location to consume learning experiences related to that specific location (Patterson, 2006). Travel, education and learning have long been associated because of the ability of travel to "broaden the mind as people learn from and interpret experiences" (Stone & Petrick, 2013:731). From its early roots, when travel and learning about other cultures was seen as an essential part of the education of European, American and Chinese scholars and aristocracy, educational travel has now evolved into a form of tourism that encompasses a variety of educational experiences (Benson, 2007). These experiences include university educational programs, school trips, seniors' educational tours and cultural educational programs. Education is defined for this research as "the organised, systematic effort to foster learning, to establish the conditions, and to provide the activities through which learning can occur" (Smith, 1982:47). Educational tourism "tells the stories of places in order to enrich the interactions of travellers with them", broadening the outlook of tourists as they learn about the global contexts of specific places and events (Wood, 2010:189). In particular, this process of learning and personal development occurs through "investigating the cultural landscapes of places" and how these cultures have evolved over time in these contexts (Wood, 2010). Educational tourism can:

> "give participants unique insights into different cultural traditions by travelling to the places where each tradition evolved, and tracing how climate, geography, demography and politics interact to create specific types of art and culture. The physical experience of different landscapes, environments and peoples with their myriad colours and scents is the first step to understanding different cultures"
> (Bennison 1999 in Wood, 2010:189).

From its beginnings, Aboriginal tourism in Australia has attracted those seeking insight into Aboriginal culture. Early tourism activities provided opportunities for travellers to visit Aboriginal people still living a traditional lifestyle and were more about viewing 'the vanishing race' than gaining understanding of their culture (Schmiechen & Boyle, 2007). Since then, tourists have moved from gazing at the 'other' to seeking a deeper knowledge and understanding of Aboriginal culture. Academic and government studies have linked Aboriginal tourism experiences to tourist preferences for learning and education (Notzke, 1999; Zeppel, 2002; McIntosh, 2004; Tourism Queensland, 2010). However, despite this link, and the potential for Aboriginal involvement in niche markets such as educational tourism as noted by Schmiechen and Boyle (2007), little examination of these markets has occurred in an Australian context. A small number of studies have been carried out in the Northern Territory (NT) on 'learning markets' for Aboriginal tourism (James, 2006; Schmiechen et al., 2010). This term was developed by Tourism NT to represent different tourist market segments that have a specific interest in learning about Aboriginal culture. James (2006:4) defines these markets as "specific segments of the broader Indigenous tourism market [comprised of]… groups or individuals who travel to learn about the culture or environment of the people and places they visit". These groups can come from educational institutions, special interest clubs and associations, government departmental cultural awareness programs and independent travellers seeking educational tourism opportunities. If Aboriginal tourism operators are to develop products for these markets, more information about the preferences of these diverse market segments for Aboriginal learning experiences is critical.

A small number of studies have examined how tourists learn about Aboriginal culture through educational tourism, and the outcome of this learning for participants. Educational tourism has been found to contribute to mutual understanding between people of different cultures and lifestyles by changing tourists' attitudes and enhancing cross-cultural understanding (Var et al., 1994). Higgins-Desboilles (2006) finds that Aboriginal educational tourism operations, such as Camp Coorong, enable tourists to gain insight into Aboriginal culture as well as personal insight, which fosters reconciliation between Aboriginal and non-Aboriginal peoples. Wright et al. (2007) describe a form of educational tourism where learning occurs between Aboriginal tour operators, university lecturers and students. The authors find that the interaction of the different perspectives of the three groups can result in a 'multi-directional' learning experience. This experience is found to transform the traditional research relationships between student, teacher and Aboriginal co-researchers, providing insight into the way in which cross-cultural learning occurs in a tourism context. In a study of Māori cultural tourism in New Zealand, McIntosh (2004) finds that learning is enhanced through interaction with Māori people, informal learning styles and the physical location where the learning takes place. However, she also finds that few existing Māori cultural tourism products are designed with these factors in mind (McIntosh, 2004). Greater understanding of the different ways in which tourists learn about Aboriginal culture, and what they are seeking from these experiences, would enable more appropriate and diverse learning experiences to be provided.

Aboriginal development aspirations

While Aboriginal tourism is often seen as way of improving economic outcomes by the government, Aboriginal individuals and communities often view tourism as a way to achieve broader development goals (Buultjens & Fuller, 2007). These goals can include, on the international scale, Indigenous aspirations to protect the natural environment, use of participatory approaches in defining development aspirations and holistic strategies to improve well-being and recognition of local diversity and culture (van Nieuwkoop & Uquillas, 2000; Giovannini, 2012). Australian Aboriginal development aspirations reflect these priorities as well as the importance of communal wellbeing and reciprocity over the individual ownership of possessions, and the intimate connection between Aboriginal identity and culture with traditional lands (Thompson et al., 2000; Dockery, 2010). The interconnectedness of these development aspirations is reflected in calls by Aboriginal organisations for the integration of economic participation with social concerns, cultural priorities, legal rights and effective governance systems (NAILSMA, 2012). Hence economic development is more than just increasing incomes, but also must provide a means of overcoming social problems and environmental issues.

Aboriginal tourism is found to contribute to development outcomes when Aboriginal people have the opportunity to exercise rights over their land, to control resources and tourism development, and to participate in decision-making (Colton & Whitney-Squire, 2010:275) In a study of Arizonian Hopi reservations, the authors argue that tourism development will not be successful unless planning activities incorporate the cultural perspectives and values of Indigenous decision-makers (Piner & Paradis, 2004). Planning processes for tourism should be inclusive and cooperative, controlled from within the Indigenous community and should incorporate cultural values and local economic practices. Matunga (2013:14) defines Indigenous planning as "a process, approach or indeed activity that links specific Indigenous communities to defined ancestral places, environments and resources". The values, ethics, concepts and knowledge used to decide planning processes must come from Indigenous people, ensuring that Indigenous ties to community, kinship and land are reflected. These studies reflect Bryant's (1999 in Buultjens & Fuller, 2007) broader findings that development outcomes can be enhanced when development is locally driven, when development paths are pragmatic and are characterized by linkages and partnerships with the wider society.

The question of whether Aboriginal tourism can contribute to development outcomes for Aboriginal people is debated in the literature. Negative outcomes from Aboriginal involvement in cultural tourism have been widely noted, including exploitation, adverse environmental or social impacts and the limited ability of tourism to fix economic and social problems for Aboriginal people (Birdsall-Jones et al., 2007; Fuller et al., 2007; Greiner, 2010). The sale of sacred lands, ceremonial sites and knowledge systems do not guarantee social and economic development for Indigenous communities according to Johnston (2006:2). On the other side, positive outcomes from Aboriginal tourism have also been identified, including broad Aboriginal community development benefits, cross-cultural understanding, cultural revival and economic development (Altman, 1989; Moscardo & Pearce, 1999; Zeppel, 2002; Colton & Whitney-Squire, 2010). However, these findings must be tempered by the realization that while Aboriginal participation in tourism 'is likely to provide a diverse range of benefits', these benefits will vary according to local contexts and histories as well as challenges such as lack of skills, cultural factors and low market profiles (Buultjens & Fuller 2007:viii).

Methods

The research presented in this chapter is part of a larger PhD project examining the supply and demand of Aboriginal educational tourism experiences. The first phase of the study involved a qualitative exploration of Aboriginal involvement in educational tourism through a case study of an Aboriginal educational tourism enterprise, Bana Yarralji Bubu, located in the Wet Tropics World Heritage area of northern Queensland. The case study approach was used to understand not only the planning and supply of educational tourism by an Aboriginal family but also the complex contextual conditions surrounding this supply. This involved a series of field trips to Shipton's Flat over a three-year period (2012-2015) to carry out observations of planning processes and workshops, as well as observations and participation in tourism experiences provided by Bana Yarralji Bubu at Shipton's Flat. The participants in this research were Marilyn and Peter Wallace, the owners and managers of Bana Yarralji Bubu and members of their family. In addition, tour operators and travel planners involved in the supply of educational tourism were interviewed to give market context to the research. Tourists visiting Bana Yarralji were also interviewed about their educational tourism experiences at the destination. The interviews were semi-structured and guided by key themes that had been uncovered during the literature review, as well as key issues that had been highlighted iteratively in the field. The data was analysed using Nvivo, a type of computer-assisted qualitative data analysis software. A set of codes was created to describe the main concepts in the data according to the themes in the research questions, ideas arising from the data as well as themes identified in the literature. The data was then organised according to these codes which allowed for relationships between data to be discovered and themes and typologies to be described.

Findings

Bana Yarralji Bubu is run by Marilyn Wallace, a Kuku Nyungkal elder and her husband Peter, who identifies as a Kuku Yalanji and Kuku Bidji elder. The Eastern Kuku Yalanji are one of the 18 rainforest Aboriginal traditional owner groups in the Wet Tropics World Heritage region of far north Queensland. The Eastern Kuku Yalanji lands are the traditional home of a number of clans, including the Kuku Nyungkal people, traditional owners of the lands of the Upper Annan River (refer to the map in Figure 3.1). The boundaries of Kuku Nyungkal land "stretch from Annan River, Kings Plain, Rossville, Shipton's Flat and Mount Amos/Archer Point to Cedar Bay and includes Hope Islands" (Bana Yarralji Bubu Strategic Plan, unpublished, 2008).

Eastern Kuku Yalanji and Kuku Nyungkal people were forcibly removed from their traditional lands in the 1950s into missions and reserves either along the Bloomfield River or further south to Yarrabah and Palm Island (Wallace et al. 2011). The forced relocations had many negative effects for Eastern Kuku Yalanji people, including the loss of culture and mobility. In a report to the Lutheran Church in 1978 they described themselves as being "like a crane standing on one leg (no room for two feet on the ground) on a little island" (Anderson, 1992). The pain caused by this government policy continues to echo in the community to this day and Yalanji people fought for many years to return to 'country'. In 2007, after fifteen years of negotiation, the native title rights of the Eastern Kuku Yalanji people were formally recognised for the first time and a consent determination was made that recognised their native title rights and interests over 126,900 hectares of land and exclusive native title rights over 30,300 hectares in the determination area.

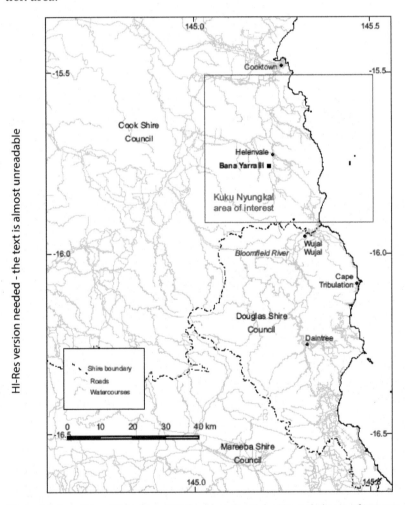

Figure 3.1: Location of Bana Yarralji Bubu, showing Kuku Nyungkal area of interest.
Source: Connect Spatial (2015)

When Marilyn and Peter moved back to Nyungkal Country, Marilyn described the importance of this move:

> *"When I came back home, this [is] my ancestral place, my parent's place... We want to go back on country, we want to live our lifestyle, exercise our native title rights, teaching language, fishing and hunting... looking after the wildlife, ...and to come back and share our knowledge. In our knowledge we see and do, and we believe that spirits are still existing, our parents our grandparents come with us, we can't see them, they can see us, and that's why going back to this, it's very important* (Marilyn, pers. comm. 2013)".

Marilyn chose the name Bana Yarralji Bubu for the tourism enterprise, which means 'cool, freshwater country' in Kuku Nyungkal language. This name reflects the importance of the waterfalls, rivers and streams that flow through their lands where they wish to restore Nyungkal lore and culture (Wallace et al., 2011).

Bana Yarralji Bubu hosts a variety of educational experiences at Shipton's Flat. The majority of their business comes directly from international or domestic travel planners at educational institutions such as universities or special interest organisations, such as conservation organisations. They also host secondary school groups who participate in week-long cultural immersion camps. Groups coming to Shipton's Flat can visit for one day, or camp for a week or longer, making use of basic campsite activities. They undertake a number of different activities during their stay. These activities are decided on, and conducted in an informal manner and can include painting and dancing workshops, collecting and cooking traditional bush foods, guided walks along bush tracks and learning about traditional ecological knowledge. The activities provided differ according to the needs and budgets of the visiting groups and what Bana Yarralji Bubu are willing or able to provide. The enterprise is small-scale and highly seasonal in nature, restricted not only by the wet season, but also by the preference of many educational groups to travel during vacation rather than term time.

When they moved back to country, Peter and Marilyn used a sustainability compass to articulate their vision of what they wanted to achieve. Their vision as described by Marilyn was:

> *"...to return back to our Nyungkal country. We feel today that it is our responsibility to return home to our custodial land to take action through traditional lore and custom to look after our land, waters, plants, and*

animals. The reason for moving back to country is to develop a better future for our families and Kuku Nyungkal warra people" (Bana Yarralji Bubu strategic plan, unpublished, 2008).

Figure 3.2: The compass of sustainability. Source: Atkisson, 1997.

The broad-based goals described in this vision were further developed using the four compass directions of the sustainability compass. The four directions symbolize the equal importance of economic, social, natural and wellbeing goals. Using this as a guide, Marilyn and Peter developed a guiding vision for their tourism enterprise with four inter-connected aims and strategies for achieving these aims:

1   The economic goal outlined the importance of bringing employment to their family and community, by providing culturally appropriate job opportunities through tourism.

2   The nature goal was to protect and manage their land, plants, animals and seal country through a country plan and using traditional ecological knowledge to manage their country.

3   The wellbeing goal was to heal their family, community and land through cultural awareness and the establishment of a healing center.

4   The society/culture goal was to protect and manage their cultural identity, history and language through rediscovering Nyungkal lore and custom.

The educational tourism enterprise is an important strategy for achieving these goals. The compass has allowed them to develop a business approach reflecting their cultural values, knowledge, land and people, in line with

Matunga's (2013) four essential conditions for Indigenous planning. The goal of the enterprise is not to accumulate profits for personal gain, but to enable Marilyn and Peter to address issues of concern to their family and community. Tourism therefore, is a means of achieving benefits such as wellbeing, cultural reconnection and spiritual healing for their family, community and land.

Marilyn and Peter view the tourism enterprise as a way to educate non-Aboriginal visitors about the importance of caring for country in traditional ways. Peter in particular is interested in using the enterprise as a way to not only protect the environment but also to find out more about it:

> *"Today we need to start moulding together the scientific knowledge and the traditional knowledge of the landscape. If we don't look after it now and do hands on stuff and working together [to] bring everything to standard today, we're lost. Everything suffers - the people suffer, the environment suffers, animals suffer and we've got a package here that… we done a business package* (Peter, pers. comm. 2014)".

Collaboration with conservation and land management groups has enabled Bana Yarralji Bubu to work with volunteers who participate in environmental protection activities as well as scientific data collection. This is an important source of labour for environmental management activities, however it does not currently constitute a significant revenue source for the enterprise. What is more important to Peter is ensuring that visitors, particularly scientists, understand that "it has rules, this countryside". So through educating scientists and volunteers about these rules, they will see "where we coming from you know" and be protected on country:

> *'[When educating tourists] we gotta take it a bit further now and add knowledge…within a 10 kilometre radius we can monitor the seasonal things you know…If you go into a sacred place, you need a 60 k. buffer radius, there are indicators that will tell you that, … but if you can't read it, you know, you gonna do more harm to that thing. So that happens sometimes, people are in that area [and] approach it the wrong way or disturb something, not singing out or things like that. Things can move around, they smell you if you going the wrong way…it's the way that you approach that place, you could get wrong data from there"* (Peter, pers. comm. 2013).

However, Marilyn and Peter have found that creating partnerships with scientific groups can be challenging, particularly given the differences between Western scientific knowledge and traditional ecological knowledge. However, it has also been a positive experience with the different participants all gaining something from their involvement:

> *"They can see a win-win-win all around; students gaining natural and cultural experiences; natural resource managers gaining valuable data; and Bana Yarralji showing themselves to be both hosts and emerging custodians of [their] lands and waters"* (White, pers. comm. 2011).

For Marilyn and Peter, the enterprise is strongly focused on educating visitors and rebuilding their own family and community knowledge about land and culture. Their vision for rebuilding this knowledge in the Nyungkal community is by having family and community members involved in the enterprise, holding cultural camps, language classes, cultural mapping exercises, and creating a database of traditional ecological and cultural knowledge. Hosting camps at the tourism enterprise is seen as a way to allow community members to reconnect with country and get away from distractions and tensions in local towns. The camps are also designed to educate the community about how to solve social issues such as drinking, gambling and poor health outcomes. In addition, cultural knowledge is rebuilt through family members being employed by the enterprise and communicating their culture to others. These jobs are also seen by Marilyn and Peter as a way to foster self-esteem and improve the well-being of family members through living on country and in this way, economic, cultural and well-being goals are simultaneously addressed:

> *"I see light at the end of the tunnel. I worked in family wellbeing for 11 years and I see the psychological problems that young people go through. It is trying to create a better position for them. The jobs have been a really good help for the young people. It is really good therapy for them. They are coming through really well"* (Peter, pers. comm. 2011).

The desire to educate others is strongly connected to their desire to fulfil their cultural obligations to live on the land and care for the land. Peter explains it as a duty of care that they have to country. For Marilyn and Peter, educational tourism is a way that they can bring together their cultural obligations to the land (nature goal), the revitalization of culture and lore (society/culture goal) and their desire to educate the wider community:

> *"With the clan group here… we have an obligation to that land. You can see the land is starting to get sick and under stress and if …people could look at the land and heal the land and learn from [it] but we need*

to educate our own mob as well...so we want to teach them about the identity, lore and custom, about their boundary and other people that come in from outside. ... People need to know about the l-o-r-e and how we in the past have sustained that place. Sometimes people go in there and they aren't respecting that. The land is about respect... that's one of the duty of care that we have to explain those sort of things. But we want to put that in some sort of an educational curriculum that can also teach about those sort of things so the land is respected" (Peter, pers. comm. 2013).

Marilyn and Peter also see the enterprise as a way to increase understanding and cultural awareness between Aboriginal and non-Aboriginal people (society/culture goal). Through fire-side stories, informal talks and discussions and participation in cultural activities, Marilyn and Peter feel pride in teaching others about their culture, while tourists gain understanding through personally connecting with them in an informal, relaxed atmosphere. The strong sense of connection that is created between tourists and Marilyn and Peter has been a highly successful outcome for the enterprise. Tourists described these experiences, including listening to stories around a campfire, or having broad-ranging conversations with Marilyn and Peter, as allowing them to get a real insight into Aboriginal life. Having the opportunity to ask questions in a friendly and open atmosphere, without 'feeling judged' allowed one tourist to "have a better understanding of walking in someone else's world from their perspective" (I2, 2014). Tourists felt that an informal style of learning encouraged a more equal exchange of knowledge between themselves and Marilyn and Peter than they would have gained from a more formal learning experience. Learning through sitting and talking on country was felt to be enriching and conducive to learning, with one interviewee noting it felt more like "we were exchanging knowledge and culture. Really that's what it felt like... [which]...from a learning perspective... was very good, and sitting around talking was very natural" (I15, 2014). It also made visitors feel that their interaction with Marilyn and Peter was characterized by a deeper cultural exchange:

"I really liked the dog and the kids. I liked that the family were there... like when you see family in a place, you can see the continuation of it and know its evolving you know...you can see the connections that are going to grow you can see the kids are going to grow up there" (I7, 2014).

A travel planner who had brought a group of students to Bana Yarralji Bubu viewed these experiences as not only enhancing understanding between Aboriginal and non-Aboriginal people through building respect, but also through presenting the realities of modern Aboriginal life:

> *"The way to do that is to get the kids out and see the realities, and they are not always going to be the romantic realities – some of it's going to be really confronting…and all in all it was a bit taxing for some students [but] many of them still point out that it was an incredibly rich experience"* (TP3, 2014).

Tourists were welcomed to Shipton's Flat with a smoking ceremony. This created a feeling of welcome and inclusiveness for tourists and a sense of being inside the culture rather than an outside observer. They felt part of 'something bigger' through participation in the ceremony and this made them more receptive to learning about Aboriginal culture. "We got welcomed to the land and felt part of it, like a spiritual connection and the Aboriginal way of life, I thought that was [a] …good thing to be a part of, a lot more authentic" (I9, 2014). Another tourist saw the ceremony as an important part of a spiritual journey because it gave him a "reason to connect with who I was…to <u>connect with the land</u> and everything else around me" (interviewee's emphasis) (I22, 2014).

Tourists also talked about having their worldviews challenged through their experience at Bana Yarralji Bubu. Some interviewees felt their experience had enabled them to see issues 'from the traditional way' and be more aware of the effect of Western academic traditions on their thinking. This affected their worldview and they talked of taking this new knowledge home with them and incorporating that knowledge in their work or study in the future. In this way tourism was seen by participants as providing wide-ranging benefits including the transfer of knowledge and transformation of worldviews. Reconciliation was seen to be a key benefit from the cross-cultural understanding achieved as part of the tourism experience. One tourist described how engaging the younger generation was particularly important:

> *"When you talk about engaging school kids, 'cause that's the next generation, and for them to get that connection with Aboriginal people …that's reconciliation. We could have hope for totally different way of having relations between Aboriginal and Torres Strait Islander peoples and mainstream Australia [through tourism]"* (I34, 2014).

Discussion

This research has described how an Aboriginal family identified a gap in the tourism market and created an educational tourism enterprise, with the aim of achieving broad-based development goals. The results from this research demonstrate that learning about Aboriginal culture and land can be achieved through a tourism enterprise and that educational tourism offers scope for achievement of broader Aboriginal development aspirations. It is important to note that a prerequisite for this achievement is undertaking planning processes for enterprise development that are local, inclusive and incorporate cultural perspectives and values, consistent with Piner and Paradiso's (2004) findings. Marilyn and Peter undertook planning activities before the start of their tourism enterprise to identify their broader vision and put strategies in place to achieve their vision. Articulating that vision first allowed them to then find ways and strategies for achieving their aims. Their enterprise, Bana Yarralji Bubu, became an integral part of this vision and allowed them to be involved in tourism in a culturally appropriate way. The enterprise was a vehicle for achieving multi-dimensional benefits, as well as a way of educating themselves and the broader community (both Aboriginal and non-Aboriginal) about their land and culture.

In articulating their vision, Marilyn and Peter affirmed the priority of being back on country, healing, re-establishing and sharing their culture. Developing an Aboriginal educational tourism business on the land they identify with has enabled Marilyn and Peter to derive an income and at the same time, fulfil their cultural obligations to live on and care for the land. However achieving economic sustainability at the same time as pursuing social, cultural, wellbeing and environmental goals has been more challenging. In part, this is due to the small-scale and seasonal nature of the tourism enterprise which means they are unable to provide jobs to all family members, or fund all the social benefits they want to provide to family and clan. In addition, trying to simultaneously achieve their multidimensional goals has been exhausting for Marilyn and Peter, who have many projects on the go, all needing time, attention and resources, and which at times, divert attention and resources away from the business. Another factor is the limited budget of some educational groups, as well as the informal nature of the educational products supplied by Bana Yarralji Bubu. Without market demand information, Marilyn and Peter have not yet developed their own product range, but rather adapt their product offering to the needs of each specific group. This makes planning for future tourism seasons difficult, however it has also resulted in spontaneous experiences that resonate with tourists. Tourists responded positively to these experiences because they felt more authentic than preplanned, scheduled activities.

The benefits of involvement in educational tourism include cross-cultural understanding as well as the re-discovery of culture. Marilyn, Peter and other family members have been able to re-connect to their culture through communicating it to tourists, and the enterprise allows them to derive a livelihood on country. In addition, by welcoming tourists in an informal atmosphere to their country and providing a space for cross-cultural learning and exchange, they have been successful in changing tourists' attitudes and ways of thinking about Aboriginal culture. The finding that cross-cultural understanding can be an outcome of an Aboriginal educational tourism indicates that this form of tourism has the potential to increase reconciliation between Aboriginal and non-Aboriginal people. Given that school groups are a major market segment for Aboriginal educational tourism, this indicates that the younger generation has the opportunity to gain a deeper understanding of Aboriginal culture by participating in this form of tourism. However, more research is needed about the needs and preferences of educational tourists for Aboriginal learning experiences. While educational tourists have been found to seek understanding of different cultures by travelling to the places where those traditions evolved, they are not necessarily all interested in Aboriginal culture, or similar types of educational experiences.

While Bana Yarralji Bubu may be only a small-scale, seasonal family business, it shows the potential for the marriage between niche forms of tourism like educational tourism and Aboriginal development aspirations. However, family-level Aboriginal tourism operators must successfully balance Aboriginal values, development aspirations and the demands of tourists to have a sustainable tourism business. Engagement between these different components and at different levels can be characterized by tensions but also by positive engagement and cross-cultural learning. Recognition of the space in which Aboriginal educational tourism interactions take place and the distinctive worldviews and practices of the different parties involved, enables better understanding of the development and operation of Aboriginal educational tourism.

Conclusion

This research has examined the motivations of an Aboriginal family for involvement in tourism and how these motivations affect the development and operation of their tourism enterprise. This was done by examining the compass of sustainability used by the Wallace family to guide the development of their educational tourism business, Bana Yarralji Bubu. Their experience demonstrates a strong link between Aboriginal control of, and planning for involvement in, tourism and the ability of tourism to be a means of Aboriginal social and economic development. This research demonstrates that educational tourism offers opportunities for achieving broad-based development goals, as well as cross-cultural education and reconciliation for both Aboriginal enterprise owners and tourists. However, simultaneously fulfilling broad-based development goals through educational tourism operators is difficult and requires the ability to balance many competing demands. Careful consideration of both internal and external factors affecting the tourism enterprise is needed for a more complete picture of how these demands are managed. Finally, given the potential of educational tourism for Aboriginal tourism, more information about the needs and preferences of educational tourists would assist Aboriginal providers to design suitable and appropriate Aboriginal educational tourism experiences for the market.

References

Altman, J. (1989). Tourism dilemmas for Aboriginal Australians. *Annals of Tourism Research* **16**, 456-476.

Anderson, C. (1992). Deaths in Custody: Kuku Yalanji and the State. *Social Analysis* **31**, 1-11.

Benson, A. (2007). Research tourism: prof essional travel for useful discoveries, in M. Novelli (ed), *Niche Tourism*, Taylor & Francis, 133-142.

Birdsall-Jones, C. ,Wood, D., & Jones, R. (2007). Great expectations: Indigenous land-based tourism in regional Western Australia. In J. Buultjens and D. Fuller (eds), *Striving for Sustainability: Case studies in Indigenous tourism*. Lismore, NSW, Australia, Southern Cross University Press, 187-210.

Butler, R. & Hinch, T. (Eds.) (2007). *Tourism and Indigenous Peoples: Issues and implications*. Oxford, Butterworth-Heinemann.

Buultjens, J. & Fuller D., (Eds.) (2007). *Striving for Sustainability: Case studies in Indigenous tourism*. Lismore, NSW, Australia, Southern Cross University Press.

Buultjens, J., Gale, D. & White, N.E. (2010). Synergies between Australian Indigenous tourism and ecotourism: Possibilities and problems for future development. *Journal of Sustainable Tourism* **18**(4), 497-513.

Colton, J. W. & Whitney-Squire, K. (2010). Exploring the relationship between aboriginal tourism and community development. *Leisure/Loisir* **34**(3), 261-278.

Dockery, A. M. (2010). Culture and wellbeing: The case of Indigenous Australians. *CLMR Discussion Papers*. C. f. L. M. Research. Perth, CLMR, Curtin Business School, Curtin University of Technology, 1-29.

Fuller, D., J. Caldicott, Cairncross, G. & Wilde, S.J. (2007). Poverty, Indigenous culture and ecotourism in remote Australia. *Development* **50**(2), 141-148.

Giovannini, M. (2012). Social enterprises for development as Buen Vivir. *Journal of Enterprising Communities: People and Places in the Global Economy* **6**(3), pre-publication article.

Greiner, R. (2010). Improving the net benefits from tourism for people living in remote Northern Australia. *Sustainability* **2**, 2197-2218.

Higgins-Desbiolles, F. (2006). Reconciliation tourism: Healing divided societies. *Tourism Recreation Research* **28**(3), 35-44.

James, D. (2006). Discussion paper on future directions for Northern Territory Indigenous tourism and learning markets. *Tourism NT Report*. Darwin: Tourism NT.

Johnston, A. (2006). *Is the Sacred for Sale?: Tourism and Indigenous people*. London: Earthscan.

Matunga, H. (2013). Theorizing Indigenous Planning. *Reclaiming Indigenous Planning*. R. Walker, T. Jojola and D. Natcher. Montreal, Canada, McGill-Queen's University Press, 3-33.

McIntosh, A. J. (2004). Tourists' appreciation of Māori culture in New Zealand. *Tourism Management* **25**(1), 1-15.

Moscardo, G. & Pearce, PL (1999). Understanding ethnic tourists. *Annals of Tourism Research* **26**(2), 416-434.

NAILSMA (2012). Indigenous futures and sustainable development in Northern Australia: Towards a framework for full Indigenous participation in northern economic development. *Northern Australia Indigenous Experts Forum*. NAILSMA.

Nielsen, R. N. (2010). *Strengths, support and self-determination: Indigenous tourism planning and the Biamie Dreaming Cooperative*. PhD, Southern Cross University.

Notzke, C. (1999). Indigenous tourism development in the arctic. *Annals of Tourism Research* **26**(1), 55-76.

Patterson, I. R. (2006). Different travel markets: Educational tourism and older adults, in I. R. Patterson (ed.) *Growing Older: Tourism and Leisure Behaviour of Older Adults*. Oxford, CABI.

Pearson, C. A. L. & Helms, K. (2013). Indigenous social entrepreneurship: The Gumatj clan enterprise in East Arnhem Land. *Journal of Entrepreneurship* **22**(1), 43-70.

Piner, J. & T. Paradis (2004). Beyond the casino: Sustainable tourism and cultural development on Native American Lands. *Tourism Geographies* **6**(1), 80-98.

Pitcher, M., van Oosterzee, P. & Palmer, L. (1999). *Choice and Control: The Development of Indigenous Tourism in Australia*. Darwin, Centre for Indigenous Natural and Cultural Resource Management and CRC Tourism.

Ryan, C. & Huyton, J. (2002). Tourists and Aboriginal people. *Annals of Tourism Research* **29**(3), 631-647.

Schmiechen, J. & Boyle, A. (2007). Chapter 5 - Aboriginal tourism research in Australia, in R. Butler and T. Hinch (eds) *Tourism and Indigenous Peoples*, Oxford, Butterworth-Heinemann, 58-70.

Schmiechen, J., James, D. & Tremblay, P. (2010). *Learning markets and Indigenous tourism*. Queensland, CRC for Sustainable Tourism.

Smith, R. A. (1982). *Learning How to Learn*. Chicago, Follett.

Stone, M. J. & Petrick, J. F. (2013). The educational benefits of travel experiences: A Literature Review. *Journal of Travel Research* **52**(6), 731-744.

Thompson, S. J., Gifford, S. M. & Thorpe, L. (2000). The social and cultural context of risk and prevention: Food and physical activity in an urban Aboriginal community. *Health Education and Behavior* **27** (6), 725-743.

van Nieuwkoop, M. & Uquillas J. E., (2000). Defining ethnodevelopment in operational terms: Lessons from the Ecuador indigenous and Afro-Ecuadoran Peoples Development Project. *Latin America and Caribbean Region Sustainable Development Working Papers*. World Bank.

Var, T. Ap, J. & Van Doren, C (1994) Tourism and world peace. In W. Theobald (Ed.) *Global Tourism: The next decade*, Oxford: Butterworth-Heinemann.

Wallace, M., White, B. & Sheer, R. (2011). On the ground: Planning on Eastern Kuku Yalanji Country. *Queensland Planner* **41**(4), 14-16.

Whitford, M. M. & Ruhanen L. M. (2010). Australian Indigenous tourism policy: Practical and sustainable policies? *Journal of Sustainable Tourism* **18**(4), 475-496.

Wood, C. (2010). Educational tourism-cultural landscapes, in B. Kent, R. Pesman and C. Troup (eds.) *Australians in Italy: Contemporary Lives and Impressions*. Melbourne, Monash University Publishing.

Wright, S. & Suchet-Pearson, S. & Lloyd, K. (2007). An interwoven learning exchange: Transforming research-teaching relationships in the Top End, Northern Australia. *Geographical Research* **45**(2), 150-157.

Zeppel, H. (2002). Indigenous tourism in the Wet Tropics World Heritage Area, North Queensland. *Australian Aboriginal Studies* **2**, 65-68

Interviews

Interviewee 2 (2014), interviewed by author, Shipton's Flat, 25/6/16

Interviewee 7 (2014), interviewed by author, Shipton's Flat, 25/6/16

Interviewee 9 (2014), interviewed by author, Shipton's Flat, 25/6/16

Interviewee 15 (2014), interviewed by author, Shipton's Flat, 26/6/16

Interviewee 22 (2014), interviewed by author, Shipton's Flat, 27/6/16

Interviewee 34 (2014), interviewed by author, Shipton's Flat, 25/6/16

Travel planner 3 (2014), interviewed by author, Cairns, 03/04/16

4 Aboriginal Tourism in Western Australia:
A case study of Yawuru Nagulagun Roebuck Bay Marine Park

Lori-Ann Shibish, Ross Dowling & Greg Willson

Introduction

The purpose of this chapter is to examine, by way of a case study, both the creation and development of an Aboriginal-led tourism initiative within a national park in the North West of Western Australia (WA), and also the key stakeholders who have worked collaboratively through a joint management framework to enable its success. The park in question is Yawuru Nagulagun Roebuck Bay Marine Park, Broome, WA. The case study illustrates the interplay of four key components and the nexus that exists through their interconnectedness: ecotourism, Indigenous people, national parks and joint management (the approach taken in the management of the natural and cultural heritage). Through the examination of Yawuru Nagulagun Roebuck Bay Marine Park as a case study, it is possible to identify these components, measure their impact and to identify where barriers and challenges exist.

The chapter examines the nature of tourism in WA and specifically ecotourism; the development of Indigenous tourism and how it has been affected by land rights issues; the role of national parks and the interplay with Indigenous tourism; and finally tourism in the Kimberley region and the emergence of Aboriginal tourism development in the case study area of

Yawuru Nagulagun Roebuck Bay Marine Park. The chapter will conclude with a look at the challenges and opportunities that have been presented, and what can be learned.

The case study formed part of a wider qualitative research project, which employed multi-method triangulation (participant observation, interviews, document analysis and case study analysis) to identify the place of Aboriginal tourism development within the new shared governance structure of Joint Management (JM). To date there have been few examples in Australia of Aboriginal tourism development occurring within a joint management governance model, as JM is relatively new. The authors discovered the emergence of a parks – tourism – Aboriginal people joint management nexus (Shibish, 2015). Moreover, the research revealed that the interface between Indigenous people and parks is a newly emerging research area (Strickland-Munro & Moore, 2013). Therefore this case study aims to extend knowledge in these areas by demonstrating, through the practical application of JM principles, how Indigenous tourism can successfully be developed whilst meeting sustainability goals and overcoming the challenges that are often faced by individual stakeholders. This may enable others working in protected areas in the drafting of park management plans, the shaping of new policies and the prioritising of future goals by giving insights into the opportunities it presents to the wider community, not only in conservation terms but for the advancement of social/cultural preservation and economic development.

For the purpose of this study, the words Aboriginal and Indigenous are used in the following context:

- Indigenous people – a global or umbrella term for all pre-colonial and/ or pre-settler societies. When referring to people who are descendants from the original inhabitants of Australia, the term will only be used if it includes both mainland Aboriginals and Torres Strait Islanders

- Aboriginal people – refers to those Indigenous people on the mainland of Australia, and does not include Torres Strait Islanders. Where the discussion pertains solely to WA, the term Aboriginal is used.

Background to the study

It is necessary to know something of the tourism framework to contextualise the development and success of Yawuru Nagulagun Roebuck Bay Marine Park. These include the tourism industry in WA and specifically ecotourism; the nature of Aboriginal tourism in WA (the cultural and historical background to Indigenous peoples); the development of tourism in the Kimberley region and the role that national parks and protected areas and their management play; and Aboriginal tourism in the region in which the case study is situated. Therefore, these aspects of tourism will be explored to provide background and meaning to the study.

Tourism in Western Australia

Australia is valued and noted for its natural environment, being one of the main reasons for visitations by tourists from overseas (Tourism Australia, 2016c) and the State and Federal government tourism bodies' key marketing messages are based around Australia's natural beauty, wide open spaces, impressive landscapes and native wildlife. Market research commissioned by Tourism Australia in 2014 revealed international visitors identified Australia's greatest strengths as its unique landscapes, safe environment and welcoming people (Tourism Australia, 2016c). Australia's natural attractions and pristine environment are well regarded by all markets and core to its global tourism offering. The greatest drivers of international visitor demand are coastal, aquatic and wildlife experiences. This is reflected in an annual visitor spend of $107.1 billion in 2014-15 from 83.2 million domestic overnight trips and 6.6 million international visitors, contributing $43.4 billion to the Gross Domestic Product (2.7%) and providing jobs for 4% of the workforce (Tourism Research Australia, 2015).

In 2016 WA received 29.5 million visitors spending $9.6 billion accounting for 10.7% of all visitors in Australia and generating approximately 97,000 jobs (Tourism Western Australia, 2016). Tourism Western Australia (TWA) has a strategy in place to increase the value of tourism in WA to $12 billion by 2020. TWA emphasises the unique features of the state for attracting visitors using its brand marketing 'Experience Extraordinary' to generate interest in tourism and leverage engagement and economic potential. The strategy earmarks the development and marketing of Aboriginal tourism as having the potential to be a key component of the WA brand image (Tourism Western Australia, 2012).

Ecotourism in Western Australia

Ecotourism has been evolving over the last 40 years and is now generally understood to encompass nature-based, low impact, sustainable, ecologically and environmentally responsible forms of tourism as opposed to conventional mass tourism (Weaver, 2008). Its primary goals are "to foster sustainable use through resource conservation, cultural revival and economic development and diversification" (Newsome et al., 2013:16).

By the 1990s, ecotourism was the fastest growing sector of tourism (Fennell, 2014). As early as 1991, an innovative not-for-profit organisation involving public and private sector individuals called Forum Advocating Cultural and Ecotourism (FACET) was formed in WA, and played a key role in supporting ecotourism development (FACET, 2012). Similarly, the Australian government recognised the value in supporting a quality ecotourism industry and in 1994 developed the National Ecotourism Strategy committing $10 million for its implementation (Ingram, 2007). At the same time, the Western Australia Tourism Commission developed a Nature Based Tourism Advisory Committee (NBTAC) which prepared a nature-based strategy for the state (WATC, 1997). Its guiding principles are conservation of the natural environment; involving and benefiting local communities; improving knowledge; providing quality products and services; and efficient and effective industry (WATC, 1997). The strategy was further updated in 2004.

An example of how the nature-based tourism strategy has been put into practice is the inception of the Naturebank program. This was initiated by the WA government in 2011 to encourage ecotourism growth through the identification of suitable sites within national parks for environmentally sensitive tourism accommodation experiences. The program is jointly managed through a partnership between the Department of Parks and Wildlife and TWA (Department of Parks and Wildlife, 2014b). Private sector developers must meet certain criteria to ensure that responsible tourism practices are adhered to whilst demonstrating a commitment to both promoting Aboriginal culture and conservation of the environment (Tourism Western Australia, 2011). This unique initiative has positioned WA as a world premier ecotourism destination and has generated interest from other states for development into a national program. It has also attracted international attention. Currently there are six locations, two of which are located in the Kimberley region (Department of Parks and Wildlife, 2014b).

The role of national parks in ecotourism development

According to Butler and Boyd (2000), protected areas are the most sought after tourism attraction. Parks, both land-based and marine, are generally regarded as a common pool resource (Adams, 2002) and have traditionally been managed by government on behalf of the public. The development of ecotourism products and the ongoing protection and management of Australia's national parks and protected areas have the potential for natural synergy. However, it has been asserted that park agencies and tourism have an ambiguous relationship (Ingram, 2007) as it is one of both symbiosis and of conflict, and this has been witnessed in WA. As nature-based tourism grew in the 1990s, park agencies needed to deal with increasing pressure on the land from growing visitor numbers and associated management issues. Within WA, this growth resulted in a significant rise in the number of licensed tourism operators in protected areas from 60 to over 400 operators (Ingram, 2007). In 2014, Parks and Wildlife recorded 16.69 million visits (Department of Parks and Wildlife, 2014a) demonstrating the enormous value of parks to the WA tourism economy and the important role that the Department of Parks and Wildlife play in managing this asset. The rapid rise in visitors and activities caused concern for park managers, some perceiving it as a threat to conservation. However within WA, the park agency viewed tourism as an 'essential partner' in achieving conservation objectives and as noted by Ingram:

> "ecotourism was seen as an opportunity for CALM [Conservation and Land Management] to develop champions for conservation within the tourism industry and assist in building a case for greater government resources for parks" (Ingram, 2007:272).

Fennell and Weaver (2005) introduced the concept of *ecotourisum* where a symbiosis of protected areas, tourism, local communities and government departments is achieved through ecotourism experiences in which visitors can directly engage in conservation. Cable Beach, Broome in WA has had some success with this through its turtle-monitoring program run jointly by Parks & Wildlife and Yawuru (the Aboriginal traditional owners of the area).

In Australia, individual States manage national parks, marine parks and other protected areas. In WA, they are managed by Parks & Wildlife. WA has

100 national parks and 13 marine parks (Department of Parks and Wildlife, 2016a) and these are created and managed under the *Conservation and Land Management Act 1984* (CALM Act). WA is Australia's largest state covering 33% of the country (Australian Bureau of Statistics, 2007). Parks & Wildlife manage lands and water totalling 28,285,218 hectares; the land area equates to 10% of the state, an area roughly the size of Italy. Of this, 22% is designated as national park. Three areas have UNESCO World Heritage status: Ningaloo Coast 2011, Purnululu National Park 2003 and Shark Bay Marine Park 1991. The creation of WA's 100th national park in 2013 - Murujuga National Park on the Pilbara coast, which is the first national park to be created on freehold land owned by an Aboriginal Corporation which has been leased back to the State and jointly managed by the traditional owner groups (employed as Park Rangers) and Parks & Wildlife (Department of Parks and Wildlife, 2016b; Figure 4.1).

Figure 4.1: Yawuru Rangers with researcher at Yawuru Nagulagun Roebuck Bay Marine Park.

Indigenous tourism and the impact of land rights

As noted by Weaver (2008), Indigenous tourism is a form of ecotourism due to the obvious links between the natural environment and Indigenous cultures. Indigenous tourism potentially enables visitors to experience and interact with authentic tourism products through traditional owner-led tours, bush-tucker experiences and exposure to Indigenous culture and her-itage. As such, the development of Indigenous tourism is inextricably tied to 'Caring for Country' as Indigenous people have a spiritual and cultural connection to the land, having inhabited Australia for at least 60,000 years (Rasmussen et al., 2011), and consequently many of the tourism offerings are either nature-based or culturally based with an emphasis on sustainability.

However, the historical legacy of land ownership in Australia has impacted greatly on what can be achieved in land access and how land is managed and used for tourism purposes. For this reason, it can be argued that Indigenous tourism is still in its infancy (Shibish, 2015). To further understand why this is so, the historical legacy of land rights needs to be explained.

The Aboriginal population of WA is around 88,000 representing 3.7% of the state's total population of 2.6 million (Australian Bureau of Statistics, 2011). The Indigenous population, which includes mainland Aboriginals and Torres Strait Islanders, have both a cultural and spiritual connection to the land and sea upon which they sustained themselves.

WA's Aboriginal population have struggled to regain their entitlement to their land, as is true for most parts of Australia. Historically, Indigenous people were dispossessed from the land during the period of early settle-ment, as land became the property of government or private landholders – a situation in which Indigenous people have and are continuing to seek redress through native title claims. As government agencies were given responsibility for conserving and protecting the native fauna and flora and creating conservation reserves, this process of creating protected areas such as national parks, largely extinguished native title claims. A watershed moment was the Mabo High Court decision in 1992 when it was acknowl-edged that the British Crown's use of the doctrine of *terra nullius* ('land belonging to no-one') had allowed it to gain absolute sovereignty and to dispossess Indigenous Australians (Lopez, 2012). Following this, the *Native Title Act 1993* (NTA) provided the legal framework to recognise Indigenous peoples' interest and rights in areas of land due to their customs and cul-tural and traditional values (Ouliaris, 2010). The NTA also recognises that Indigenous people were disadvantaged by the dispossession of their land (Storey, 2012).

Native title can now be determined through the jurisdiction of the Federal Court of Australia by way of negotiation or litigation. It allows payment of compensation to the native title holders or for native title to be transferred by traditional law or custom. Native title may include occupation, rights of possession, use and enjoyment of traditional country, the right to access an area of land or the right to participate in decisions concerning how other people use the land and waters. It may exist along with other rights called co-existence (Federal Court of Australia, 2015). Since the amendment to the NTA in 1998, Indigenous Land Use Agreements (ILUA) have been enabled to allow Aboriginal people to negotiate practical and flexible arrangements about the use and management of land and waters to suit their particular circumstances, regardless of whether native title has, or has not yet, been determined.

Land dispossession, massacres, slavery, use of indentured workers, imprisonment and harsh government policies relating to the removal of mixed race children from families over several generations caused enormous upheaval and dislocation of Aboriginal societies. The legacy of these actions and policies are still evident today. Rates of literacy and numeracy in Indigenous people are far lower than the average population (Ferrari, 2013). Indigenous people have poorer health, shorter life expectancy, higher rates of infant mortality and rates of incarceration are far higher (Australians Together, 2014).

Government strategies for Indigenous tourism and addressing visitor perceptions

The national and several state tourism strategies make reference to the importance of preserving, protecting and honouring Indigenous culture using tourism development as a vehicle. Such strategies recognise the need to involve and provide opportunities for Aboriginal people to increase self-determination, self-management and economic self-sufficiency through the development and implementation of ecotourism programs (Tourism Australia, 2016a). Most emphasis so far has been placed on the international visitor market although research on the domestic market profiles undertaken by Tourism Research Australia (2010) noted that in fact there is a demand for interaction with Indigenous tourism by the domestic market but that it is often overlooked. In 2009, three million visitors participated in an Indigenous tourism activity in Australia and 71% of these were domestic overnight visitors spending $3 billion whilst travelling in Australia. For both markets, whilst participating in Indigenous tourism activities is important, it is not regarded as a primary motivator or a 'must see' attraction, but rather a desirable component of the total holiday (Tourism Research Australia, 2010). Furthermore, research has shown that there are some issues with perception by domestic tourists, who may view the Indigenous product to be contrived, lacking authenticity and developed solely for the international market. Similarly, there appears to be a lack of understanding by domestic tourists as to the complexity of what constitutes an Aboriginal experience, and scepticism for products claiming to offer Aboriginal cultural experiences (Tourism Research Australia, 2010). Consequently, research suggests that the Indigenous tourism product is relatively underdeveloped with a mismatch between experiences sought and product offered (Tourism Research Australia, 2010).

In the State Government Strategy for Tourism in Western Australia 2020, Aboriginal tourism was recognised as one of the seven strategic pillars for tourism growth in WA (Tourism Western Australia, 2012) with the vision to "provide every visitor with the opportunity to have an Aboriginal tourism experience" (p.7). TWA reports that research conducted in 2010 indicates that Aboriginal tourism experiences are highly sought after with survey statistics recording that 66% of all visitors and 83% of international visitors are seeking to participate in Aboriginal tourism activities in WA.

Another key player in the development of Aboriginal tourism in WA is the Western Australian Indigenous Tourism Operators Council (WAITOC), a non-profit organisation representing the Aboriginal tourism industry. It is the only state-based Indigenous tourism body in Australia. WAITOC assists the development of existing and emerging Aboriginal tourism operators and also develops collaborative and joint venture opportunities within Aboriginal and non-Aboriginal tourism. The Aboriginal Tourism Strategy 'Making a Difference' recognises the need to assist Aboriginal tourism businesses in the areas of business development; planning; marketing; access to funding and support, as well as employment and training. This is necessary in order for successful integration into mainstream tourism and allowing for integration of Aboriginal culture into tourism events and activities (Western Australian Indigenous Tourism Operators Council & Tourism Western Australia, 2011). Previous strategies resulted in achievements in quality (49 Aboriginal businesses gaining formal accreditation for quality) and employment and training (38 Aboriginal people were placed in traineeships and eight in cadetships) in the tourism and hospitality industry, whilst 28 visitor centres employed 30 Indigenous trainees (Tourism Western Australia, 2006).

As of 2014, WAITOC listed 119 Aboriginal tourism operator members who offer either mainstream or Aboriginal cultural tourism experiences - an increase from 65 operators in 2006 (Western Australia Indigenous Tourism Operators Council, 2014), ten of which have been selected by Tourism Australia (TA) as Indigenous Tourism Champions (see Table 4.1) (Tourism Australia, 2016b). Tourism Champions are a selection of Indigenous 'export ready' businesses offering experiences delivered by Aboriginal people, as nominated by their State and Territory tourism organisations. It is TA's aim to build a reputation amongst Indigenous tourism operators of reliability and quality in service delivery by meeting stringent criteria, so that the businesses being promoted meet the needs and expectations of tourists.

Tourism operator name	Region
Barradict Sport Fishing Charters	Kimberley, North-West
Brian Lee Hunters Creek Tagalong Tours	Kimberley, North-West
Bundy's Cultural Tours	Kimberley, North-West
Kimberley Wild Expeditions	Kimberley, North-West
Kooljaman at Cape Leveque	Kimberley, North-West
Koomal Dreaming	Margaret River, South-West
Shark Bay Coastal Tours	Shark Bay, Coral Coast
Uptuyu Aboriginal Adventures	Kimberley, North West
Urban Indigenous Culture	Perth
Wula Guda Nyinda Eco Adventures	Shark Bay, Coral Coast

Table 4.1: Indigenous tourism champions in Western Australia (Tourism Australia, 2016b)

In partnership with WAITOC, the State government's $4.6 million Aboriginal Tourism Development Plan will deliver business development training and marketing over three years to 2018, to support a sustainable Aboriginal tourism sector (Commonwealth Government of Western Australia, 2016). In its budget for 2007-8, the Federal government also allocated $3.8 million over four years from 2007 onwards to its Business Ready Program for Indigenous Tourism (BRPIT) through AusIndustry. This program is designed to provide existing and newly created Indigenous Tourism businesses with business skills and knowledge through mentoring schemes (Commonwealth Government, 2007).

Indigenous tourism in national parks

Indigenous tourism and protected areas are inextricably linked by their legacy of land tenure, and thus many of the Indigenous tourism opportunities remain within national parks or have protected area status. Research on Indigenous people, and their role in national parks generally, is relatively new (Shibish, 2015). In fact, the empowerment of Indigenous peoples as stakeholders in the management of their land and its development for sustainable tourism practices and mutual benefit is a recent development and there are few case studies which can illustrate this. However, even before the legislative framework was already in place, Parks & Wildlife and its predecessors were already working with Aboriginal traditional owners on a variety of projects on conservation lands, strengthening relationships and creating more opportunities for Aboriginal involvement. For example, in the 1990s two Aboriginal Park Councils were created at Purnululu National Park and Karijini National Park; an Aboriginal ranger program was initiated and Aboriginal ecotourism ventures were supported (C. Ingram, personal communication, 6 January 2014). As of 2012, changes in the CALM Act allowed Parks & Wildlife to enter into formal joint management arrangements with traditional owners.

Joint management of protected areas and national parks

JM is the result of the decentralisation of power from a top-down, government led, authoritarian style of management of land and assets to a more liberal, inclusive, bottom-up, participatory approach to the management of protected areas, in which all parties benefit from shared information, values and experiences. JM has been defined as:

> "A partnership by which two or more relevant social actors collectively negotiate, agree upon, guarantee and implement fair share of management functions, benefits and responsibilities for a particular territory, area or set of natural resources." (Borrini-Feyerabend et al., 2004:69).

Although JM is still in its infancy, Ross et al. (2009) argue that Australia is a world leader in the use of JM in protected areas involving Indigenous people. Such negotiations resulted in the creation of JM arrangements between Aboriginals and government for Kakadu National Park and Uluru-Kata Tjuta National Park and this management model (freehold and lease back to Government) has been sought after by other Aboriginal groups.

In WA, key drivers that facilitated the shift from top-down management of parks to JM are illustrated in Figure 4.2. The factors which enabled this to happen included Aboriginal groups expressing a strong desire to be involved in the management of their traditional lands; native title claims; changes in attitudes by park staff following many years of working with Aboriginal people and the recognition of the value they could bring to land management; the development of ILUAs which required a more collaborative approach; and changes to the CALM Act including the objective of managing the land for the culture and heritage of Aboriginal people, thereby recognising the significance of Indigenous cultural heritage in environmental management (Shibish, 2015).

Figure 4.2: Drivers of JM in WA (Parks & Wildlife)

Tourism in the Kimberley Region, WA

Of the 29.5 million visitors to WA, 6% visited the tourism region known as Australia's North West (Tourism Western Australia, 2016) in which this case study is situated (Figure 4.3). This tourism region covers over one million square kilometres or four times the size of the United Kingdom (Australia's North-West, 2016). The area is known for its natural beauty, ancient landscapes, geological formations, unexplored islands and reefs, as well as the flora and fauna endemic to this region.

The region is marketed under three sub-regions: Broome, The Pilbara and The Kimberley. The Kimberley covers an area of 424,500km² which is approximately twice the size of the Australian State of Victoria and attracts around 300,000 visitors each year (Government of Western Australia, 2011). The region has a varied climate from high rainfall tropics to semi-arid deserts. The region contains 22 Aboriginal language groups, which account for nearly half the population of the Kimberley region which totals 34,794.

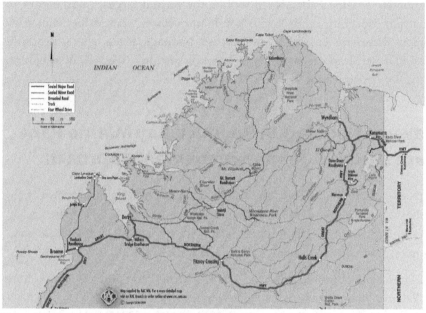

Figure 4.3: Map of the Kimberley Region (RAC, 2015)

Land use consists of pastoral, mining and other leases (58%), unallocated Crown Land (25%), Aboriginal reserves (12%) and national parks and conservation reserves (5%). This is changing rapidly with native title claims being settled. Agriculture, resource extraction and tourism all make significant contributions to the state's economy. The Kimberley is internationally known for its natural landscapes and is named as one of Australia's 15 National Biodiversity Hotspots (Commonwealth Government of Australia, 2016) due to the terrestrial and marine ecosystems, making it a focus of conservation initiatives by the state government. The Kimberley region contains two sites made available for development through the state's Naturebank program. These are located at Purnululu and Windjana Gorge national parks (Tourism Western Australia, 2011).

In 2011, the WA Government released the Kimberley Science and Conservation Strategy (KSCS) and committed $63 million over 4 years for the purposes of protecting and conserving the State's unique natural and cultural values, and to promote nature-based tourism opportunities in regional WA (Government of Western Australia, 2011). Further indication of the government's support for tourism development was revealed in the 2016-17 State budget. The WA government has committed, through its Royalties for Regions program, $22 million for establishing and managing new Kimberley national and marine parks, including the proposed Great Kimberley Marine Park, which will be the second largest marine park in Australia, covering more than 3.5 million hectares. Within the Kimberley region there are currently one World Heritage listed site (Purnululu National Park) and two National Heritage listings (West Kimberley and Dampier Archipelago).

Yawuru Nagulagun Roebuck Bay Marine Park case study: A joint management approach

This case study highlights how the instigation and establishment of a JM initiative has allowed for differing needs to be met whilst fostering an ecotourism and conservation perspective for the benefit of the wider community, the traditional owners (Yawuru) and visitors alike.

The town of Broome is located 2,240 km from Perth and sits on the shore of Yawuru Nagulagun Roebuck Bay (Figure 4.4). Broome is the coastal gateway city to the Kimberley (Australia's North-West, 2016) and it has had a long history of identity as a popular tourism destination. However, recently Broome's tourism visitation has been showing signs of decline (ABC News 2013a). As a result, a Broome Tourism Strategy was launched by TWA to develop a sustainable tourism future for Broome. One important aspect of the strategy was to progress the development of Yawuru Nagulagun Roebuck Bay Marine Park, which was a long-standing proposal. Prior to the native title agreement, and as part of the KSCS the WA government planned to create four new marine parks in the Kimberley including Yawuru Nagulagun Roebuck Bay Marine Park. Yawuru Nagulagun Roebuck Bay was declared a Ramsar Convention wetland of international significance as early as 1990 and was also listed on the National Heritage Register in 2011 due to the high biodiversity it supports (Yawuru Nagulagun Roebuck Bay Working Group, 2012) such as the intertidal mudflats attracting migratory shorebirds as well as providing a home for many species of invertebrates, crustaceans and fish. There are also mangrove forests, which attract mud crabs, prawns, fish and marine conservation species such as turtles, sawfish, snub nose dolphins and dugong, as well as migratory humpback whales.

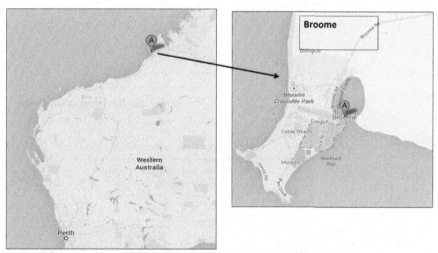

Figure 4.4: Location of Broome, Western Australia (Google Maps, 2015)

The traditional owners of the Broome area are the Yawuru people. During colonization in the 1860s, the Yawuru were denied access to their land, denied equal rights and were treated disrespectfully (Yawuru RNTBC, 2014). Since NTA came into being, claims have been made to regain lands but it has not been a straightforward process as claimants have to be able to provide evidence of a continued connection with their land and/or waters – a process which took 12 years through the courts and two years in appeal court. The Yawuru native title claim included the township of Broome. Native title was granted over large sections in and around the Broome town site. An ILUA and Area Agreements were set up and finalised in 2010 (Department of Premier and Cabinet, 2015).

These agreements cover approximately 5,300 square kilometres of land in and around Broome, resolving heritage and land development issues. Benefits of $56 million were provided to the Yawuru for housing; to establishing a conservation estate; for capacity building; for preservation of cultural heritage; and for economic development. A Joint Management Agreement was initiated in 2010 enabling the Yawuru to become directly involved in the creation and management of Yawuru Nagulagun Roebuck Bay Marine Park (Figure 4.5).

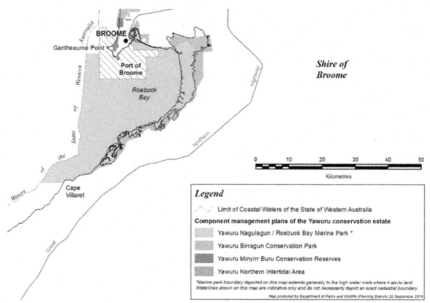

Figure 4.5: Yawuru Nagulagun Roebuck Bay Marine Park (Department of Parks and Wildlife, 2016c).

As part of the terms of the ILUA, a Yawuru Park Council (YPC) was established (a formal body consisting of the Shire of Broome, Yawuru and Parks & Wildlife). The YPC is responsible for the management of the jointly managed lands and waters and is tasked with undertaking the drafting of park management plans and is the decision making group for the area under Native Title. The YPC are responsible for:

- the conservation and protection of the environment and wildlife therein;

- the preservation of Aboriginal heritage and culture directly through the land and sea for its cultural and spiritual significance to the Yawuru people;

- sustainable development as a vehicle to creating jobs, injecting wealth into the local economy and providing social wellbeing benefits for the community as a whole.

Joint management in practice: Challenges and opportunities

JM has not been without its challenges, as members of the YPC have discovered. For example, westerners tend to interpret land and sea areas as separate and therefore have structured their management separately by appropriate agencies. Yawuru's view is tenure blind, believing the land and sea need to be managed holistically, with a single management plan over all the marine, intertidal and land areas (Shibish, 2015).

Further, bureaucratic difficulties arise when Shire Council members, whose responsibility lies with representing all of Broome's population, are unable to make decisions as members of the YPC without first taking all matters back to the Shire for approval. This has caused lengthy delays in the planning and decision-making process. Nevertheless, interviews conducted with all three stakeholders (Yawuru, Parks & Wildlife and the Shire), as part of this case study, revealed that all agreed tourism development is high on the list of development priorities (Shibish, 2015).

One such priority tourism project was the redevelopment of the adjacent Minyirr Park near Cable Beach, which has numerous walk trails through bushland and dunes, and is of spiritual significance to the Yawuru as their birthplace. A second tourism project was the development of a jetty-to-jetty interpretive walk trail (Shibish, 2015). While many tourism development opportunities exist, tourism has been unavoidably delayed until the creation of the marine park management plan has been finalised and put into effect. JM partners have also held different views on what kinds of tourism development would be appropriate for the region. However all recognised the need for tourism development to provide an economy to support other JM projects (Shibish, 2015).

Another challenge for the YPC has involved partners trying to find ways to satisfy their own objectives, which were often in conflict with others, and having ulterior agendas. Initial teething problems involved gaining trust, understanding other's perspectives and creating mutually beneficial outcomes. Government and Shire planning approval processes also created delays and restrictions in what could be achieved easily. Cultural differences, and the management and administrative inexperience of some representatives, prior prejudices and the lack of shared vision created further challenges (Shibish, 2015).

Previous research has shown that parts of the tourism industry have not yet adapted to the reality of Aboriginal land ownership arising from native title settlements, and there have been issues whereby tourists and tour operators have been accessing Aboriginal controlled country without the permission of traditional owners, creating management issues (Scherrer & Doohan, 2013); (Smith et al., 2009); (Wunambal Gaambera Aboriginal, 2000).

However, opportunities through the creation of JM do exist. These include capacity building for partners, improving cross-cultural understanding and appreciation, better conservation outcomes through shared knowledge, access to conservation and land management legislation to assist in managing visitors and tour operators on Yawuru conservation estate and revenue sharing. Additionally JM allows structures to exist which enable access to external funding not available to individuals or government agencies (Shibish, 2015).

Conclusions

It can be argued that tourism plays a role in incentivising stakeholder participation in conservation, whilst providing tangible outcomes such as the opportunity for social, economic, ecological and cultural benefits to be harnessed. The development and marketing of Indigenous tourism attractions and experiences presents some unique challenges, unknown to other forms of tourism. These relate to the legacy of land ownership, claims to native title, styles of management, differences in approaches to ongoing day-to-day site operations, language and education issues and knowledge transfer methods. Additionally sensitivity, appreciation and awareness of cultural differences in respect of differing worldviews in what 'country' means to Indigenous people and their spiritual connection to their ancestry, and also how problems are approached and dealt with tribally. These issues all have a bearing on the success of Indigenous tourism operations and increase the propensity for failure if not taken into account. This case study illustrates how the JM approach towards developing and managing a tourism asset can offer a high degree of success if the partners share a common goal, and the dynamics of working together focus on attaining mutual benefits, irrespective of their own agendas.

There is much to be gained from the successful development and operation of Indigenous tourism products, not least for the Aboriginal community as it provides them with the capacity to manage and care for country in keeping with their traditions, maintaining their connection to their spiritual home, retaining cultural values whilst potentially leveraging economic and social benefits particularly employment for the Aboriginal community. This is crucial in sparsely populated, remote areas where employment options are limited. For the broader community it provides a deeper understanding of the Indigenous cultural heritage of the region in which they live, fosters better cross-cultural relations, broadening knowledge of customs, increases awareness of the value of the natural environment and flora and fauna whilst preserving and maintaining the land and seascape sustainably for future generations. For the visitor they have the opportunity to experience and learn something about Australia's unique cultural heritage, landscape and wildlife, which cannot be experienced anywhere else in the world. Partnering with other stakeholders through the JM framework assists Indigenous people to build capacity which enables them to provide some level of authenticity and offer a richer more rewarding tourism experience, satisfying the visitor need to gain a deeper understanding of what makes Australia unique as a tourism destination.

Acknowledgements

The lead author wishes to acknowledge support from the Australian Commonwealth Government's Research Training Scheme; Edith Cowan University Postgraduate Research Scholarship; Graduate Women WA; the WA's Department of Parks & Wildlife's Nature-based Recreation and Tourism Award; and Zonta International's Jane M. Klausman Scholarship. The authors also acknowledge the contribution of Sharon Lamb, Research Assistant, Edith Cowan University, to this chapter.

References

Adams, M. (2002). National Parks as Common Pool Resources: Scale, Equity and Community. http://www.researchgate.net/ publications/42761667_National_Parks_as_Common_Pool_Resources_ Scale_Equity_and_Community

Australia's North-West (2016). About the North-West. http://www. australiasnorthwest.com/About_the_North_West

Australian Bureau of Statistics (2007). Yearbook. http://www.abs.gov.au/ ausstats/abs@.nsf/7d12b0f6763c78caca257061001cc588/DA1C7F83FF19B 91DCA257235008133DC?opendocument

Australian Bureau of Statistics (2011). Estimates of Aboriginal and Torres Strait Islander Australians, June 2011. http://www.abs.gov.au/ausstats/ abs@.nsf/mf/3238.0.55.001

Australians Together (2016). The Gap: Indigenous Disadvantage in Australia. http://www.australianstogether.org.au/stories/detail/ the-gap-indigenous-disadvantage-in-australia

Borrini-Feyerabend, G., Pimbert, M., Farvar, M.T., Kothari,A. & Renard,Y. (2004). *Sharing Power : Learning by doing in co-management of natural resources throughout the world*. Cenesta, Tehran: IIED and IUCN/CEESP/CMWG.

Butler, R. & Boyd, S.W. (2000). *Tourism and National Parks: Issues and implications*. Chichester: Wiley.

Commonwealth Government (2007). Trade, Business, Tourism and Investment: Initiatives. http://www.budget.gov.au/2007-08/ministerial/html/dotars-30.htm

Commonwealth Government of Australia (2016). Australia's 15 National Biodiversity Hotspots. https://www.environment.gov.au/biodiversity/conservation/hotspots/national-biodiversity-hotspots

Commonwealth Government of Western Australia (2016). 2016-17 Budget: Broadening the State's economy through tourism. http://www.static.ourstatebudget.wa.gov.au/16-17/factsheets/tourism.pdf?

Department of Parks and Wildlife (2014a). Annual Report. Retrieved from http://www.dpaw.wa.gov.au/about-us/annual-report-and-yearbook

Department of Parks and Wildlife (2014b). Naturebank Perth, Australia: http://parks.dpaw.wa.gov.au/for-business/naturebank

Department of Parks and Wildlife (2016a). About Us. https://www.dpaw.wa.gov.au/about-us

Department of Parks and Wildlife (2016b). Murujuga National Park. https://parks.dpaw.wa.gov.au/park/murujuga

Department of Parks and Wildlife (2016c). Yawuru Nagulagun / Roebuck Bay Marine Park: Joint management plan 86. https://www.dpaw.wa.gov.au/images/documents/parks/management-plans/ynrbmp_mangement_plan_web.pdf

Department of Premier and Cabinet (2015). Yawuru Agreements. http://www.dcp.wa.gov.au/lantu/Agreements/YawuruAgreements/Pages/Default.aspx. Perth,Australia:DCP.

Federal Court of Australia (2015). Native Title. http://www.fedcourt.gov.au/law-and-practice/national-practice-areas/native-title

Fennell, D.A. & Weaver, D. (2005). The ecotourisum concept and tourism-conservation symbiosis. *Journal of Sustainable Tourism*, **13** (4), 373-390. doi: 10.1080/09669580508668563

Fennell, D.A. (2014) *Ecotourism*, 4th edn, Oxford: Routledge.

Ferrari, J. (2013). Lift in Indigenous literacy. Weekend Australian. http://ezproxy.ecu.edu.au/login?url=http://search.proquest.com/docview/1467657757?accountid=10675.

Government of Western Australia (2011). Kimberley Science and Conservation Strategy. https://www.dpaw.wa.gov.au/images/documents/conservation-management/kimberley/kimberley_science_conservation_strategy.pdf

Ingram, C. (2007). Certification in protected areas: A Western Australian case study. In B. Crabtree (Ed.), *Quality Assurances and Certification in Ecotourism* (pp. 266-298). Oxford: CAB International.

Lopez, D. (2012). Mabo: A fundamental truth and a basis for justice. *Indigenous Law Bulletin*, 8(2), 3-4.

Newsome, D., Moore, S.A. & Dowling, R.K. (2013) *Natural Area Tourism: Ecology, impacts, and management*, 2nd edn, Bristol: Channel View Publications.

Ouliaris, J. (2010). *The Legal Maze*, 7th edn,. South Yarra, Victoria: Macmillan Education Australia.

Rasmussen, M., Guo, X., Wang, Y., Lohmueller, K. E., Rasmussen, S., Albrechtsen, A. & Willerslev, E. (2011). An Aboriginal Australian genome reveals separate human dispersals into Asia. *Science*, **334** (6052), 94-98. doi: 10.1126/science.1211177

Ross, H., Grant, C., Robinson, C.J., Izurieta, A., Smyth, D., & Rist, P. (2009). Co-management and Indigenous protected areas in Australia: Achievements and ways forward. *Australasian Journal of Environmental Management*, **16** (4), 242-252. doi: 10.1080/14486563.2009.10648783

Scherrer, P., & Doohan, K. (2013). It's not about believing: Exploring the transformative potential of cultural acknowledgement in an Indigenous tourism context, *Asia Pacific Viewpoint*, **54**, 158-170. doi: 10.1111/apv.12016.

Shibish, L.-A. (2015). *The evolution of Joint Management in Western Australia Parks and the Indigenous Tourism Nexus*, Perth: Edith Cowan University.

Smith, A. J., Scherrer, P. & Dowling, R.K. (2009). Impacts on Aboriginal spirituality and culture from tourism in the coastal waterways of the Kimberley region, North West Australia, *Journal of Ecotourism*, 8(2), 82-98

Storey, M. (2012). 20 years after Mabo v Commonwealth, *Alternative Law Journal*, **37** (3), 190-191. Strickland-Munro, J. & Moore, S. (2013). Indigenous involvement and benefits from tourism in protected areas: A study of Purnululu National Park and Warmun Community, Australia, *Journal of Sustainable Tourism*, **21**(1), 26-41. doi: 10.1080/09669582.2012.680466

Tourism Australia (2016a). Aboriginal Tourism. http://www.tourism.australia.com/aboriginal.aspx

Tourism Australia (2016b). Indigenous Tourism Champions. http://www.tourism.australia.com/programs/indigenous-tourism-champion-program.aspx

Tourism Australia (2016c). Understanding Tourism Australia's International Consumer. http://www.tourism.australia.com/documents/Statistics/TASI10578_Aggregate_CDP_Fact_Sheet_Web.pdf

Tourism Research Australia (2010). *Indigenous Tourism in Australia: Profiling the domestic market.* Canberra: Tourism Research Australia.

Tourism Research Australia (2015). *State of the Industry 2015.* Canberra: Tourism Research Australia.

Tourism Western Australia (2006). *Listening, looking, learning: An Aboriginal tourism strategy for Western Australia, 2006-2010.* Perth: Tourism Western Australia.

Tourism Western Australia (2011). *Naturebank: Exceptional ecotourism opportunities in Western Australia'.* Perth: Tourism Western Australia & Department of Environment and Conservation.

Tourism Western Australia (2012). *State Government Strategy for Tourism in Western Australia 2020.* Perth: The Government of Western Australia.

Tourism Western Australia (2016). *Fast Facts Year Ending June 2016.* Perth: The Government of Western Australia.

WATC (1997). *Nature Based Tourism Strategy for Western Australia.* Perth: Western Australian Tourism Commission.

Weaver, D. (2008). *Ecotourism,* 2nd edn, Milton, Qld: John Wiley & Sons.

Western Australia Indigenous Tourism Operators Council (2014). Exciting times for Aboriginal tourism in WA. www.waitoc.com/announcements/waitoc-media-release-november-2014-adoption-of-a-new-constitution

Western Australian Indigenous Tourism Operators Council, & Tourism Western Australia. (2011) *Making a difference: Aboriginal tourism strategy for Western Australia 2011-2015.* Perth: WAITOC & TWA.

Wunambal Gaambera Aboriginal Corporation (2000). *Land of Wandjina and Wunggurr: Ngauwudu management plan Wunambal people: Mitchell Plateau north-west Australia.* Kalumburu, WA: Wunambal Gaambera Aboriginal, Corporation.

Yawuru Nagulagun Roebuck Bay Working Group, (2012). Roebuck Bay Working Group. http://www.roebuckbay.org.au

Yawuru RNTBC (2014). *2014 Annual Report: Strengthening governance, strengthening country and culture, strengthening community.* http://www.yawuru.com/wp-content/uploads/2014/12/YAWURU-ANNUAL-REPORT-2014-FINAL-ID-105622.pdf

5 First Things First: The foundations of organisational development

Gabrielle Russell-Mundine

Introduction

Tourism has long been promoted as a powerful and dynamic industry which can help alleviate poverty, enhance cultural pride, reduce economic vulnerability through diversification, and which also supports the development of skills and entrepreneurial capacity (WTO, 2002). In Australia, Indigenous tourism is seen to be a market segment that can capitalise on these particular characteristics of tourism and which could lead to economic development as a pathway to greater independence, increased employment opportunities and less reliance on Government transfers. Indigenous tourism is not a new concept (Altman, 1993; Altman, 2001; Whitford et al., 2001), however it gained more impetus in the early 1990s when Aboriginal economic development was identified as a key recommendation arising from the 1991 *Royal Commission into Aboriginal Deaths in Custody* (Royal Commission into Aboriginal Deaths in Custody, 1991; Birdsall-Jones et al., 2007) with tourism promoted as a particularly viable option for Indigenous communities. Despite the promise of Indigenous tourism and expectations that the market would grow, there has been a small but steady decline since 2005 to 13% of international visitors in 2010, which is the last year that statistics were collected for this market (Ruhanen et al., 2015).

Developing Indigenous tourism product can be difficult and there is limited research that engages with this market segment from Indigenous perspectives. The majority of recent research on Indigenous tourism has focused on integrating sustainability in areas such as branding (i.e. for festivals and events), visitor impacts and satisfaction, research methods, heritage management, and policy and empowerment (Whitford and Ruhanen, 2016). Whitford and Ruhanen (2016:1091) state that "it is imperative that academic researchers gain a more comprehensive understanding of Indigenous tourism from the perspective of Indigenous stakeholders."

This chapter seeks to address this paucity of research from the perspective of Indigenous stakeholders and reports on results of a study undertaken with the Jubal Aboriginal Corporation (Jubal), in Northern NSW. The aim of the study was to gain clearer insights into the needs of Aboriginal communities in developing a tourism business and what capabilities are required to develop a sustainable tourism business. Importantly, the study focuses on the Bundjalung Nation of Northern NSW, which is a region that is not well represented in existing research about Indigenous tourism development.

At the commencement of the study Jubal was in the process of identifying options for development. Tourism was one viable development option identified. However, as this study shows, such an aspiration was premature and would have failed if Jubal had not first attended to its organisational development. This study highlights the difficulties and lack of practical support available to Indigenous organisations to develop viable tourism businesses. Schaper et al. (2007 cited in Higgins-Desbiolles, 2014) identify the importance of studying failure to identify barriers to successful business venture formation, growth and management. The Jubal story is not a story about failure; rather it is one that shows a strong belief in the community's sovereign rights to make development decisions that suit their aspirations and where they are in the process. Jubal decided that tourism was not the right pathway to development for them at the time. At a very practical level, their experience highlights barriers to the successful development of business ventures and provides insight into the factors necessary for success.

Barriers to development

Indigenous tourism businesses often fail for the same reasons that non-Indigenous ones fail (Pitcher et al., 1999). These can include inadequate market research, absence of a detailed business plan, inadequate funding, lack of business advisory support, inexperienced managers and poor marketing skills (Bell, cited in Pitcher et al., 1999, Birdsall-Jones et al., 2007).

However, nascent Indigenous businesses can also encounter barriers specific to their context as shown in Table 5.1.

Table 5.1: Barriers to tourism enterprise development in Indigenous communities

Economic barriers

- Difficulty accessing required capital;
- Community ownership requires wide distribution of profits;
- Financial success can lead to a reduction in program support resulting in negative net benefit;
- Lack of control in joint ventures;
- Lack of access to land tenure.

Resource barriers

- Lack of adequate managers;
- Lack of access to appropriate legal advice;
- Lack of skills and training in tourism jobs;
- Insufficient infrastructure;
- Lack of interest in interactions with tourists;
- Individuals choosing not to work;
- Community conflict and lack of understanding about its causes.

Industry barriers

- High expectations of the mainstream industry regarding professional delivery of product;
- Conflict between the tourism industry's reliance on tight itineraries and the observance of cultural and social protocols;
- Conflict between industry requirements for volume products and the tendency of Indigenous enterprises to accommodate small numbers for limited periods;
- Concern about pricing and whether it is possible to be competitive and viable;
- Disconnect between Aboriginal culture and the economic and political structures involved in tourism;
- Remoteness and cost of travel;
- Lack of networks between Indigenous and mainstream tourism businesses.

Cultural barriers

- Concern that in the process of customising Indigenous culture to attract and entertain tourists that culture may be distorted, exploited and undermined;
- Reduced lack of access to land utilised by tourists.

Source: Altman, 1983, 1989; Birdsall-Jones et al., 2007; Commonwealth, 2008; Craik, 2001; Rooke, 1993.

One of the key barriers for Indigenous entrepreneurs, identified over decades, is difficulty accessing capital and adequate finance and land tenure (SCRGSP, 2007, Altman, 1993, Commonwealth, 2008). This situation arises primarily because significant amounts of Aboriginal owned land is held by inalienable and communal title, a legacy of colonisation which has resulted in the inability of communities to use property to raise capital (Altman, 1993; Commonwealth, 2008). Also, many communities are in a situation where the productive market in their location is relatively small, resulting in a lack of viable enterprises as well as a disproportionately high level of government influence; and communities are often dependent on government finance to start projects, resulting in management structures that can be stifling to Indigenous enterprise development (Altman, 1993). Lack of financial literacy is a further barrier and is considered a key first step in developing Indigenous business; additionally, the Law Council of Australia considers that lack of access to appropriate legal advice and assistance creates substantial risks for Indigenous entrepreneurs (Commonwealth, 2008).

Kin and cultural obligations can also prove difficult to manage (Commonwealth, 2008; Altman, 1993). For example, the expectations and obligations of relationships can limit the ability of individuals to accumulate their own wealth and to invest in the business (Altman, 1993). Community ownership of the venture can also mean that the profit must be distributed widely and not used for reinvestment in the business (Altman, 1993). As well, a culture of using resources for community benefit can stifle the entrepreneurial drive for individual achievement and acquisition of wealth (Commonwealth, 2008). Another disincentive to business development can occur when the venture is financially successful and causes a reduction in Government program funding, resulting in a negative net benefit (Altman, 1989). In other words, the community may lose some Government funding as it is expected that the community will be able to use income generated by the business to pay for services or programs that had previously been provided for by Government funding.

To balance these barriers however, recent evidence shows that there is a growing interest in developing Indigenous business in general. This rising interest is attributed in part to demographic shifts. With 60% of the Aboriginal population under 25 there is an increased concern about providing a future for families that does not include the hardship experienced by previous generations (Commonwealth, 2008). There is also more interest from younger people who are able to balance community obligations with business demands (Commonwealth, 2008). Additionally, Indigenous people are creating new models of business. For example, creating businesses that only operate for six months of the year to enable the owners to have time for cultural practices (Commonwealth, 2008).

Methodology

This study was undertaken with Jubal by incorporating an Indigenist research paradigm with ethnographic and participatory action research (PAR) methodologies. Indigenous academics argue that by privileging Western methodologies, non-Indigenous researchers continue to deny others their culture, their voice and the ability to express their understanding of the world through Indigenous ways of knowing, being and doing (Martin, 2001). As a non-Indigenous researcher I was guided by principles espoused by Indigenous academics. In particular, my research approach was informed by Judy Atkinson (2001), Karen Martin (2001, 2002, 2008), Martin Nakata (2004 ; 2007), Lester Irabinna Rigney (1996, 1999) and Linda Tuhawei Smith (2003). As a result, the research was intentionally critical, recognising social, political and historical contexts. It aimed to privilege Aboriginal voices and the agenda was set by the community participants and focused on issues that were important to them. The methodology was centred on cultural protocols, social mores and behaviours of the Jubal community.

I undertook this research as a 'participating observer' (Bernard, 2006:347) and was immersed in particular aspects of Jubal's activities and day to day life, mostly in terms of financial administration, community planning and development activities. Much of the evidence was gathered through yarning, which in this context meant sitting together and listening to each other's stories. Through yarning we talked, analysed and delved into the issue at hand in order to examine our options for action. Through yarning I also learnt about the broader context and was able to position the enterprise and community development within an historical and social context of the people and place.

Evidence was also gathered at formal community meetings, board meetings and meetings with other agencies. In order to ensure that I was representing the participants correctly I regularly talked through my observations with them, for example, after meetings or while we were working on specific activities. Participants names are used in this paper as agreed to at the time of the research.

Jubal case study

The Jubal Aboriginal Corporation (Jubal) is located near the township of Tabulam in Northern NSW.

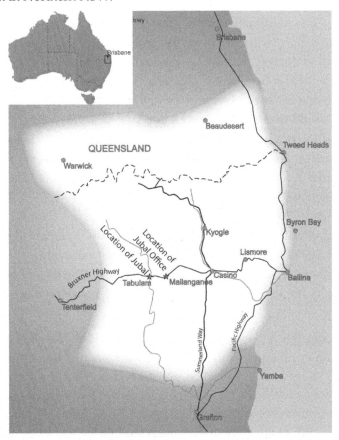

Figure 5.1: Locations of Jubal and Jubal Office

It grew out of a community desire:

> To look after all our members by ensuring a proud Bundjalung way of life as equal partners in Australia. To provide our members with good housing, health services, work, freedom and safety, and to work to protect our history, culture and our land for our children and all their future children (Collaborative Solutions, 2000: 12).

To achieve their goals the community recognised the need for a place:

> *Our ideal is to own a large property in the area that some of us can live on, where we can teach our young people about the land, and on which we can make a living. We have applied to the ILC to support us in this. If this land is bought by us then there will be considerable activity in respect to employment, cultural activity and enterprises that will be based on that land* (Collaborative Solutions, 2000:12).

The community successfully applied to the Indigenous Land Corporation (ILC) under their cultural acquisition program, to purchase a 525 hectare property five kilometres east of Tabulam and 50 kilometres west of Casino (LPM Qld Pty Ltd, 2006). The Jubal Aboriginal Corporation (Jubal) was registered in 1999 and ownership of the property was transferred from the ILC to Jubal in the same year. Jubal comes under the regulations of the Office of the Registrar of Indigenous Corporations (ORIC) which is governed by the Corporations (Aboriginal and Torres Strait Islander) Act 2006 (CATSI Act) (www.ORIC.gov.au). The property was named Jubal because the word 'jubal' is a Bundjalung word for witchetty grubs, which are in abundance on this property.

When Jubal took over the property there was no infrastructure on it. Over the years, the community built an ablutions block, a machinery shed and some individual cabins. Jubal successfully hosted events and groups, such as church gatherings, and education and immersion tours for schools, churches and university groups. Jubal had also developed events, such as the Annual Jubal Country Retreat where they hosted a large group of people for Church fellowship. In school holidays they held camps which catered for up to one hundred children. People who needed somewhere to stay were also welcomed. For example, a new jail was being built nearby and a need for a place for people to stay while visiting their relatives was identified:

> *Tourism was prompted by church groups so they had somewhere to stay. We knew that the jail was going up – rather than have families travel back to visit their kids every day. I know how they feel, they are broke and have no money and have to sleep out in parks. We felt for the people – at least they know there is somewhere to stay, they can't even afford to pay $50 a night*
>
> (Kevin Torrens, personal communication, 2006).

Jubal was considering how best to develop the markets they had already tapped into but which remained underdeveloped. They were also grappling with several issues which were integral to their ability to develop tourism ventures. First, the lack of infrastructure, such as adequate accommodation, meeting rooms and enough toilets and showers (existing ones were also used by resident community members) was impacting on the services that Jubal could provide. Second, there were financial barriers, particularly in regard to finding funding for the building of infrastructure such as accommodation. Third, there were problems with the administration systems, particularly accounting systems. Related to this was a need for training of community members in all facets of running a business.

Despite Jubal's intent and targeted support for tourism development from Government and local development organisations, it was apparent that Jubal's primary need was to attend to its own capacity to operate such a business. As Board member Norm Torrens indicated, to go ahead with tourism enterprises at this stage in Jubal's development would be a mistake:

> It's put on the back burner - we're not in a position to. If we got pushed ahead we'd be biting off more than we can chew. We are battling where we are at the moment. Eventually 5-6 years down the track. We would prefer drop ins and school groups. Big bus loads of people - no we are not interested

(personal communication, 2007).

Therefore, in response to the needs of the community at that time, this study became very much about the practical aspect of developing Jubal's foundations and its capacity for further community and economic development.

According to Fine et al. (2003:186), researchers often focus too much on the great stories and ignore the "mundane rituals of daily living". Brewer (2000) suggests identifying focal events for the people under study, and to develop comprehensive descriptions. This was the approach taken in this study. There were three focal events which formed the basis of the evidence. These areas of activity were: the process of entering into a Shared Responsibility Agreement (SRA); the process of developing a Property Management Plan (PMP); and the establishment of proper accounting practices.

Focal events

In 2004, the Federal Government announced its intention to dismantle the Aboriginal and Torres Strait Islander Commission (ATSIC) (Vanstone, 2005), through which it had administered funding since 1990. The intention was to deliver policy related services through the establishment of Indigenous Coordination Centres (ICC) (ATSIC, n.d.).

A key platform of the policy changes was the concept of mutual obligation, which according to the Federal Government meant that in return for the provision of funding and services, Indigenous communities would be expected to take responsibility to ensure the proper use of funds and implementation of programs (Vanstone, 2005). To enable this concept of mutual obligation, communities would be required to sign Shared Responsibility Agreements (SRAs) that were agreements between communities and the Federal Government. SRAs set out a series of responsibilities and mutual obligations in return for funding and were expected to result in the development of integrated and flexible programs and services for Indigenous peoples (Vanstone, 2005).

> *Signing an SRA required serious contemplation for Jubal. The Board members wanted Jubal to be independent and not reliant on Government 'hand-outs' but they also recognised that Government funding in the immediate future was necessary. We like to think we are on the way. We like to think we're almost in the position to be independent. We will continue along those lines. But we will have to go along for a while getting 'handouts'. If we do things right and hang in there we are strong enough to become independent* (Norm Torrens, 2007).

Considerations for Jubal centred on whether they would lose control over their community and whether the Government could understand the context it was operating in. However, the SRA would facilitate a better relationship with Government and would provide funding for short term programs for youth.

At the same time, the ILC who had funded the purchase of the Jubal property were requesting a Property Management Plan (PMP). The ILC had funded some remedial projects. These projects included installing fencing around the dam used for domestic water to prevent contamination from animals, and the construction of a new entrance to Jubal. However, further funding was contingent on a PMP to detail future needs and plans for the use of the Jubal property.

As well as the PMP and SRA, there was another component to the work Jubal needed to do, and this became the most challenging and time consuming issue during this study. Jubal was not in compliance with ORIC's regulations which require Aboriginal corporations to submit annual reports and audited financial statements to ORIC. Although Jubal had individually audited and acquitted every grant they had received, they were not aware that they also had to provide ORIC with annual audited financial statements. There was no suggestion that anything untoward had occurred, but Jubal had received no governance training and had only received limited help from a person who assisted the community, generally in a volunteer capacity, but who did not have appropriate accounting or regulatory knowledge or experience. The situation needed rectifying urgently as funding agencies would not fund an organisation that was deemed to be not compliant. In order to facilitate a solution I reconstructed five years of accounts from receipts and submitted them for auditing, at the same time establishing proper accounting systems. This process took some months as we had to find all the receipts and reconcile five years of accounts. However, the process became very drawn out when it came to auditing the accounts. There were a range of issues impacting on the audits, none of which related to the actual account statements (Russell-Mundine, 2010). It was hard to find an auditor in the area, and there were a range of assumptions made that meant the wrong items were taken to the auditor, who failed to communicate this. There was obfuscation by the auditor and lack of respect for the community as clients. The delays were for the most part outside of the control of Jubal and pointed to the difficulties that an Aboriginal organisation in a country area faces when it has limited access to appropriate professional accounting and auditing services (Russell-Mundine, 2010).

Discussion

> "Jubal's motivation for enterprise development was to gain more control over their lives and future. Owning land was always seen as integral to the community's future: Our ideal is to own a large property in the area that some of us can live on, where we can teach our young people about the land, and on which we can make a living ."
> (Collaborative Solutions, 2000).

The ILC program, together with the ongoing funding and support that the ILC provided, was the single most practical and valuable program with which Jubal engaged because it provided the most tangible and long-term benefits to Jubal. They had a physical place to hold events and develop future projects. The land provided intangible benefits such as pride, a connection to their culture and Spirit and a sense of ownership. Most importantly, owning the land allowed the community the opportunity to regain some of what had been lost through colonisation.

> [B]ut eventually when Jubal came along we reunited as one body and as one family… as a body we are making our own decisions for ourselves but in other places the Government tells us what to do
> (Norm Torrens, 2007).

However, as found elsewhere (Finlayson, 2007; Cornell & Kalt, 2004; Jorgensen & Taylor, 2000; Dodson & Smith, 2003), the property on its own was not enough to achieve self-determination. Although Jubal did develop a forestry agreement and gained some independent income from that, for the most part there was reliance on Government funding.

This created a crucial tension between Jubal's plans and Government funding priorities. It is necessary to foster autonomy and protect the organisation's vision as a core capability for development (Morgan, 2006b). Otherwise the funding priorities of an external agency can lead to a deprioritising of the community's own development agenda. To illustrate this point, Jubal obtained funding to buy tents for holiday camps and to run a women's project, which were both in alignment with the objectives of the SRA to address family violence. Obtaining funding for family violence related programs met Government funding priorities but neglected Jubal's priorities, such as building cabins, as identified in the PMP. The building of cabins was seen by Jubal as important to fulfil its community-identified objective to be a place of safety, thereby contributing to its own vision of violence mitigation programs. However, the building of cabins was not recognised by Government as a priority for violence mitigation programs. The Jubal experience highlights that there is a missing link between the development of plans which identify the community's aspirations and ways of developing solutions to the issues they face, and projects they are able to develop because of Government funding priorities. The Jubal experience also highlights a lack of linkages between Government departments, in this case between the Federal Government's SRA and the ILC's PMP. Clearer integration between agencies, policies and programs which lead to more flexible funding regimes would be beneficial to communities.

Systems and processes

Establishing effective human, financial and institutional procedures helps separate the management of the business from community management and helps protect board members from community politics and competing demands for the use of resources (Cornell & Kalt, 2004; Finlayson, 2007). Establishing formal decision making rules and procedures as well as instigating professional personnel and record keeping systems are essential to ensure an enterprise's success (Morgan, 2006b; Cornell & Kalt, 2004; Dodson & Smith, 2003; Hunt & Smith, 2007). While it is clear that not being compliant, and a lack of proper financial systems has a negative impact on an organisation's stakeholder perceptions and confidence (Cornell & Kalt, 2004; Jorgensen & Taylor, 2000; Hunt & Smith, 2007), what is perhaps less understood is the impact of not being compliant on the Board members. In Jubal's case the lack of compliance was identified as a stressful situation and caused problems for the Board amongst the wider membership who questioned the Board's actions. For example, the membership were worried that the delays to the audit were due to Board actions (Russell-Mundine, 2010).

The experience of Jubal and the failure of any agency to provide adequate advice or training supports Hunt and Smiths' (2007) findings that there is a greater need for long term, place based training and mentoring to ensure long term, sustainable outcomes. Trainers and mentors need to be hands on and involved in the day to day operations in order to really assist the community to develop sustainable systems and processes. Community access to skilled people, with whom they can build a relationship of trust and who are committed for a long period of time, is essential.

Governance

Successful organisations have culturally legitimate governance arrangements (Hunt & Smith, 2007). This was true of Jubal's governance structure. Jubal elected Board members from within each family group, thus ensuring that each family was represented at the Board level. This governance arrangement is particularly effective if conflict arises. Although conflict is addressed as a whole group, each Board member was responsible for dealing with conflict created by, or affecting, their own family. This system of governance was perceived by the Board members as being an appropriate way to manage the community.

There is nothing we would do differently - we deal with the conflict, we sit down and discuss it, we bring it up at general meeting, and in most cases the committee is supportive of each other. (Norm Torrens, 2007).

Jubal Board members found the language of ORIC requirements difficult to decipher, but their model of governance was congruent with ORIC regulations as well as being culturally legitimate. They have an appropriate and functional system of choosing their Board and have clear functions and responsibilities for those Board members. To ease Board concerns about whether they are compliant with ORIC it was necessary to identify the common ground between what the community see as a culturally appropriate form of governance and ORIC's requirements and governance practice in general.

Leadership

Successful organisations have strong leadership (Finlayson, 2007). Hunt and Smith (2007) identified certain characteristics of Indigenous leadership which they found were less about individual characteristics and more about a process and relationship negotiated between a group of people that focused on consensus building and which depended largely on networks and relationships. Leadership may be transmitted to particular people due to their knowledge, personal qualities, experience, and or social place within the community (Hunt & Smith, 2007).

Where leaders are respected for their cultural attributes as well as their management abilities the organisation is more successful (Hindle et al., 2005). At Jubal, leadership was largely conferred on its Elders who are also the Board members. The Chairperson of the Board was proud of the way that the community in general were involved in decision making at Jubal. He attributed the high participation rate to the fact that Board members were constantly telling the rest of the community what was going on and that they intended to be inclusive:

At Jubal people are pulling together now, I think it's because we have regular meetings and we take the time to explain everything to people. We say to them you are part of here, come to the AGM and make sure we have representatives from each family on the committee. I'm not the boss, I'm there looking after them…and we update them all the time.
(Kevin Torrens, 2006).

Although an identified strength at Jubal was the involvement of people from the community at meetings, in terms of day to day operations the load was mostly on the Chairperson. This highlights an issue of sustainability and the need to build on the strength of family structures to ensure the administration and management of Jubal is sustainable. In order to do this Jubal needs to address its succession planning and make sure that they are training and giving experience to a new generation of leaders.

Succession can be an issue for any organisation, but Hindle et al. (2005) found that Indigenous organisations are more vulnerable to generational changes than others. This vulnerability relates to passing on leadership to successors as well as vulnerability to political succession. For example, annual appointments of Board members can potentially result in a high turnover of Board members and lack of consistency (Hindle et al., 2005, Hunt & Smith, 2007).

For Jubal, the political succession has been stable. While this allows for consistency and for the continuation of corporate knowledge, it also creates a problem as it does mean that the organisation is overly reliant on a small group of people. The Board members all identified concerns about passing on responsibility to the younger generations.

> *It worries me, bothers me, who's going to take over… They are capable, but goes back to understanding responsibility and that worries me* (Kevin Torrens, 2006).

Conclusion

The Jubal case study highlighted some clear factors that enable and empower Indigenous communities to develop enterprises, whether in tourism or other industries. In particular, the study showed how difficult it can be for Aboriginal Controlled Community Organisations to develop entrepreneurial activities. Despite various programs that are designed to support Indigenous tourism development (Buultjens et al., 2005), organisations may not be in the right phase of their own development to access those programs. Assistance is more readily available for feasibility studies and business/property management plans. But in this case there was no program available which could have met Jubal's need to develop the organisation itself. Support was necessary not only to develop a business plan but most importantly, to implement the plan effectively. A lack of support in this area continues despite a recommendation from the Government's own review (IBR, 2003), that a more hands-on approach is required, which recognises the lack of business skills and in many cases the lack of educational attainment amongst those now developing businesses.

As the study identified, there is a need for governments to more closely understand the individual context of communities. This will require governments to genuinely listen to community priorities and aspirations and then (with proper consultation and negotiation) to develop programs flexible enough to accommodate the needs and aspirations of each individual community. Funding regimes must also accommodate the development priorities of individual communities and recognise and support the community's own responses to issues, rather than impose a uniform approach to dealing with such issues. Any development should be about regenerating communities, where communities themselves are identifying and using their own assets (Dodson, 2003).

Another key outcome of this study was to demonstrate the benefits of developing community skills rather than bringing in external consultants on short term contracts. Developing community skills is a longer, but ultimately a more sustainable, way to develop the community. Governments would achieve greater outcomes from program funding by taking a more holistic view to development and committing long term funding to support and develop those aspirations including funding administration and coordination of the community itself, rather than focusing only on discrete project funding.

A fundamental challenge that this study highlighted is that organisations need to focus on the development of the actual organisation, rather than direct all their attention to Government-funded projects. Organisations should focus on those areas over which they can have the greatest control and where their efforts will have the greatest effect (Dodson & Smith, 2003) and use their resources more effectively. The consequences of focusing primarily on Government-funded projects is that organisational structures, policies and procedures tend to be neglected as the community focuses on delivering program outcomes and generating reports and financial statements for the funding body. The results of this study highlighted that a disproportionate amount of time was spent by Jubal Board members responding to external influences created by pursuing project-based funding opportunities. Less time was spent on issues pertaining to developing the entity itself in line with its vision statement and enabling individual community members to better participate in the running of the organisation. The effect of this was to leave Jubal vulnerable in several areas of governance and internal structures.

Although Jubal decided not to proceed with tourism at that time, their experience illuminates a realistic approach to development that puts the community needs and aspirations at the centre of decision making and highlights a strengths-based approach to development. It also, importantly, explores some of the external factors that can make the difference between a measured approach to tourism development and a business that fails because of a rush to develop something without first addressing the foundations of the organisation.

References

Altman, J. (1989). Tourism dilemmas for Aboriginal Australians. *Annals of Tourism Research*, **16**, 456-476.

Altman, J. (1993). *Indigenous Australians in the National Tourism Strategy: Impact, Sustainability and Policy Issues*. Centre for Aboriginal Economic Policy Research. Canberra: ANU.

Altman, J. (ed.) (2001). *Sustainable Development Options on Aboriginal Land: the Hybrid Economy in the Twenty-First Century,* Canberra: Centre for Aboriginal Economic Policy Research.

Atkinson, J. (2001). *Lifting the Blankets: The Transgenerational Effects of Trauma in Indigenous Australia*. Doctoral Thesis, Queensland University of Technology.

ATSIC. n.d. New Arrangements in Indigenous Affairs. Available: http:// pandora.nla.gov.au/pan/41033/20060106/ATSIC/ATSIC_ATSIS_Closure/ Default.html. Accessed 23rd March 2007.

Bernard, H. R. (2006). *Research Methods in Anthropology: Qualitative And Quantitative Approaches,* Lanham, AltaMira.

Birdsall-Jones, C., Wood, D. & Jones, R. (2007). Great expectations: Indigenous land-based tourism in regional Western Australia. In: Buultjens, J. & Fullers, D. (eds.) *Striving for Sustainability: Case Studies in Indigenous Tourism*. Lismore: Southern Cross University Press.

Brewer, J. D.(2000). *Ethnography,* Buckingham: Open University Press.

Buultjens, J., Waller, I., Graham, S. & Carson, D. (2005). Public sector initiatives for Aboriginal small business development in tourism. In: Ryan, C. & Aicken, M. (eds.) *Indigenous Etourism: The commodification and management of culture*. Oxford: Elsevier.

Collaborative Solutions, (2000). *Jubal Country Report*, unpublished

Commonwealth (2008). Open for business: Developing Indigenous enterprises in Australia. In: *House of Representatives Standing Committee on Aboriginal and Torres Strait Islander Affairs* (ed.). Commonwealth.

Cornell, S. & Kalt, J. P. (2004). Reloading the dice: Improving the chances for economic development on American Indian Reservations. Los Angeles: American Indian Studies Center. www.ksg.harvard.edu/hpaied/docs/reloading%20the%20dice.pdf. Accessed 1st September 2004.

Craik, J. (2001). Tourism, culture and national identity. In T. Bennett & D. Carter (Eds.), *Culture in Australia: Policies, Publics and Programs* (pp. 89-113). Cambridge: Cambridge University Press.

Dodson & Smith, D. E. (2003). *Governance for sustainable development: Strategic issues and principles for Indigenous Australian Communities.* Centre for Aboriginal Economic Policy Research, Discussion paper 250, 21.

Fine, M., Weis, L., Wessen, S. & Wong, L. (2003). For whom? Qualitative research, representations and social responsibilities. In: Denzin, N., K. & Lincoln, Y., S. (eds.) *The Landscape of qualitative research: Theories and issues*. Thousand Oaks: Sage.

Finlayson, J. (2007). *Organising for success: Successful strategies in Indigenous organisations,* Canberra: Australian Collaboration, AIATSIS.

Higgins-Desbiolles, F. (2014). The Coorong Wilderness Lodge: A case study of planning failures in Indigenous tourism. *Tourism Management,* **44**, 46-57.

Hindle, K., Andersn, R., Gibersno, R. J. & Kayseas, B. (2005). Relating practice to theory in Indigenous entrepreneurship: A pilot investigation of the Kitsaki Partnership Portfolio. *American Indian Quarterly,* **29**, 1-23.

Hunt, J. & Smith, D. E. (2007). *Indigenous community governance project: Year two research findings.* CAEPR Working Paper No. 36/2007. Canberra: Centre for Aboriginal Economic Policy Research ANU.

Jorensen, M. & Taylor, J. B. (2000). What determines Indian economic success? Evidence from Tribal and Individual Indian Enterprises. *Harvard Project on American Indian Economic Development.* Malcolm Weiner Center for Social Policy, John F. Kennedy School of Government, Harvard University.

Martin, K. (2001). Ways of knowing, ways of being and ways of doing: developing a theoretical framework and methods for indigenous re-search and indigenist research. *The Power of Knowledge, The Resonance of Tradition - Indigenous Studies*: Conference 2001, ANU - Canberra. AIATSIS.

Martin, K. (2002). Ways of knowing, being and doing: a theoretical framework and methods for indigenous and indigenist re-search. *Journal of Australian Studies*, **76**, 203-214

Martin, K. (2008). *Please Knock Before you Enter: Aboriginal regulation of Outsiders and the implications for researchers*, Teneriffe, Qld:Post Pressed.

Morgan, P. (2006b). The Concept of Capacity. In: Europena Centre for Development Policy Management (ed.) *Study on Capacity, Change and Performance.*

Nakata, Martin (2004) Ongoing conversations about Aboriginal and Torres Strait Islander research agendas and directions. *Australian Journal of Indigenous Education*, **33**, 1-6.

Nakata, M. (2007). *Disciplining the Savages: Savaging the Disciplines*, Canberra: Aboriginal Studies Press.

Pitcher, M., Van Oosterzee, P. & Palmer, L. (1999). *Choice and Control: The development of Indigneous Tourism in Australia.* Darwin: Centre for Indigenous Natural and Cultural Resource Management, Cooperative Research Centre for Sustainable Tourism.

Rigney, L.-I. (1996). Tools for an Indigenist research methodology: A Narungga perspective. World Indigenous Peoples Conference: Education, 15 - 23 June 1996 1996 Albuquerque, New Mexico.

Rigney, L.-I. (1999). The first perspective: Culturally safe research practices on or with Indigenous peoples. Chacmool Conference, 1999 Calgary, Alberta Canada. 1 - 26.

Rooke, B. (1993). Finance: The Umorrduk experience. Paper presented at the *Indigenous Australians and Tourism: A Focus on Northern Australia Conference*, Darwin.

Royal Commission into Aboriginal Deaths in Custody. (1991). Report Available: http://pandora.nla.gov.au/pan/41033/20060106/ATSIC/issues/Law_and_Justice/rciadic/Overview_and_Recommendations/RCIADIC_RECS.pdf. Accessed 5th October 2006.

Ruhanen, L., Whitford, M. & McLennan, C.-L. (2015). Indigenous tourism in Australia: Time for a reality check. *Tourism Management*, **48**, 73-83.

Russell-Mundine, G. (2010). From pumpkins to property management: Developing the organisational capacity of the Jubal Aboriginal Corporation. PhD, Southern Cross University.

SCRGSP (2007). Overcoming Indigenous Disadvantage: Key Indicators 2007. In: Steering Committee for the Review of Government Service Provision. (ed.). Canberra: Productivity Commission.

Smith, L. T. (2003). *Decolonizing Methodologies: Research and Indigenous Peoples*, London, Zed Books.

Vanstone, A. (2005). Address to the National Press Club. Canberra: National Press Club.

Whitord, M., Bell, B. & Watkins, M. (2001). Indigenous tourism policy in Australia: 25 Years of rhetoric and economic rationalism. *Current Issues in Tourism*, **4**, 151-181.

Whitford, M. & Ruhanen, L. (2016). Indigenous Tourism research, past and present: where to from here? *Journal of Sustainable Tourism*, **24**, 1080-1099.

WTO (2002). *Tourism and Poverty Alleviation*, Madrid: World Tourism Organisation.

6 Native Foods in Australian Restaurants: How to ensure Indigenous Australians benefit?

*Freya Higgins-Desbiolles, Tricia Vilkinas,
Gayathri Wijesinghe and Stuart Gifford*

Introduction

> *"Many whitefellas just don't realise that it's so important to have Aboriginal people involved in the industry... If you lose that link between Aboriginal people and bush food, then you lose everything. It's hollow. It's nothing"*
> Rayleen Brown (cited in Merne Altyerre-ipenhe et al., 2011:26).

A recent news article carried the headline 'who owns a plant?' (Newton, 2016). This follows recent media interest in native foods, with headlines declaring 'foraging is the new black', 'advance Australia fare' and 'an all-consuming quest for a native cuisine'. Celebrity chefs such as Jock Zonfrillo are feted for making the world's oldest cuisine our trendiest (Sebag-Montefiore, 2015; Brearley, 2015; Lovitt, 2014). The Australian food industry is working to create brand identity through developing a unique national cuisine. As the Restaurant Australia tourism campaign demonstrates, the food sector can also deliver significant tourism branding opportunities for countries such as Australia (Tourism Australia, n.d.). The Australian cuisine of distinction is that based on native foods, and chefs such as Mark Olive, Clayton Donovan, Peter Gilmore, Andrew Fielke, Shannon Bennett, Kylie Kwong and Jock Zonfrillo are creating excitement by placing native or bush foods on their menus. Arguably, it is the emerging interest in local foods that has opened up the opportunity for renewed appreciation of native foods in Australia. Additionally, as sustainability and climate change emerge as serious concerns, native foods are promoted as more sustainable in terms of conserving biological diversity and more compatible with Australia's fragile ecology. But the opening question of 'who owns a plant' draws our attention to the question of whether Indigenous Australians have any special rights and roles in the native foods industry and what benefits they should derive from its prospering as a result of these.

This chapter analyses the native food industry in Australia, particularly the niche featuring in Australian restaurants and catering. It examines the capacity for Indigenous Australians to supply native foods to the restaurant sector and argues that proactive efforts must be made to ensure Indigenous Australians can better benefit from this emerging and important opportunity. This approach is based on an Indigenist philosophy and reflects changes inaugurated with the advancement of Indigenous rights under the United Nations Declaration on the Rights of Indigenous Peoples (UNDRIP) and other international protocols. Our findings indicate that the interface between native foods and Indigenous tourism offers the most promising opportunities for economic and cultural self-determination; a case study of Koomal Dreaming in Western Australia is presented as an example. Decolonising this culinary space opens up possibilities for building Indigenous Australian futures and bridging Australian divides.

Background and literature review

According to recent research, Indigenous Australian societies practiced sophisticated agriculture, aquaculture and land management, including sustainably secured nourishing food from difficult ecologies (Pascoe, 2014). It has been estimated that "there are up to 5,000 native food species (almost 20% of Australia's native flora and fauna) that were utilised by the Aboriginal people" (SBS Food, n.d.). These extensive practices, developed over millennia, have resulted in a knowledge base and expertise on native foods and medicine that is of enormous value to present day Australians.

In recent decades, numerous efforts have been made to feature native foods in Australian cuisine. Beginning in the 1980s, with outback stereotypes such as Paul Hogan and Les Hiddens (the 'bush tucker man'), native foods slowly evolved in the public consciousness from disrespect to slowly gaining attention and more sophisticated engagements (Cleary, 2013). Non-Indigenous celebrity chefs such as Jean-Paul Bruneteau, Andrew Fielke and Vic Cherikoff have been inspired by native ingredients and featured these in their dishes. More recently, Scottish-born celebrity chef, Jock Zonfrillo opened Orana Restaurant in Adelaide and challenged Australia and the world to embrace native ingredients as the true Australian cuisine, stating: "Our food celebrates post settlement Australia while cooking with respect to Country and the culture of the First Australians" (quoted in Welch, 2016: 31). Additionally, world renowned chef Rene Redzepi of Noma Restaurant in Copenhagen hosted a pop-up of 'Noma in Sydney' in early 2016 which created a fever pitch around native foods in Australia; it was held at the newly launched, prestige development at Barangaroo and supported by Tourism Australia (Thomsen, 2016). White (2014) noted that the use of native spices has created a bush tucker brand and built an identifiably Australian national cuisine that suggests that these efforts are, in part, directed at branding through commercial nationalism. The Noma pop-up in Sydney in 2016 supports White's claim, and it is clear that Australian native foods are being embraced for branding and tourism marketing purposes.

Simultaneously, Indigenous chefs have made notable contributions and raised the profile of native foods. Rayleen Brown, co-founder of the catering business Kungkas Can Cook in Alice Springs, has been a leader in advocating the benefits available to Indigenous communities through the native foods industry. Similarly, Pat Torres from the Kimberley region of Western Australia has presented a television series called *Kriol Kitchen* and has been instrumental in forming the Indigenous Harvest Australian Co-operative to secure access to the native foods industry for Indigenous community benefit. Celebrity chef, Mark Olive presented the television series *Outback Café* and acted as an ambassador for native foods in Australian cuisine, recently appearing on the international road shows of Restaurants Australia. Thus, a number of Indigenous-led initiatives have been undertaken to build Indigenous opportunities, share Indigenous knowledge and foster respect (Sleath, 2015; Torres, 2010). Notably, some of these Aboriginal leaders responded to the Noma in Sydney event with developing a collaboration under the title 'the Five Kungkas' (kungkas being the word for women from the Pitjantjatjara language) and challenging Redzepi and his team to source some of his native ingredients from them rather than non-Indigenous distributors (see http://5kungkas.com.au).

Janer's (2007) cultural studies analysis calls for a 'decolonization of culinary knowledge'. She advocates a move away from culinary nationalism to a state where we can appreciate the 'culinary epistemology' of Indigenous cultures on their own terms and the multiple benefits this may open up. When leaders such as Torres (2010) describe the knowledge derived from the Dreaming and the ancestors, which informs the use of native plants such as gubinge (kakadu plum), she is in fact demonstrating this culinary epistemology and inviting her audience to thereby engage and learn.

The profile of Indigenous Australian foods varies, with some well-known and appropriated by non-Indigenous people, some in restaurants and others provided for export, some emerging into mainstream awareness as tasty and/or healthy products, and others known mainly to Indigenous communities and enjoyed in Indigenous cultural settings. These foods range from meats and seafoods that are not particularly viewed as 'native foods', including kangaroo and abalone, to others seen as more exotic such as wallaby, emu and crocodile; to spices long loved, including lemon myrtle, and fruits such as bush tomatoes and quandongs; to native ingredients that are debuting on novel menus of hot restaurants (see Restaurants Australia, n.d.). Perhaps the most lucrative niche is that labelled superfoods such as kakadu plum which are in demand amongst health-conscious and wealthy consumers. Lastly, there are foods, such as the macadamia nut, which were taken for cultivation in other places in the late 19th century and are now no longer exclusive to Australia.

There is a growing consumer awareness of the unique nature of Australian bush foods and a desire to understand the origin and provenance of the menu offerings that incorporate these foods. Discerning consumers are also willing to pay high prices for such products (Hurst, 2007). Harvesting from the wild remains the predominant means of supplying fruit and seed to the bush food industry. Of 13 main fruit and seed species, six or more are presently supplied to the market in this manner (Rural Industries Research and Development Corporation (RIRDC), 2008). Many of the bush foods used in restaurants are sourced from non-Indigenous distributors such as Creative Native, Australian Functional Ingredients, Outback Pride and Outback Spirit; however a small number of Indigenous distributors, providers and harvesters also supply the restaurant sector such as the Five Kungkas, Mayi Harvests and Indigiearth. In relation to some Indigenous providers (particularly in remote Australia) concerns have been raised about how the food supply is being used, who uses it and where it goes (Cleary, 2012). Further, at present, the benefits derived by Indigenous providers from the bush foods industry are minimal with the primary benefits accruing to providers outside of remote Australia (Bryceson, 2008; Cleary, 2012; Cleary et al., 2008). However, most concerning is the fact that the supply chain issues disadvantage Indigenous remote and regional communities and have, for the most part, led to the dominance of non-Indigenous distributors. Research by Cleary (2013) showed that:

> ICT and transport systems are usually designed and managed by those largely external to remote regions, and…these systems are more likely to be based in urban centres. Urban-based actors are more likely to be positioned to control supply chains, and consequently to use the technology to exploit remote businesses (2013: 23).

Even for Indigenous Australians in non-remote locations, access to the native foods industry is not easy. Non-Indigenous initiatives have largely driven the development of the industry and use cultivated systems rather than wild-harvesting; for example, while Jock Zonfrillo has worked with Elder Bruno Dann to source native ingredients from the Kimberley for his restaurants in Adelaide, his approach has been described as follows:

> Each ingredient is known by the name given by the community it comes from and they receive direct payment for the wild ingredients they harvest. Jock has had to overcome deep mistrust with some Indigenous communities to even get close to talking to them about their native ingredients in their regions, so he believes ensuring acknowledgement and payment is given respectfully is essential. He has also established the Orana Foundation to give chefs and farmers access to detailed information about ingredients, flavour profiles and cultivation
> (Welch, 2015: 17).

This chapter shows why this seemingly innocuous statement of giving chefs and farmers access to these things is problematic from an Indigenous rights point of view. It argues, that while non-Indigenous involvement in the native foods industry is inescapable, much more must be done to protect the rights of Indigenous Australians and ensure they benefit from this emerging sector. Thus the question 'who owns native foods' has more depth and meaning than is first apparent.

Methodology

This chapter is based on the conceptual analysis for a pilot study entitled from 'Bush to Table' which examines the access of Indigenous Australian harvesters and providers to the supply chains of Australian restaurants. This project is a qualitative study undertaking semi-structured interviews with leading experts, chefs, restaurateurs, native foods distributors and native foods providers to identify the best practice guidelines that could be implemented to ensure Indigenous Australians benefit from the use of native foods in Australian cuisine. This analysis required a philosophical interrogation as to why Indigenous harvesters and providers should be prioritised in these activities. This chapter's insights are derived from the analysis of primary and secondary literature and applying a critical methodology to develop understandings of this interface.

It is important to acknowledge the tricky space that Indigenous research occupies currently and the problematic nature of relations between Indigenous and non-Indigenous Australians at the cultural interface. Trust is difficult when the context is recovering from invasion, dispossession and marginalisation in settler-colonial societies such as Australia. As Māori Indigenous scholar Linda Tuhiwai Smith has stated:

> "... scientific research is implicated in the worst excesses of colonialism...the word itself, 'research', is probably one of the dirtiest words in the indigenous world's vocabulary" (2003: 1).

The research team (of both Indigenous and non-Indigenous researchers) approached this topic from a critical, Indigenist standpoint and engaged with Indigenous communities from a position of solidarity. Critical theory contends that "claims to truth are always discursively situated and implicated in relations of power" (Kincheloe & McLaren, 2005:327). Adopting the approach of Denzin (2005:950), this work respects and follows an Indigenous research ethic that aims to support Indigenous self-determination. Denzin noted that the Indigenous research ethic calls for:

> "a collaborative social science research model that makes the researcher responsible not to a removed discipline...but to those studied...it forcefully aligns the ethics of research with a politics of the oppressed, with a politics of resistance, hope, and freedom" (2005:952).

Indigenous rights and Indigenous foods

'Knowledge about bush foods belongs to Aboriginal people'
(Merne Altyerre-ipenhe et al., 2011: 3).

Native foods may appear to represent commercial opportunities for Indigenous and non-Indigenous peoples alike; however, such a view ignores the fact that knowledge of the use of Indigenous plants derives from tens of thousands of years of Indigenous cultivation and cultural wisdom. As Pat Torres (2010) recognised in her Barrgana Lecture, her knowledge of the native foods of the Kimberley has been passed down through generations and has deep spirituality encompassed in the fullness of the Dreaming. Certainly, ethics and fairness must prohibit the appropriation of this knowledge from some of the most disadvantaged Australian communities that continue to suffer from indicators of poverty, marginalisation and exclusion more typical of people in the developing world. Further, there is also a growing legal imperative resulting from the concerted efforts of Indigenous peoples.

Indigenous peoples around the world resisted colonisation from the outset; however, since the 1960s, Indigenous peoples have begun to assert their rights to self-determination and called for reparations and solutions for the dispossession, exploitation and marginalisation they suffered. The new millennium inaugurated a new era of Indigenous rights that followed decades of work by Indigenous leaders and Indigenous communities around the world. Fora (such as the United Nations) were used by Indigenous people to press for recognition of their rights and these efforts culminated in the 2008 UNDRIP.

Notably, UNDRIP's Article 31 on 'Cultural and Intellectual Property' states:

> *Indigenous peoples have the right to maintain, control, protect and develop their cultural heritage, traditional knowledge and traditional cultural expressions, as well as the manifestations of their sciences, technologies and cultures, including human and genetic resources, seeds, medicines, knowledge of the properties of fauna and flora, oral traditions, …They also have the right to maintain, control, protect and develop their intellectual property over such cultural heritage, traditional knowledge, and traditional cultural expressions* (United Nations, 2008:11).

Further, UNDRIP requires that "states shall take effective measures to recognize and protect the exercise of these rights" (United Nations, 2008:12).

However, current practices in the native foods industry create limited opportunities for Indigenous Australian harvesters and providers and may be leading to what could be labelled appropriation or, even worse, biopiracy. Indigenous communities have numerous stories of how researchers have taken their traditional knowledge for use in pharmaceutical patents or taken plant seeds and cuttings to develop products in other places (Robinson, 2015). According to Robinson (as cited in Mills, 2015), "bio-piracy is... where people haven't sought consent and haven't agreed to share benefits where they've used both a biological resource and or traditional knowledge from a traditional group. There's been many cases globally and we're just uncovering some now in Australia". The biopiracy threatening Indigenous knowledge and Indigenous foods emerges from a potent mix of destructive forces that have structured the scene of Indigenous disadvantage, including invasion, colonisation, attempted assimilation and now a strict disciplining to the dictates of a neoliberal and globalised market.

Robinson (as cited in Mills, 2015) addressed the biopiracy of an American cosmetics company who patented an extract from kakadu plum and stated:

> "This is a massive loss of opportunity. It will mean that our biological resources could be exploited overseas without the opportunity for small start-up companies and Indigenous enterprises to exploit their natural assets in the country... It's also potentially culturally offensive to certain Indigenous groups to be using these things and patenting them without their consent, particularly where their knowledge may provide a lead to the research."

This kakadu plum (or gubinge in one of its custodial language) has been identified as a significant superfood with health, cosmetic and medicinal value and is in demand for restaurants and food exporters. Thus, Robinson's concerns, voiced in relation to pharmaceutical and cosmetic usages, are relevant to this discussion on the native foods industry. The use of such plants as 'genetic resources' and the traditional knowledges associated with them are now coming under the Nagoya Protocol, the first international instrument of particular relevance to Indigenous communities negotiated since the adoption of the UNDRIP. It sets out requirements for prior informed consent and benefits-sharing (Convention on Biological Diversity (CBD), n.d.). The native foods industry does not enjoy such legal protections and this is a key vulnerability.

In her work to ensure Indigenous Australian benefit from native foods, Pat Torres (as cited in Martin, 2015) made the following comment on gubinge:

> So much has been taken from Indigenous people, and this is one of the few things left where we can do business with it. We understand the tree, we understand the seasons, we know how to protect it, we know how to collect the fruit. This industry can provide us with honest, hard work that we can connect to.

With these comments in mind, it would seem the most promising space for Indigenous Australian control and benefit from the use of native foods would be in the tourism space. Native foods have been a feature of Indigenous Australian tourism experiences for decades because these foods are integral to Indigenous Australian life, culture and connection to country. In order to gain an understanding of the empowerment to be found in this space, we offer a case study of Koomal Dreaming.

Case Study of Koomal Dreaming

Aboriginal people were farming the native plants and animals that were already here for thousands of years. Being the oldest living culture, they had that deep connection to country. Laws, customs, spirituality, beliefs and Dreaming; it was really a unique way of life and social system and economic system that extended for thousands of years (Josh Whiteland, in Carter, 2013a).

Josh Whiteland has created a tourism business called Koomal Dreaming which offers cultural experiences based on his knowledge of Wadandi and Bibbulman culture and country. Josh has been a leader in the tourism industry in the South West region of Western Australia (WA) and thinks tourism offers a good opportunity:

> I think tourism is quite good for Aboriginal people. It gives them the opportunity to continue cultural activities, to go back to country, to run and have their own business, to be confident and proud of who they are, and it's a vehicle for continuation of these cultural practices... they can also have a better lifestyle... by going back to the land

(pers. comm. Josh Whiteland, 4 August 2016).

He originally did not feature food and food experiences in his tourism offerings but as he looked to create compelling experiences, the attraction and value of foods became clear. Josh explained how his multiple skills and talents led him to feature native foods in the cultural experiences he offers:

> To begin with it was mostly about creating tourism experiences and I guess all that complements that. I'm a musician and artist, and I love public speaking. But I also had a passion for cooking and foraging and hunting and farming, because I have a farming background
> (pers. comm. Josh Whiteland, 4 August 2016).

The Koomal Dreaming website shows how these multiple talents of cultural story-teller, artist, chef, and custodian come together to create the Koomal tourism offering:

> Be moved by the skill and intensity of Josh's didgeridoo playing and fire-making, taste native foods, discover bush medicine and meet the animals, plants and Dreaming spirits that have enriched the lives of Wadandi and Bibbulman people since time began (Koomal Dreaming, n.d. a).

Under the section on food on the Koomal Dreaming website, it states:

> The Wadandi people 'forest people by the sea' live within the 'Cape to Cape' 'Warren Blackwood' region. They maintain an intricate system and way of life living by the six seasonal rotation, and have done so for over 50,000 years. Learning to live by these seasons Josh developed a passion for foraging, hunting and cooking. Experimenting with local foods and native flavours has led to a flair and passion for cooking. Josh cooks traditional food out on country and often blends these flavours with contemporary foods and cooking styles at home for visitors.

Over the last couple of years Josh has been sharing this knowledge and passion for food with visitors and chefs from around the world. This has led to opportunities to connect and work with leaders in this field both on film, on location and at events (Koomal Dreaming, n.d. b).

Josh views learning about native foods on country through food tourism experiences as essential and surpasses what can be gained from restaurants. He stated "if you're out talking about the plant, looking at the sky and the land and the trees and forest, and then going into a beautiful setting and having a nice meal, it's a journey" (pers. comm. Josh Whiteland 4 August 2016).

Josh has tried to impact international chefs and transform their appreciation of native foods and the Aboriginal custodians of these foods. Josh has hosted a group of world renowned chefs, including Peter Gilmore and Jock Zonfrillo, and took them foraging for bush foods and later cooking together (Koomal Dreaming, n.d. b). He also hosted the famous chef Rene Redzepi of Noma Restaurant fame in 2012 (mentioned earlier) when he took him foraging for native foods in the South West region of Western Australia (Carter, 2013a). Josh stated:

> For the individual to create the awareness about the bush plants and fruits and vegetables and spices, they would really need to immerse themselves within the culture and land and be able to connect to the land, connect to the people and connect to the fruits and vegetables and the food that comes from the land. Then you'll have a really clear understanding of what is available and what [are] our national foods
> (Josh Whiteland in Carter, 2013a).

Josh argues that these experiences are essential to gaining a genuine sense of place and securing a sense of identity. As Josh explained in an interview that aired on radio:

> Those sorts of recipes and foods I just think [give an] amazing connection back, from understanding the bulya which is the rock, understanding the fire, the kala which is the warmth and how it relates to the family, culture and kindship of Aboriginal people
> (Josh Whiteland in Carter, 2013b).

It is in the niche of food tourism experience that Aboriginal people can assert advantages over native foods that non-Indigenous people have difficulty infringing on. The advantage comes from the cultural knowledge that Aboriginal tourism operators have gained from their cultural upbringing and that gives them access to the stories of the native foods. Josh stated:

> Everything's about the food stories. You may be explaining about a certain plant that flowers and fruits in a certain time of year, or talking about animals that have nesting periods. You want to be able to forage and hunt and gather sustainably, the food stories are a big part of food tourism… quite often the audience is intrigued by the food story. More and more people want to learn more about sustainable foods and also healthy foods with medicinal properties. They want to just be able to connect to the area with the stories, the food and the culture; there's a whole experience available and that's what I like offering the most
> (pers. comm. Josh Whiteland, 4 August 2016).

Josh has also been instrumental in co-creating a unique event as part of the Margaret River Gourmet Escape event in Western Australia. It is called Kambarang South West Aboriginal Gourmet Experience, and together with renowned Aboriginal Chef Mark Olive (aka the Black Olive), a top food experience is offered for some 100 guests with native ingredients being the feature. However, what is most outstanding about this initiative is the experience and training it gives to Aboriginal hospitality students from various high schools, and apprentices and students from the Outback Academy; all proceeds from these events went to the Outback Academy's Hospitality Program, which encourages Aboriginal people to train for careers in hospitality, tourism and events (Koomal Dreaming, n.d. c).

Koomal Dreaming has won numerous awards, including the Indigenous Tourism Award at the West Australian Tourism Awards in multiple years, resulting in its induction into the WA Tourism Awards Hall of Fame in 2016. Josh has also gained an international profile through his dedicated work to enhance the profile of Australian native foods, including presenting on foraging for native foods at the MAD [food] Symposium in Copenhagen in 2013 on the invitation of Chef Rene Redzepi (see Carter, 2013c).

Indigenous Australian-led futures in native foods

Because of a growing concern about the rapid development of the native foods industry and lack of proper legal protection, the Merne Altyerre-ipenhe (Food from the Creation Time) Reference Group intervened with a call for the 'bush foods industry [to] grow to be equitable and fair' (Merne Altyerre-ipenhe et al., 2011: 4) and suggested guidelines and principles to shape the sector for ethical outcomes and benefits for Indigenous Australians, stating:

> For bush foods, medicines and other produce and products we want to see:
> - *RECOGNITION of Aboriginal knowledge, skills and practice*
> - *RESPECT for Aboriginal elders, workers and youth*
> - *ROLES and RESPONSIBILITIES chosen by Aboriginal people*
> - *RETURNS and BENEFITS to Aboriginal custodians and knowledge holders*
> - *RESTORATION and CARE for Aboriginal land, ecosystems and plants*
> - *REPATRIATION of knowledge and support to intergenerational knowledge transfer*
>
> (Merne Altyerre-ipenhe et al., 2011: 4).

The set of guidelines recommended an ethical approach, ensuring fair returns to Indigenous Australians, offering training and employment opportunities, restoring native foods' ecologies and improving governance roles for Indigenous Australians in the industry (Merne Altyerre-ipenhe et al., 2011:25).

While there are in place these two pillars – the UNDRIP (and other international protocols) as well as these ethical guidelines – it is also necessary to re-affirm that there are Indigenous Australian laws, protocols and custodial obligations that derive from the web of relationships between the Dreaming, the native plants and animals, the Country and the people (Merne Altyerre-ipenhe et al., 2011:14-17). This is the foundation of Indigenous Australian engagement with the native foods industry, but because Australian governments and the private business sector do not fully recognise and respect these, Indigenous Australian organisations are working to inform Indigenous Australians so they can protect their knowledges and advance their interests. An example is the publication *'Know your rights to your Aboriginal plant knowledge'* (Morse, 2010). This document recommends a range of options in a weak legal context including protocols, written agreements, copyright, trademarks, geographic indications and their own customary laws and processes to protect their Indigenous knowledges (2010:22). This work is supported by international efforts to negotiate in fora such as the CBD, where strategies, guidelines and protocols are being developed to help realise the UNDRIP rights. The Nagoya's protocols on benefits-sharing and securing prior informed consent provide a useful guide for the native foods industry and have led to resources that could guide best practices, for example, the detailed list of monetary and non-monetary benefits that could be considered in benefit-sharing agreements found in the Bonn Guidelines (Secretariat of the CBD, 2002), affiliated with the CBD.

In summary, an analysis of the current state of play in the native foods sector finds Indigenous Australians asserting their law and custodial responsibilities over native foods and their use, some non-Indigenous industry leaders responding with respectful approaches, but with no assurance that the native foods industry will not progress by appropriating native foods and Indigenous knowledges without proper engagement and benefits-sharing with Indigenous Australians. A key failing in this network of stakeholders is the role of governments. The question arises as to whether the native foods industry can be left to the ethics and goodwill of the non-Indigenous sector, or should governments play a greater role –

and should this role be regulatory, advisory, enabling or a combination of these? Currently Australian governments demand economic advancement for Indigenous Australians as they remove welfare supports, but largely leave them to their own devices to find their pathways in the native foods industry in cooperation with non-Indigenous business interests. However, given that Australia is a signatory to UNDRIP and has policies such as 'Closing the Gap', it is recommended that Australia take a policy approach in prioritising Indigenous Australian interests in the native foods industry and facilitating their access through all levels of action possible.

The benefits that supporting the prioritisation of Indigenous Australians in the native foods industry could deliver are numerous. As Pat Torres noted, it not only provides important business opportunities, but also opportunities to maintain and practice culture, be on Country, foster land management capacities, continue custodianship and gain important skills, and thereby gain respect for Indigenous ecological knowledges and capacities (Torres, 2010). The benefits for non-Indigenous stakeholders in native foods could be equally impressive. Governments could find a positive pathway to 'Closing the Gap' by providing Indigenous Australians with a competitive advantage and thus securing recognition for Australia as a progressive country in relation to Indigenous rights. Further, non-Indigenous business stakeholders would be required to access native foods in an ethical and fair manner, which in turn could create multiple positive outcomes, including gaining access to the stories of native foods and the knowledge that this might unlock; assuring discerning consumers of the ethical and fair provenance of the foods; distinct branding opportunities because of the ethical positioning; developing sound strategies of corporate social responsibility; and thus building a more prosperous future for all stakeholders. For such a positive transformation to occur, Indigenous Australians need both practical support and accessible guidelines on how to better grasp opportunities to get involved in the supply chain at points of enhanced value, and how to build business opportunities through partnerships and networks. Finally, educating consumers to value and support the role of Indigenous Australians as custodians of these native foods will harness their support to motivate the other stakeholders outlined above.

Figure 6.1 provides a model for the transformation of the native foods industry that delivers respect for Indigenous Australian rights, addresses Indigenous Australian disadvantages and potentially promotes elements of reconciliation. Such a transformation would require a three-pronged approach; that is, it would need to be Indigenous-led, work in joint part-nership with non-Indigenous experts and businesses, and be supported by governments at all levels.

In relation to Indigenous-led approaches, Torres and Brown have offered Indigenous leadership to turn native foods opportunities into Indigenous Australian benefits; Torres' Indigenous Harvest Australian Co-operative demonstrates a model of structural cooperation, while Brown's work through her catering business includes supporting local 'wild harvest' initiatives and advocacy for Indigenous involvement and benefits from the growing native foods industry.[1]

In terms of joint partnerships, non-Indigenous chef Andrew Fielke has a vision of developing partnerships with Aboriginal communities for supply-ing native foods to restaurants and for export, and through his leadership of Australian Native Foods Industry Ltd (ANFIL) tried to foster Indigenous Australian community involvement and benefit from this emerging sector (personal communication, 26 August 2015). Similarly, Mike and Gayle Quarmby of Outback Pride are non-Indigenous cultivators and distributors who claim working with Indigenous communities for decades to assist them to enter the supply chain of the native foods industry (Outback Pride Fresh, n.d.). There also business philanthropists supporting cooperative projects, for example the Kindred Spirits Foundation and its work on kakadu plum with Wadeye and other Aboriginal communities (http://kindredspiritsfoun-dation.org.au/).

However, it is the role of governments at all levels to better support Indigenous Australians to ensure that they prosper from the native foods industry. The Western Australian government is leading the way in this with its recent work with Mamabulanjin Aboriginal Corporation giving a lease on more than 600 hectares of state government land to establish a native foods plantation, featuring kakadu plum (Brann, 2016). However, for government intervention to be effective, a key requirement will be ensuring that proper processes of prior informed consent and benefits-sharing are followed. As the Commonwealth government considers implementing its policy of 'Closing the Gap' to address disadvantage Indigenous Australians, the native foods industry should be prioritised.

---

1   Brown has done this by serving on the Merne Altyerre-ipenhe Reference Group
    to develop the ethical guidelines for the bush foods industry and the Board of
    ANFIL (Sleath, 2015)

Figure 6.1: A model of a native foods industry geared to Indigenous Australian benefit

Returning to the work of Jock Zonfrillo in sourcing native foods (discussed above), the question arises as to whether such non-Indigenous stakeholders are aware of these current circumstances. Many Indigenous Australians are distrustful of non-Indigenous stakeholders in the native foods industry, as they fear losing custodial rights over Indigenous foods. Simultaneously, legal contexts established by the UNDRIP, the CBD and other protocols are not being effectively applied to protect the interests of Indigenous Australians in this sector. The wider cultivation of native plants may better secure a reliable supply of native ingredients; however, it may also inadvertently undermine the window of opportunity for Indigenous harvesters and providers to supply native foods and thus secure sustainable futures.[2] Accordingly, information campaigns (paralleling those mentioned above) need to be run to inform non-Indigenous stakeholders in the native foods industries of their obligations to secure prior informed consent and negotiate meaningful benefits-sharing agreements that honours not only financial obligations to give fair returns, but also ethical obligations to respect Indigenous rights and honour the Indigenous knowledges that set the foundations of the native foods industry. This emerging area needs concerted action to direct opportunities and benefits to Indigenous Australians.

---

2   Similar to the Orana Foundation advocates, Outback Pride cultivates its own plants at its Reedy Creek Nursery in South Australia, but also works with Indigenous Australian harvesters and producers in communities around the country (Outback Pride Fresh, n.d.).

Conclusions and implications

> *"It is about us growing up as a nation and that means evolving our own culture and food"*
> Chef Andrew Fielke (as cited in Bonney, 2012:53).

Janer's (2007) analysis of decolonising culinary knowledge invites us to imagine what a critical and ethical approach to native foods might offer the Australian community, while cautioning us about what a lack of respect for the Indigenous culinary epistemology might bring. This paper outlined the dynamics of Australia's native foods industry that is currently dominated by non-Indigenous stakeholders; however, it noted that important interventions have been made by Indigenous Australian leaders who are eager to build a space for Indigenous Australian engagement and benefit through initiatives such as the ethical guidelines developed by the Merne Altyerre-ipenhe Reference Group (2011). Given Australia's commitment to Indigenous rights (as evidenced by Australia's signing the UNDRIP), the significance of Indigenous Australian knowledge in relation to promoting native foods and the considerable disadvantages experienced by Indigenous Australians, it is imperative that concerted efforts be made to prioritise Indigenous Australian access to the opportunities offered by the emerging native foods industry. In our current research project, we are working to support improved access and opportunities for Indigenous Australian providers in the native foods supply chain and thus exploring the space available for reconciliation, Indigenous self-determination and dialogues between cultures across the medium of native foods.

Acknowledgements

This chapter is derived from a conference paper presented at the Council for Australasian Tourism and Hospitality Education annual conference in 2016 (see Higgins-Desbiolles et al., 2016). The research was made possible by a grant from Le Cordon Bleu Australia and the School of Management, University of South Australia. We wish to thank all the people who supported this research project and agreed to be interviewed. Any faults, errors or omissions are the responsibility of the authors and we invite ongoing feedback and advice.

References

Bonney, N. (2012). *Edible wild native plants in Southern Australia,* Tantanoola, SA: Openbook Howden.

Brann, M. (2016). *Unique land deal near Broome paves way for major Kakadu plum,* http://www.abc.net.au/news/rural/2016-12-05/land-deal-near-broome-paves-way-for-kakadu-plum-plantation/8084786.

Brearley, M. (2015). Advance Australia fare. *The Australian.* http://www.theaustralian.com.au/life/food-wine/advanceaustralia-fare-indigenous-food-past-present-and-future/story-e6frg8jo-1227530412175. Accessed 27/09/2015

Bryceson, K.P. (2008). *Value chain analysis of bush tomato and wattle seed products. Research Report 40,* Alice Springs, NT: Desert Knowledge Cooperative Research Centre.

Carter, J. S. (2013a, 7 August). Should kangaroo be our national meat? ABC Rural News, http://www.abc.net.au/news/2013-08-07/indigenous-disconnect/4869184. Accessed 05/12/2016.

Carter, J.S. (2013b). The fine art of local food foraging. *ABC Radio National,,* 10 August. http://www.abc.net.au/radionational/programs/rnfirstbite/josh-whiteland/4871582. Accessed 09/01/2017.

Carter, J.S. (2013c, 27 August). The fine art of local food foraging. RN First Bite, http://www.abc.net.au/radionational/programs/rnfirstbite/art-of-foraging/4911976. Accessed 09/01/2017.

Cleary, J. (2012). It would be good to know where our food goes: Information equals power? In P. Drahos & S. Frankel (eds.). *Indigenous Peoples' Innovation, Intellectual Property Pathways to Development,* Canberra, ACT: ANU EPress, 53-71.

Cleary, J.A. (2013). Cultural icons and cash commodities: The two-world story of Australian bush foods. Unpublished PhD thesis, University of South Australia.

Cleary, J., McGregor, M.J., Bryceson, K.P. & James, C.D. (2008). *Bush to bottle: Development of a value-driven bush foods chain that rewards Aboriginal people.* Proceedings of 15th Biennial Conference, Australian Rangelands Society, Charters Towers, Qld.

Convention on Biological Diversity (n.d.). *About the Nagoya Protocol.* https://www.cbd.int/abs/about/. Accessed 20/08/2015

Denzin, N. K. (2005). Emancipatory discourses and the ethics and politics of participation. In N. K. Denzin & Y. S. Lincoln (eds.) *The Sage Handbook of Qualitative Research, 3rd ed.,* Thousand Oaks, C.A.: Sage Publications, 933-958.

Higgins-Desbiolles, F., Vilkinas, T., Wijesinghe, G., Akbar, S. & Gifford, S. (2016). Indigenous foods benefiting Indigenous Australians. In M. Scerri & L. Hui (eds.), CAUTHE 2016 conference proceedings: *The changing landscape of tourism and hospitality: the impact of emerging markets and emerging destinations,* Blue Mountains International Hotel Management School, pp. 527-542.

Hurst, B (2007). Accreditation: Is it really worth it? *Just Food.* http://www.just-food.com/comment/is-it-really-worth-it_id97896.aspx. Accessed 03/11/2015.

Janer, Z. (2007). (In)Edible nature: New world food and coloniality. *Cultural Studies,* **21**(2-3), 385-405.

Kincheloe, J.L. & McLaren, P. (2005). Rethinking critical theory and qualitative research. In N. K. Denzin & Y. S. Lincoln (eds.) *The Sage Handbook of Qualitative Research, 3rd ed.,* Thousand Oaks, C.A.: Sage Publications, 303-342.

Koomal Dreaming (n.d. a). *Aboriginal tours, art and culture.* www.koomaldreaming.com.au/. Accessed 03/12/2016.

Koomal Dreaming (n.d. b). *About us.* www.koomaldreaming.com.au/. Accessed 03/12/2016.

Koomal Dreaming (n.d. c). *Gourmet Escape.* www.koomaldreaming.com.au/gourmet-escape-aboriginal-gourmet-food-event/. Accessed 03/12/2016.

Lovitt, Z. (2014). Jock Zonfrillo's all-consuming quest for an Australian cuisine. *Australian Financial Review,* 1 November, http://www.afr.com/lifestyle/arts-and-entertainment/art/jock-zonfrillos-allconsuming-quest-for-an-australian-cuisine-20141031-11fatn. Accessed 27/09/2015

Martin, L. (2015, 19 May). Gubinge: Kakadu plum 'superfood' set to lead expansion of Kimberley bush fruit industry. ABC News, http://www.abc.net.au/news/2015-05-19/gubinge-industry-set-to-take-off/6480204 . Accessed 14/09/2015.

Merne Altyerre-ipenhe (Food from the Creation Time) Reference Group, Douglas, J. & Walsh, F. (2011). *Aboriginal people, bush foods knowledge and products from Central Australia: Ethical guidelines for commercial bush food research, industry and enterprises.* Desert Knowledge CRC Report, 71, Alice Springs, NT: Ninti One.

Mills, V. (2015, 5 February). *Favourite Kimberley bush foods and medicine targeted by bio-pirates.* ABC News, http://www.abc.net.au/local/stories/2015/02/05/4174920.htm. Accessed 28/09/2015.

Morse, J. (2010). *Know your rights to your Aboriginal plant knowledge*. http://www.terrijanke.com.au/documents/Know_your_rights_may2010.pdf. Accessed 03/09/2015.

Newton, J. (2016, 30 November). Who owns a plant? *SBS Online,* http://www.sbs.com.au/food/article/2016/11/30/who-owns-plant. Accessed 20/12/2016.

Outback Pride Fresh (n.d.). Communities. http://www.outbackpridefresh.com.au/about/communities/. Accessed 04/10/2015.

Pascoe, B. (2014). *Dark Emu Black Seeds: Agriculture or accident?* Broome, WA: Magabala Books.

Restaurants Australia (n.d.). Contemporary bush tucker in Australian restaurants. http://restaurant.australia.com/en/explore/National/Produce/contemporary-bush-tucker-in-australian-restaurants.html. Accessed 15/09/2015.

Rural Industries Research and Development Corporation (RIRDC) (2008) *Native foods R&D priorities and strategies 2007 to 2012*, Canberra, ACT: AGPS.

Robinson, D.L. (2015). *Biodiversity, Access and Benefit-sharing: Global case studies*, London: Routledge.

SBS Food (n.d.). Native Australian recipes and Native Australian Food. http://www.sbs.com.au/food/cuisine/native-australian. Accessed 03/09/2015.

Sebag-Montefiore, C. (2015). Foraging is the new black in Australian cuisine. BBC, 25 September, http://www.bbc.com/news/world-australia-34332885. Accessed 27/09/2015.

Secretariat of the CBD (2002). Bonn Guidelines on Access to Genetic Resources and Fair and Equitable Sharing of the Benefits Arising out of their Utilization. Appendix 2, https://www.cbd.int/doc/publications/cbd-bonn-gdls-en.pdf. Accessed 03/09/2015.

Sleath, E. (2015). *Native foods specialist wants Aboriginal involvement in industry*. ABC Alice Springs, 22 June, http://www.abc.net.au/local/stories/2015/06/22/4259530.htm. Accessed 02/09/2015.

Smith, L. T. (2003) *Decolonizing methodologies: Research and Indigenous Peoples*. London: Zed Books.

Thomsen, S. (2016, 16 February). Review: Noma in Sydney takes Australian cuisine to the next level, but hits one crucial hurdle. *Business Insider Australia*, http://www.businessinsider.com.au/review-noma-australia-does-a-danish-chef-really-know-us-better-than-we-do-2016-2. Accessed 22/12/2016.

Torres, Pat (2010). Can bush tucker provide meaningful lives and a path for Aboriginal people into the modern economy? Barrgana Lecture, http://www.abc.net.au/local/photos/2010/07/26/2964154.htm. Accessed 03/03/2015.

Tourism Australia (n.d.). Food and Wine. http://www.tourism.australia.com/campaigns/Food-Wine.aspx. Accessed 18/11/2015.

United Nations (2008). Declaration on the Rights of Indigenous Peoples. http://www.un.org/esa/socdev/unpfii/documents/DRIPS_en.pdf. Accessed 03/06/2014.

Welch, L. (2015). Jock Zonfrillo. *Adelaide Dining Magazine*, 17-18.

Welch, L. (2016). Jock Zonfrillo, *Adelaide Dining Magazine,* 31.

White, L. (2014). Australian native spices: Building the 'bush tucker' brand. In L. Jolliffe (ed.) *Spices and Tourism: Destinations, Attractions and Cuisines,* Bristol: Channel View, 153-168.

7 Closing the Gap?
Transforming Indigenous tourism through recognition, redistribution and representation

Rob Hales and Freya Higgins-Desbiolles

Introduction

Fifty years ago Australia's Indigenous people gained full citizenship rights in a public referendum. Whilst this event afforded citizen rights under Australian law, the constitutional recognition and questions of a treaty for the First Peoples of Australia still remain at the forefront of public debate. First Peoples and Aboriginal and Torres Strait Islander people are accorded certain rights, which play out in various ways in the law, political economy and public sphere of Australia. Indigenous people are also culturally different and have experienced historical (and present) trauma, marginalisation and neglect as a result of colonial and post-colonial domination (Atkinson, 2002). Recently Indigenous people have (erroneously) become a 'problem' to Australian society and governments (Altman, 2009). The agenda of manufacturing Indigenous Australians, as a problem, is multifaceted including a perennial effort to assimilate them in Australia's body politic. However more recently, the 'problem' of Indigenous Australians has been articulated through comparison of Indigenous socio-economic indicators such as child mortality, incarceration and unemployment with similar figures of white Australia. The lack of progress in key indicators prompts public policy responses and media attention to create a discourse of 'closing the gap' (see the Australian Prime Minister's, *Closing the Gap* reports 2009-2017).

As a consequence of such conditions, a dominant political and discursive view has emerged in Australia that Indigenous people should not be seen as citizens with structural rights, but rather they should be seen as citizens predominated by a sense of individual agency and personal responsibility for their living conditions (Altman, 2014). The latter view sees solutions to the gap sourced in neoliberalism. Under the neoliberal approach, 'closing the gap' is about new ways of schooling, working, spending, home owning and mobility for Indigenous people, which disciplines them to the dictates of the market economy; these initiatives are akin to the assimilation strategies of the 1950s with a contemporary veneer. Adopting these new ways means that the interrelated (Indigenous) ways of being: kinship, language, ceremony, ties to country (place) and law are devalued or eroded as the primacy of the individual is key focus of improvement. This view is held by both conservative and liberal based political parties in Australia and has the support of some Indigenous Australian leaders. Altman (2014) argues that the three interrelated concepts of recognition, redistribution and representation (see Fraser, 1999, 2009) may be a more useful frame to reconfigure the so-called 'close the gap problems' of Indigenous Australians.

What does this have to do with tourism? Tourism, despite its apparent carefree nature, is an ideological concept and practice. The discourse of tourism as an industry is a recent phenomenon and has usurped the discourse of tourism as a social force (Higgins-Desbiolles, 2006). Indeed the 1980 Manila Declaration on World Tourism, with its emphasis on social justice and inclusion, seems out-moded with the discourses on tourism as an industry predominant today. The Declaration stated that "In the practice of tourism, spiritual elements must take precedence over technical and material elements" (UNWTO, 1980). At the heart of the Declaration is the affirmation of the originality of cultures and respect for the moral heritage of peoples.

The timing of the Declaration ironically heralded the development of mass tourism. In the mid-1980s the global airline industry was deregulated and this afforded opportunities for greater tourism industry development. Neil Leiper in 1979 (see Leiper, 1995) identified that there was a concerted effort by tourism businesses prior to the 1980s to argue that tourism was a serious industry worthy of government support and facilitation. Simultaneously, tourism morphed into an individualistic and hedonistic pursuit of the consuming tourists, who could demand any product and experience that their money could purchase; thus diminishing the earlier forms of, say, pilgrimages and social tourism, where social and spiritual values prevailed.

At the risk of oversimplification, there appears to be a duality of tourism as both a burgeoning industry and a smaller, socially-oriented leisure activity with certain socio-ecological underpinnings; both with quite different purposes. While a niche segment for responsible tourism remains evident and tourism is still used as a space of intercultural contact, this is only a very small niche market and is seen to be an odd outlier, for the most part. The impacts of this shift have been recently framed as structural violence which impacts on both humans and non-human natures through the systematic production of inequalities, excessive waste and 'spaces of exception' – i.e., a tourism bubble where normal local socio-environmental rules are not applicable (Büscher & Fletcher, 2016). Indigenous tourism falls into this category, as demonstrated in some recent studies where it is analysed as: inauthentic (Reisinger & Steiner, 2006), mutually beneficial exploitation (Whyte, 2010), cultural exploitation (McLaren, 1998) and a source of environmental injustice (Higgins-Desbiolles et al., 2013) to name a few.

How might Indigenous tourism negotiate the dominant tourism frame, and for what purpose can Indigenous tourism be conducted? Is Indigenous Australian tourism about 'closing the gap', and what exactly might that mean?

Based on Fraser's (1999, 2009) justice framework, we offer tourism cases where the justice frames of recognition, redistribution and representation are present in the Indigenous tourism contexts. These cases exemplify how attention to each element of the justice frame is important in maintaining tradition and livelihoods in ways determined by Indigenous people. This framework counters neoliberal logic which does little for Indigenous traditions and self-determination.

Neoliberal commodified Indigenous tourism and the alternative

Indigenous tourism does not necessarily privilege Indigenous engagement and benefit. One of the most used definitions of Indigenous tourism comes from Butler and Hinch (1996:10) who define it as "tourism activities in which Indigenous people are directly involved either through control and/ or by having their culture serve as the essence of the attraction". They offer a matrix to illustrate the categories this definition describes, with variations based on the level of Indigenous control and the cultural content of the tourism products. This matrix demonstrates that Indigenous tourism may involve varying levels of Indigenous ownership, management and cultural content and that it can exist without Indigenous involvement at all. This model therefore demonstrates the capacity for some forms of 'Indigenous tourism' to dispossess Indigenous peoples through tourism, taking their cultures and exploiting it for non-Indigenous benefit (see Hollinshead, 2007; Jacobsen, 2016). We suggest legitimate forms of Indigenous tourism must overturn the possibilities of such exploitation and dispossession. In this work, we recognize as Indigenous tourism, all activities and operations that advance Indigenous Australian engagement and benefit from tourism activities.

Some of the benefits Indigenous Australian tourism may deliver, when done under circumstances of Indigenous engagement and benefit, include: employment, the capacity to make a living off their lands, securing inter-generational legacies, maintenance or revival of culture, ability to protect country, building of self-esteem and pride, supporting self-determining futures, protecting languages and valuing cultures/knowledges. For non-Indigenous Australians and/or Others, the benefits include: cross-cultural engagement and learning opportunities, reconciliation between Indigenous and non-Indigenous Australians, transformations in environmental con-sciousness and for Australia as a nation – improved standing in the interna-tional community.

From these brief introductory words, it is clear that Indigenous Australian tourism is a promising endeavor that delivers more than just individual benefits to Indigenous people and other Australians associated with these businesses. However, such benefits presume perfect and seamless co-option of Indigenous ways of doing and being into the market economy.

Space does not permit a full analysis of the ways in which the perfect co-option does not occur, but Dean MacCannell's *Empty Meeting Grounds* (1992) provides a background to such issues. He discusses the cannibal incorporation into the capitalist market economy. He describes a globalisa-tion that allows an illusion of harmony as we all become one by becoming regimented to the systems and structures of the market. Indigenous peoples are invited to be performative primitives, staging culture for the tourists for profit, but the essence of their culture and their spirituality is leeched out as market values dictate the exchange. Commodification through tourism hollows out any possibility of cross-cultural engagement as differences in cultural values are disappeared by imposed market values. This perspective is important in the discussion below about justice and self-determination in tourism.

Recognition, redistribution and representation in Indigenous tourism in Australia

Recognition is meant here as restructuring of symbolic order (Fraser & Honneth, 2003). In terms of recognition for Indigenous people in Australia, recognition in the Australian constitution and a signing of a treaty would be two actions that would be considered as a symbolic restructuring of social order. One symbolic recognition process that has occurred and will continue to develop in Australia is reconciliation within Indigenous tourism (Higgins-Desbiolles, 2003). The reconciliation movement in Australia advanced during the time of the Sydney Olympics of the year 2000. Its opening and closing ceremonies featured Indigenous Australians prominently. The pressure of the spotlight that hosting this global event placed on Australia made the country self-reflexive in a way arguably not undertaken to that point. It was followed by thousands of Australians showing commitment through Reconciliation Bridge Walks across Australia as the reconciliation decade came to its end. The Australian community seemed open to changing its relationship with its Indigenous Australian communities and it was a time of optimism.

At this time, Indigenous Australian tourism came in for strong support from organisations ranging from the Australian Tourism Commission (now Tourism Australia) to state and territory authorities around Australia. As a result, a number of Indigenous Australians were trained and supported to enter tourism and their products and experiences marketed partly in order to be ready for the tourism bonanza that allegedly spins off from major events such as the 2000 Olympics. Indigenous Australian tourism operations popped up all over the country, including in cities and remote regions and those that already existed were lauded and supported. Outstanding examples included Camp Coorong, Desert Tracks, Tjapukai, Manyallaluk, and Umorrduk Safaris (see *A Talent for Tourism*, Office of National Tourism, 1994).

Redistribution is more easily understood than recognition but is fraught with moral philosophical and legal issues. The rise of ownership of traditional lands in various ways in Australia has led to Indigenous people connecting with their country in greater numbers (this is not without problems, see Altman & Markham, 2015). Native title legislation and land rights legislation, as well as increased joint management of parks, has led to Indigenous people having various forms of access or ownership over those lands. Benefits of the resultant joint management of the lands occurs particularly if there are community controlled management systems in which preservation and maintenance of knowledge systems upon which the livelihoods of Indigenous people depends (Langton et al., 2014). Such joint management has been promoted as having co-benefits but in terms of monetary outcomes, there are few examples of joint management leading to significant benefits to traditional owners involved with tourism (see Wearing & Wearing, 2016). At the heart of the issue is control, and land tenure is fundamental to the power which Indigenous people can exercise in relation to the development of tourism activities.

Rights afforded by native title, land rights, and Aboriginal trusts are different to that of private property and thus involve a problematic process for 1) self-determined Indigenous tourism development and 2) partnerships with other tourism operators. Such tourism development requires particular frameworks that dictate collective negotiations of the Indigenous people of Australia with the state in order for tourism development to occur on the land in question, whether that is for self-controlled tourism development or partnerships with other tourism organisations. Such negotiations are critical for increasing benefits from a community development perspective, as local tourism needs to be reflexive to the context of the external policy changes which dictate how local communities may engage with – and variously benefit from – development (Jamal & Dredge, 2014). For an overview of factors influencing Indigenous engagement in tourism development see Fletcher et al. (2016).

Representation is an important issue for Indigenous tourism. Ensuring Indigenous people are engaged through appropriate levels of participation in the various facets of Indigenous tourism activities is fundamental to ensuring the rights of Indigenous people. Article 18 of The United Nations Declaration on the Rights of Indigenous Peoples states that "Indigenous peoples have the right to participate in decision-making in matters which would affect their rights, through representatives chosen by themselves in accordance with their own procedures, as well as to maintain and develop their own indigenous decision-making institutions" (2007:6). Self-determination of Indigenous people lies at the heart of representation in tourism (Johnston, 2003). Additionally, the issue of consent is fundamental to tourism operations that require involvement of indigenous people (Hales et al., 2013; Robinson, 1999).

To illustrate the importance of recognition, redistribution and representation we will offer case studies below.

Camp Coorong (Recognition – reconciliation)

Camp Coorong was founded in 1985 as a place for South Australia's school children to come and learn about Ngarrindjeri culture and history with the long-term aim that this experience will contribute to reconciliation between Indigenous and non-Indigenous Australians. Founded by George Trevorrow, a cultural educator within the South Australian school system, Camp Coorong was planned to use cultural education to end the racism and oppression that Ngarrindjeri suffered in their daily lives. Camp Coorong is a community-based education facility and tourism enterprise. Its aim, as stated by Tom Trevorrow:

> We don't put a value on the dollar - we put education and love and understanding first, and I suppose that's what may make us different compared with other businesses…We're not doing this to get rich - we're doing it to help solve a problem
> (A Talent for Tourism, 1996:7&9).

Camp Coorong offer a range of opportunities to learn about Ngarrindjeri culture and history which include: a cultural museum sharing insights into Ngarrindjeri people, cultural education through workshops on language, a walk through native bushland demonstrating Ngarrindjeri knowledges of food and medicines and first hand exposure to the camps as a symbol of Ngarrindjeri sustainable lifeways in the face of the damages of dispossession.

Since its founding in 1985, Camp Coorong has educated thousands of youth and adults from around South Australia and the world. Its impact has been profound. Some statements made in the visitors' book include:

> "Education is the key to reconciliation – may the stories live forever
> May this Camp prosper and teach Australia its forgotten history
> Reconciliation is a difficult process. Camp Coorong helps to overcome our ignorance

Thank you for teaching me not to feel guilty but to seek awareness instead"

(Higgins-Desbiolles, 2003:40).

Camp Coorong has hosted: groups of South Australian school children; specialist groups interested in environment; university students studying health, education, law, ecology, architecture; international groups of tourists and students; government bureaucrats and political leaders from local, state and federal levels; Indigenous peoples from around Australia and the world; and Ngarrinderi people who want to return to country and practice culture on country. Its impact has not been adequately measured but is no doubt an agent of profound transformation.

Reconciliation is an important part of recognition of Indigenous culture and history in Australia. In the case of Camp Coorong, the concept of recognition has been linked to redistribution and representation. The land of the camp is administered by the Ngarrindjeri Lands and Progress Association and the land tenure is an Aboriginal Land Trust. Recently, the 25 year lease of the property was renewed, which also includes the large area of land (Bonney Reserve) where cultural activities are undertaken. Additionally, the revised 2014 Aboriginal Land Trust Act increases the autonomy and decision making power of Aboriginal communities associated with these lands (South Australian Government, 2014). Increased security of tenure will allow the camp to continue their important work of promoting cross-cultural awareness and reconciliation.

One of the reasons for Camp Coorong's success may stem from the justice framework of Fraser (1999, 2009) in which the three frames are present (in varying degrees) in the context of this venture.

Garma Festival (Redistribution – land)

A case which highlights redistribution and the implications for Indigenous tourism is an annual event, located in the remote Arnhem Land of the Northern Territory of Australia. Garma, an annual 'cultural festival and political' event, was started by the Yothu Yindi Foundation 18 years ago. According to Phipps:

Garma is an intercultural gathering of national political, cultural, and academic significance, and simultaneously a very local gathering of Yolngu clans on Yolngu land for Yolngu purposes" (Phipps, 2010:227).

On the 2016 website, Garma is described as:

> *"Australia's Leading Cultural Exchange event. It is held annually onsite at remote Gulkula, a traditional meeting ground in Arnhem land"* (www.yyf.com.au).

In 2016, the theme of the festival was land rights (i.e., the 'land is our backbone'), as Australia was celebrating the 40th anniversary of land rights. Themes of each festival do not follow the standard festival focus of entertainment but rather, meaningful issues to be contemplated, commemorated and debated to bring the Australian nation into a dialogue with its Indigenous peoples.

This vision of cultural exchange, and even spiritual engagement, was expressed by Djawa Yunupingu at the 2013 event when he stated:

> *"To my countrymen and women I want to say to you that the Yolngu people do not stand apart from you – we stand with you and you stand with us. Our ceremonies link with you throughout the country".*

Djawa Yunupingu, Garma Key Note Speech, 9 August 2013.

Since its founding, Garma has been an invitation to the country of the Yolngu peoples and a chance to be educated and engaged with Yolngu culture and Yolngu country on their terms. And come they have: political leaders, artists, community leaders, activists and visionaries. It is almost a must attend event on the diaries of prime ministers and ministers of Australian governments; Yolngu leaders have demonstrated that a cultural event can be an opportunity to re-cast the relationship between Yolngu and Balanda (or Indigenous and non-Indigenous) on Yolngu terms and values.

While clearly something uniquely cultural for Yolngu people, it is also important to note that Garma stands as a major event in Australia's calendar, promoted by Tourism Australia. Additionally, Garma efforts have also recently generated a great community-initiated tourism strategy and initiative called Lirrwi Tourism (see http://www.lirrwitourism.com.au/). As Yolngu people prepare for a post-mining and self-determining future, tourism and event tourism have been used to powerful effect for Yolngu engagement and thriving. Without land rights and the creation of Arnhem Land as Aboriginal land, the certainty of such an event would be jeopardised. The celebration of land tenure in a festival is symbolic of the importance of the redistribution of land to Indigenous people of that country.

Uluru (Representation – consent)

Uluru is the ultimate site of division in Australia on Indigenous matters. Formerly known as Ayers Rock, the site was returned to Anangu custodianship in 1985 under land rights legislation and they were required to promptly lease it back to the Commonwealth National Parks and Wildlife service under a 99 year lease. It was declared a UNESCO World Heritage site in 1987 for both its natural and cultural values. Since then the guidelines for the inclusion of properties on the World Heritage List incorporate the concept of free prior informed consent (UNESCO, 2016). If Uluru was to be nominated today we suggest that the representation of Indigenous people and their power in the management of the park would be different to the current system of management and land tenure.

The key issue through which the aspect of consent comes to the surface is the tourist summit climb of Uluru. Despite the stated wishes of the Anangu, there are a considerable number of non-Indigenous tourists who climb Uluru each year. The Anangu request visitors not to climb in order to respect their law and culture because the climb follows a sacred route used by ancestral Mala men when they arrived at Uluru. Additionally, tourists often injure themselves and deaths sometimes occur which leads to the Anangu people to feel responsible under customary law (more than 30 people have died on the Climb). As traditional owner Kunmanara says:

> That's a really important sacred thing that you are climbing... You shouldn't climb. It's not the real thing about this place. The real thing is listening to everything. And maybe that makes you a bit sad. But anyway that's what we have to say. We are obliged by Tjukurrpa to say. And all the tourists will brighten up and say, 'Oh I see. This is the right way. This is the thing that's right. This is the proper way: no climbing

(Parks Australia, n.d.)

Tour companies continue to market the climb and tourists arrive still expecting the chance to conquer Uluru and see the sites from the top. Souvenir shops sell stickers with 'I climbed Uluru' on them and bloggers blog about their exploits. However, after educational effort and strategic planning, in 2007 it was thought the time was arriving to phase the climb out. Alternatives to the climb were developed, including base walks and a viewing platform. Recent news though noted the Turnbull Government and his Environment Minister have no plans to ban the climb and this was followed by the Northern Territory Chief Minister Adam Giles (a man of

Aboriginal descent) stating his opposition to ending the climb and said it was not different than climbing the Sydney Harbor Bridge or Paris' Eiffel Tower. Giles' statements were based on his argument that the tourism industry is vital and that the jobs from tourism should not be endangered by a ban (see Davidson, 2016). This gives weight to the proposition (Büscher & Fletcher, 2016) that tourism enables spaces of exception in the pursuit of economic growth.

As the metaphorical heart of the country, this struggle for cultural respect is also emblematic of the struggle for ensuring tourism serves meaningful cross-cultural engagement rather than merely the market imperatives set for tourism by neoliberal governments, tourism industry interests and tourists of a consumer mindset.

Further evidence of spaces of exception impacting on redistribution despite acknowledgement of the need for consent can be found in the Park authorities' management planning for the climb. The Park's authorities have decided the climb will be permanently ended when three conditions are met. Firstly, the board, in consultation with the tourism industry, must be satisfied that adequate new visitor experiences have been successfully established. Alternatively, the proportion of visitors climbing falls below 20% [the current level]. Or that the cultural and natural experiences on offer are the critical factors when visitors make their decision to visit the park (Maher, 2013).

However, recent events suggest it is not that simple, and a good deal of politics from governments, the tourism industry and tourists will continue to feature vocal opposition the ban of the climb, superficially resting on economic grounds but underpinned by deep cultural divides in understanding. Space limitations do not permit an extensive exploration of the issues surrounding consent.

Recent Indigenous lobby groups called for the World Heritage Nomination Guidelines to include Free Prior Informed Consent (FPCI). The result of this lobbying was that the nomination guidelines now include FPIC (UNESCO, 2016). Representation issues surrounding World Heritage and Indigenous people's involvement still exist and result from the fact that previously nominated areas (such as Uluru) have management plans which were created without the power that free prior informed consent affords (see The International Expert Workshop on the World Heritage Convention and Indigenous Peoples that was organized by the International Work Group for Indigenous Affairs, 2012).

Dreamworld (Representation – consent)

Dreamworld is another iconic tourism attraction that highlights the importance of representation. Dreamworld is a large tourism theme park on the Gold Coast, Queensland, Australia. The recently opened Corroboree exhibit has a number of key components which acknowledge the frames of recognition and representation. The creation of the exhibit took several years as a result of the consultation with the traditional owners of the land on which Dreamworld is located (the Yugambeh People) and also consultation with other traditional owners whose cultural property was used in the exhibit.

Consent was a key component of the development of the exhibit. Representation is also a component of the exhibit. The creation of the exhibit prompted Dreamworld to further develop their Reconciliation Action Plan aimed at improving employee access for Equal Employment Opportunity target groups. Although the exhibit does not explore post-settlement issues like other cross-cultural tourism ventures in Australia, the creation of such an exhibit in one of the largest theme parks in Australia is significant in terms of representation.

Conclusion and future directions

With such promising examples (with the exception of Uluru), one would think that recognition, redistribution and representation has advanced Indigenous tourism in Australia. But this would unfortunately be wrong. Despite mainstream and niche Indigenous tourism development in Australia, Indigenous communities have yet to achieve widespread visibility and can be considered as 'the visited Other' rather than as leaders in the tourism sector (Carr, Ruhanen & Whitford, 2016).

Since the 2000s, the promise of Indigenous tourism has declined and the signs are not positive for those who hope to harness its capacities. We could speak about some technicalities, such as the fact that the market has always been focused more strongly on the international visitor than the more difficult, yet perhaps more societally important, domestic market, or the fact that many businesses started in the heady days of the late 1990s are now closed (such as the Coorong Wilderness Lodge and Desert Tracks). But instead of this picture, wider societal dynamics are an important context in which Indigenous tourism and its social capacities can either thrive or falter.

In making sense of these scenes we have shared with you, we must note that Australia is a settler-colonial country and the terms of living together are by no means settled and resolved. In our view, the settler-colonial stain of invasion, dispossession, attempted genocide, taking of children, attacks on culture, rapes of women and usurping of the wealth of the land remains clearly unhealed; Australia is divided and in an arrested state of development as a result, despite the 1967 referendum, the implementation of full citizenship rights, the reconciliation movement, the Apology to the Stolen Generations and now the Recognize movement.

How can Australia as a nation and the tourism sector negotiate a settlement between ourselves and the 'Other' with whom we live and work to build a shared future? Indigenous cultures and lifeways offer a lesson in the acceptance of diversity. The world recognised Indigenous peoples, their cultures and rights, with the 2007 United Nations Declaration on the Rights of Indigenous Peoples (UNDRIP). In tourism, the Larrakia Declaration on the Development of Indigenous Tourism (2012) offers the foundations for a tourism that fosters cross-cultural engagement and learning. The Larrakia Declaration was created in Darwin, and Australia has much to gain by ensuring the tourism industry leads the way in Indigenous rights in tourism for self-determining futures. Taken together, UNDRIP and the Larrakia Declaration offer unsettled settler-colonial societies tools to negotiate and build a shared future.

Due to constraints, we have only offered a brief comment on cases that evidence success and failure of recognition, redistribution and representation in the broader sphere of Indigenous issues in Australian. The importance of integration of these three facets of justice are important for Indigenous people, particularly because of the interrelationship between the Indigenous ways of being: kinship, language, ceremony, ties to country (place) and law.

The Indigenous values introduced here, such as the custodianship and cultural-sharing demonstrated in the cases presented illuminate other possibilities and challenges to overcome. Economist Jon Altman:

> "cautions against policies which seek to enforce neo-liberal economics as normal, arguing that Aboriginal economies have their own dynamic logic. The way forward is a hybrid economy, which provides room for economic vitality grounded in Aboriginal culture alongside western capitalism" (2010).

References

Altman, J. (2009). *Beyond closing the gap: Valuing diversity in Indigenous Australia*, Canberra: Centre for Aboriginal Economic Policy Research.

Altman, J. (2010). What future for remote Indigenous Australia? Economic hybridity and the neoliberal turn. In Altman, J. & Hinkson, M. (eds), *Culture Crisis: Anthropology and politics in Aboriginal Australia*, Sydney: UNSW Press, pp. 259-280.

Altman, J. (2014). Indigenous policy: Canberra consensus on a neoliberal project of improvement. In Miller, C. & Orchard, L. (ed.) *Australian Public Policy: Progressive ideas in the neoliberal ascendency*. Bristol: Policy Press.

Altman, J. & Markham, F. (2015). Burgeoning Indigenous land ownership: Diverse values and strategic potentialities. In Brennan, S., Davis, M., Edgeworth, B. & Terrill, L. (eds.) *Native Title from Mabo to Akiba: A vehicle for change and empowerment?* Sydney: Federation Press.

Atkinson, J. (2002). *Trauma Trails, Recreating Song Lines: The transgenerational effects of trauma in Indigenous Australia*, Melbourne: Spinifex.

Büscher, B. & Fletcher, R. (2016). Destructive creation: Capital accumulation and the structural violence of tourism. *Journal of Sustainable Tourism*, **25**(5), 651-667.

Butler, R., and Hinch, T. (1996) *Tourism and Indigenous Peoples*, London: International Thomson Business Press.

Carr, A., Ruhanen, L. & Whitford, M. (2016). Indigenous peoples and tourism: The challenges and opportunities for sustainable tourism. *Journal of Sustainable Tourism*, **24**(8-9), 1067-1079.

Davidson, H. (2016). Uluru: Northern Territory chief minister opposes climbing ban. www.theguardian.com/australia-news/2016/apr/20/dont-stop-tourists-climbing-uluru-says-northern-territory-chief-minister. Accessed 23/04/2017.

Department of the Prime Minister & Cabinet (2017). Closing the Gap reports. https://www.dpmc.gov.au/indigenous-affairs/closing-gap. Accessed 25/04/2017.

Fletcher, C., Pforr, C. & Brueckner, M. (2016). Factors influencing Indigenous engagement in tourism development: an international perspective. *Journal of Sustainable Tourism, **24**, 1100-1120.

Fraser, N. (1999). Social justice in the age of identity politics: Redistribution, recognition, and participation. In Ray, L. and Sayer, A. *Culture and Economy after the Cultural Turn*. London: Sage, pp. 25-52.

Fraser, N. (2009). Social justice in the age of identity politics. In G. Henderson & M. Waterstone (eds.), *Geographic Thought: A Praxis Perspective*, London: Routledge , pp. 72-90.

Fraser, N. & Honneth, A. (2003). *Redistribution or Recognition?: A political-philosophical exchange*, London: Verso.

Hales, R., Rynne, J., Howlett, C., Devine, J. & Hauser, V. (2013). Indigenous free prior informed consent: A case for self determination in World Heritage nomination processes. *International Journal of Heritage Studies*, **19**(3), 270-287.

Higgins-Desbiolles, F. (2003). Reconciliation tourism: Tourism healing divided societies? *Tourism Recreation Research*, **28**(3), 35–44.

Higgins-Desbiolles, F. (2006). More than an industry: Tourism as a social force. *Tourism Management*, **27**(6), 1192-1208.

Higgins-Desbiolles, F. Whyte, K.P. & Tedmanson, D.J . (2013). Tourism and environmental justice. In K. Schwab & D. Dustin, (eds.) *Just Leisure: Things that we believe in*. Illinois: Sagamore, pp. 91-100.

Hollinshead, K. (2007). Indigenous Australia in the bittersweet world: The power of tourism in the projection of 'old'and 'fresh'visions of Aboriginality. In R. Butler & T. Hinch (eds.) *Tourism and Indigenous Peoples: Issues and Implications* (2nd ed.). Amsterdam: Butterworth-Heinemann, pp. 281-304.

Jacobsen, D. (2016). Worldmaking and domestic tourists: Critical insights from philosophical hermeneutics. *Tourism Analysis*, **21**(2), 309-324.

Jamal, T. & Dredge, D. (2014). Tourism and community development issues. In R. Sharpley & D. Telfer (eds.). *Tourism and Development. Concepts and Issues*, London: Channel View, pp.178-204.

Johnston, A. (2003). Self-determination: Exercising Indigenous rights in tourism. In Singh, S. Timothy, D. & Dowling, R. (eds.) *Tourism in Destination Communities*, London: CABI, pp. 115-133.

Langton, M., Palmer, L. & Rhea, Z, (2014). Community-oriented protected areas for indigenous peoples and local communities. In S. Stevens. (ed) *Indigenous Peoples, National Parks, and Protected Areas: A new paradigm linking conservation, culture, and rights*, Arizona: University of Arizona Press, pp. 84-107.

Leiper, N. (1995). *Tourism Management*. Melbourne: RMIT Press.

McLaren, D. (1998). *Rethinking Tourism and Ecotravel*. West Hartford: Kumarian.

Maher, L. (2013). The message is clear: please don't climb Uluru. www.abc.net.au/news/2013-06-03/maher-please-don27t-climb-uluru/4728726. Accessed 23/04/2017.

Office of National Tourism, (1994). *A Talent for Tourism,* Canberra: Commonwealth of Australia.

Parks Australia (n.d.) Please don't climb Ulur. http://www.parksaustralia. gov.au/uluru/do/we-dont-climb.html. Accessed 23/04/2017.

Phipps, P. (2010). Performances of power: Indigenous cultural festivals as globally engaged cultural strategy. *Alternatives, 35,* 217-240.

Reisinger, Y., & Steiner, C. (2006). Reconceptualizing object authenticity. *Annals of Tourism Research, 33*(1), 65-86.

Robinson, M. (1999). Collaboration and cultural consent: Refocusing sustainable tourism. *Journal of Sustainable Tourism, 7*(3-4), 379-397.

South Australian Government (2014). Aboriginal Land Trusts. http:// statedevelopment.sa.gov.au/aboriginal-affairs/aboriginal-affairs-and- reconciliation/initiatives/aboriginal-lands-trust. Accessed 23/03/2017.

UNESCO (2016). World Heritage Operational Guidelines. http://whc. unesco.org/en/guidelines/. Accessed 15/04/2017.

United Nations (2007). United National Declaration on the Rights of Indigenous People, http://www.un.org/esa/socdev/unpfii/documents/ DRIPS_en.pdf. Accessed 15/04/2017.

UNWTO (1980). Manila declaration on world tourism. Madrid: United Nations World Tourism Organization. http://www.world-tourism.org/ sustainable/concepts. Accessed 03/03/2017.

Wearing, S. & Wearing, M. (2016). Decommodifying Grassroots Struggle Against a Neoliberal Tourism Agenda: Imagining a Local, Just and Sustainable Ecotourism. In Mosdale J. (ed) *Neoliberalism and the Political Economy of Tourism,* London: Routledge, pp. 139-153.

Whyte, K. (2010). An environmental justice framework for Indigenous tourism. *Journal of Environmental Philosophy, 7*(2), 75-92.

Yunupingu, D. (2013). Garma Key Note Speech, 9 August,by Djawa Yunupingu [in Gumatj Matha]. https://www.youtube.com/ watch?v=4qEHq3AUdFI. Accessed 20/04/2017.

8 Understanding Tourism through an Indigenous Lens of New Zealand and Aboriginal Australian Cultures

Freya Higgins-Desbiolles, Sharleen Howison and Zexuan Sun

Introduction

This interface between tourism and indigenous peoples is a complex and fraught space due to the history of colonisation, exploitation and denigration that many indigenous peoples have suffered in the global community. Nonetheless, in recent years indigenous communities around the world have embraced tourism for its potential value in offering economic, social, cultural, environmental and political opportunities. Specifically in the settler colonial nations of Australia and New Zealand, positive tourism initiatives have been harnessed as these countries have worked to come to terms with tourism as an internal and external driver of community development.

In this chapter we explore the values that could reshape our understanding of tourism and its cultural interface. In part this exploratory work was inspired by the challenge set by Peters and Higgins-Desbiolles (2012:79) who noted:

> *"The profit-driven focus of tourism under global economic conditions of capitalism runs counter to the shared, community/group-based ideals of Indigenous cultures. As such ... many Indigenous Australians struggle to have a major impact on an industry that is focused on Western ways, disregards Indigenist thought, and has success determined by Western (capitalistic) measures.*

In today's era options for Indigenous engagement with tourism are rather limited; increasingly there is the assimilationist model where Indigenous peoples join tourism on the tourism industry's terms of economic rationalism and market values (see Whitford *et al.*, 2001).

Our hypothesis in this exploratory work is that Indigenous tourism which is operationalised adhering to Indigenous cultural values can offer cultural encounters that make a difference in terms of cross-cultural understanding and respect. Understanding these underpinning cultural values is important as it enables this work to be valued and continued. We also propose that tourism viewed through a prism of Indigenous values illuminates a different paradigm for tourism that is worth considering. First we will briefly contextualise this discussion in terms of the social values of cultural tourism before moving on to Indigenous peoples' engagement with tourism and the particular cases of Aotearoa/ New Zealand and Australia.

The enduring social values secured by cultural tourism

Cultural tourism is a lucrative special interest niche of tourism and has been studied extensively since the 1980s. As Richards (2003) noted, cultural tourism has a long history and in its western form it can be traced back to the European Grand Tour. Cultural tourism can be defined as "all aspects of travel, whereby travellers learn about the history and heritage of others or about their contemporary ways of life or thought" (McIntosh & Goeldner, cited in Richards, 2003). While cultural tourism has been subject to critical scrutiny in order to identify its boundaries and parameters, we are concerned here with it specifically as a place for cultural encounter and learning. Sociologist George Ritzer (2016:56) asserted that, in essence, culture encompasses "the ideas, values, norms, practices, and objects" and it allows a group of people or a society to live collectively with a maximum of harmony. Based on this assumption, culture in a tourism context plays a fundamental rule in shaping the attitudes of people and communities, both as visitors and hosts, and thereby providing a possibility for comprehension from cross-cultural encounters.

However as Higgins-Desbiolles (2006) has argued, the social capacities of tourism niches such as cultural tourism have been inadvertently narrowed as tourism has increasingly been approached as an industry and promoted for its contributions to economic growth. While it is impossible to ignore the business aspects of tourism in today's market society, it should not be allowed to erase tourism's vital social and cultural capacities. As Tribe (2002) confirmed, tourism stakeholders should foster both the vocational and the philosophical aspects of tourism so that we can reflect on the kinds of worlds we wish to foster through tourism. In an increasingly cosmopolitan world in need of creative answers to numerous challenges, the insights and perspectives of many cultural worldviews are vital to creating a shared future. With the industrial view of tourism, we are beginning to forget the powerful capacities of tourism to connect people and foster creative dialogue.

An example of the bold expectations of tourism from the earlier era can be found in this statement from McKean (1989:133) who asserted:

> "Underlying tourism is a quest or an odyssey to see, and perhaps to understand, the whole inhabited earth, the oikumene. Tourism can be viewed as not an entirely banal pleasure-seeking escapism ... but as a profound, widely share d human desire to know 'others,' with the reciprocal possibility that we may come to know ourselves."

In her analysis of tourism as a social force, Higgins-Desbiolles (2006:1202) argued:

> "The contemporary, 'western' understanding of tourism comes from a rather narrow set of experiences and philosophies, which results in its emphasis on a highly individualistic and marketised tourism. In the mainstream tourism literature it is difficult to find academic contributions to the critique of tourism that approach the topic from a 'non-western' perspective "

This chapter offers an opportunity to consider the tourism cultural encounter through the lens of the Indigenous peoples of New Zealand and Australia, the Māori and Indigenous Australians. We will briefly overview the context of Indigenous peoples' engagement with tourism in order to situate our discussion before moving to our study context in the Antipodes.

Tourism and Indigenous peoples

Understanding the interface between tourism and Indigenous peoples requires awareness that the Indigenous view of, experience of and engagement with, the forces of tourism may be entirely different from those of Western peoples. In countries such as Australia and New Zealand, tourism was often imposed on Indigenous communities as a part of the process of conquest and colonization. Non-Indigenous peoples came to triumphantly gawk at Indigenous people as remnants of primitive and dying cultures of interest in effectively a human zoo situation; for instance, Indigenous peoples were presented at world fairs as tokens of the wars of conquest in the imperial age (see for example Welch, 2011). Frequently, creation of national parks for the enjoyment and recreation of mobile middle classes resulted in the dispossession of Indigenous peoples and their exile from their country in the interest of conservation of the last 'wilderness' areas (Mowforth & Munt, 2003). Tourism has also been used as a cover for biopiracy of Indigenous traditional ecological knowledge on plant use for medicines and incorporated into the commercial pharmaceutical industry with little recognition of or returns to Indigenous custodians (McLaren, 2003). These are only a few of the experiences that have resulted in many Indigenous peoples holding great suspicions of tourism.

Despite these suspicions, some Indigenous communities decided to assert control over tourism by building ventures themselves and seizing its capacities for autonomy. As Smith et al. (2000:14-5) argued:

> "...for many Indigenous communities, cultural tourism and art production offer a way to achieve economic empowerment. This is not an arena into which Indigenous peoples have been unwillingly dragged, but rather one to which Indigenous peoples who have been unwillingly colonized have turned as a means of asserting their rights and autonomy."

It is also important to understand that principles of Indigenous rights and self-determination have gained greater status following the promulgation of the United Nations Declaration on the Rights of Indigenous Peoples and are now challenging the tourism status quo (Johnston, 2003; Higgins-Desbiolles, 2007). Outcomes from these developments are well exemplified in "the Oaxaca Declaration of the International Forum on Indigenous Tourism (IFIT)" of 2002, which resulted from a gathering of Indigenous peoples of the Americas who came together to challenge the United Nations'

International Year of Ecotourism. This declaration stated "tourism is only beneficial for Indigenous communities when it is based on and enhances our self-determination" (IFIT, 2002).

More recently, the Pacific Asia Travel Association convened a conference on Indigenous tourism in Darwin, Australia, which resulted in the Larrakia Declaration on the Development of Indigenous Tourism (Pacific Asia Indigenous Tourism Conference, 2012). In its preamble, this document points to the profound possibilities of Indigenous tourism when done from an approach of respect for Indigenous values and worldviews:

- Recognizing that for Indigenous tourism to be successful and sustainable, Indigenous tourism needs to be based on traditional knowledge, cultures and practices and it must contribute to the well-being of Indigenous communities and the environment;

- Recognizing that Indigenous tourism provides a strong vehicle for cultural understanding, social interaction and peace;

- Recognizing that universal Indigenous values underpin intergenerational stewardship of cultural resources and understanding, social interaction and peace.

This preamble outlining the norms and values that should underpin Indigenous tourism suggests that Indigenous peoples are demanding their rights in tourism, have much to offer tourism and its practice through Indigenous knowledges and are open to working towards more harmonious relations with non-Indigenous peoples using tourism as a tool for building understanding. For this work, it intimated to us that an understanding of who the Indigenous 'hosts' are and what their relationships are, what their cultural values are and what their cosmo-visions are that result from these, may offer us an approach to tourism that is different to western approaches and thereby holds great value in opening up tourism disciplinary knowledge.

Māori and tourism

There has been a good deal of academic analysis of Māori engagement with tourism (e.g. Amoamo & Thompson, 2010; Barnett, 2001; Carr, 2007; Ryan, 2002; McIntosh et al., 2004). As McIntosh et al. (2004) noted, Māori have been engaged in tourism for an extensive period of time and this has been largely based on the principle of *manaakitanga*, requiring Māori hospitality and care for the guest. A key catalyst to recent Māori engagement in tourism has come from the opportunities that language revival, cultural revitalisation and the resources provided by the Treaty of Waitangi settlements; as Love and Love have noted, "the Treaty of Waitangi Act 1975 became the basis for Crown acknowledgement and resolution of Māori historical grievances. Treaty settlements have provided an investment base and allowed Māori to be more self-reliant" (2010).

Known as *tangata whenua* (people of the land), Māori comprise a number of *iwi* (tribes), *hapu* (subtribes), and *whanau* (extended family units) but they share in the rich tradition of songs, dance, art and oral literature (Butler, 2010). In order to construct an appropriate understanding of Māori culture of high significance for cultural tourism, three values call for attention: *whanaungatanga* (relationship), *manaakitanga* (hospitality) and *kaitiakitanga* (guardianship of natural resources). With these cultural and spiritual values, we clearly see how the complex and deep relationships between peoples, the land and all beings coexisting on this land are interwoven and meaningful. This is demonstrated in Māori introductions, or *pepeha*, where a person introduces themselves through their genealogies, their associations with place (including a mountain and a river) and their relations with others; through such an approach people can meet on terms of building webs of relationships (in both space and time).

Whanaungatanga acknowledges the significance of attaining and maintaining relationships and may be defined as "a relationship through shared experiences and working together which provides people with a sense of belonging" (Boulten & Brannelly, 2015). O'Carroll (2013) stated that *whanaungatanga* is a process in which people collectively get involved in order to enhance relationships. This is important to Māori who value relationships both within and outside of the business context (McNatty & Roa, 2002, as cited in Boulten & Brannelly, 2015). *Whanaungatanga* is not excluded from the modern Māori business setting and may be expressed in many ways, such as in: the design of systems and structures, the development of plans and strategies, the use of networks, or the management of human resources, all in such a way that people are placed at the centre of concern (Spiller, 2012). But it should be noted that *whanaungatanga* is never limited to a linear relationship that confines the connection between one person and another; rather it reviews and renews the shared experience of Māori people, including those of the past, the present and the future (Mitchell & Mitchell, 2007).

One important aspect of managing and sustaining *whanaungatanga* is *manaakitanga*, which is also one of the most important values in understanding the Māori culture on *marae* (a Māori meeting house serving for social and ceremonial functions). Gagné (2013:152) suggested that *manaakitanga* refers to "befriending holistically and demonstrating extreme kindness with the utmost respect", which begins when the guests arrive and finishes when all guests depart. Gifford and Boulton (2015) pointed out that the concept of *manaakitanga* is well entrenched in Māori society and is manifested as caring and/or sharing with others: being generous, taking care of others' needs, and fostering relationships. In the 2015 New Zealand Tourism Strategy, the Ministry of Tourism (2007) defined it as "sharing exceptional and natural hospitality, knowledge, and beliefs, on the basis of mutual respect between host and visitor". Huia and Liu (2012) further illuminated understanding by stating that *manaakitanga* reveals the importance of interdependence between hosts and guests in Māori culture, exemplified by the proverb '*he tangata takahi manuhiri, he marae puehu*' (p.141), that proper and kind treatment of guests is vital for maintaining the life force of a *marae*. In summary, *manaakitanga* is characterised as an amalgam of responsibility, hospitality and mutual respect.

According to Rhodda (2012:120), *kaitiakitanga* is a "Māori philosophy describing guardianship, care and protection, and providing a basis for our approach to sustainably managing our natural, cultural, and built environment for current and future generations". Underneath this philosophy is the traditional Māori belief that people are a part of the natural order and are therefore, not superior to it (Te Ahukaramu, 2009). *Kaitiakitanga*, as a traditional value, underscores the importance of responsible and respectful interactions between people and offers guidance to issues and challenges facing today's Māori people (Mcintosh *et al.*, 2014). It should be noted that *kaitiakitanga* both "had inspired a range of conservation and restoration efforts throughout New Zealand" and "remains a major source of conflict" arising from different interpretations of it by the English and the Māori (McGrinnis, 2016:80). Nonetheless, after exploring a great diversity of business practices fostered by *kaitiakitanga*, from the radically designed eco-lodges to cutting-edge ventures, Bangs (2008) concluded that this ancient Māori concept has given rise to a very prominent and popular eco-friendly movement that characterises the modern identity of New Zealand, as well as an outstanding ecotourism offering.

The New Zealand Māori Tourism initiative illustrates the articulation of these values and how these shape the aims, goals and objectives of Māori tourism. On their 'about us' segment of their webpage they stated:

> *"Māori tourism, as the first impression and final exclamation mark for visitors to Aotearoa New Zealand visitors, is important to NZ Māori Tourism.*
>
> *The Māori world provides a key point of difference for visitors and entering this world offers a fascinating first impression, a unique connection, and everlasting memories.*
>
> *NZ Māori Tourism works collaboratively with the Māori tourism sector to ensure visitors arrive as strangers but leave Aotearoa New Zealand as members of our whānau (family)."* (NZ Māori Tourism, n.d.)

The page continued by articulating these values specifically:

> ⟩ *"**Ngā Mātāpono** or The Values we uphold:*
>
> **Mana Tangata***: This term refers to the prominence of a person - mana tangata - and expresses the 'people first' approach in all we do.*
>
> **Manaaki Manuhiri***: Māori culture places great emphasis on hospitality. The care of visitors - manaaki manuhiri - is important to our culture and in providing the best tourism experiences.*
>
> **Rangatiratanga***: The leadership we practice - rangatiratanga - stems from our knowledge of our world and the ability to meet our responsibilities. We aspire to develop exemplary governance, and leadership.*
>
> **Kaitiakitanga***: Our country is the life source of our people. The guardianship - kaitiakitanga - of this land requires that we maintain and protect our environment for future generations.*
>
> **Whanaungatanga***: We have developed a close relationship with the Māori tourism sector - whanaungatanga - through shared experiences and working together collaboratively and collectively."*

With this simple content on its' 'about us' webpage, NZ Māori Tourism affirms the centrality of *te reo*, or Māori language, and thus invites potential tourists to engage on the hosts' terms. The outline of concepts here asks visitors to enter the space of sharing that can place them in relationships, eventually through hospitality to become family and to also become custodians of the precious New Zealand environments they have come to visit. It also suggests a different form of tourism: where people of the land and the land itself are placed first above all else, where leadership is exercised for long-term responsibility and well-being; and where the tourism sector is built on cooperation and not relentless competition.

In Aotearoa/ New Zealand, the Māori are in a very strong position to assert their values in their engagement with tourism in a way that would be the envy of others. As Love and Love (2010) have noted, *"in tourism – the largest single contributor to export earnings – the Māori culture was increasingly seen as one of the defining points of difference for visitors who wanted an authentic 'Kiwi experience'. Only Māori could deliver a Māori cultural experience"*.

Indigenous Australia

Indigenous Australia is more difficult to describe in terms of cultural values that may be shaping Indigenous Australian engagement in the tourism space. This is because Indigenous Australia is comprised of two main groupings (Aboriginal and Torres Strait Islander peoples) that are vastly different and these main groupings are subdivided into hundreds of individual nations with their own languages, protocols and cultures. As a result, it is not possible to write about Indigenous Australian engagement with tourism in terms of cultural values in a comparable way to the Māori case that has been outlined above. However, there are some commonalities that can be used to explain how these cultures might engage with tourists and tourism differently and this is best accomplished through an examination of illustrative examples. Before doing this, we will provide a brief context for understanding Indigenous Australian tourism.

Indigenous Australians have had a long engagement with tourism and cross-cultural engagement over millennia (Peters & Higgins-Desbiolles, 2012) and as these authors document, there were frequent gatherings, exchanges, ceremonies and trade between the nations of Indigenous Australia. As they noted: "Travel and movement was based on such things as Elders' leadership decisions, kinship, seasonal availability of resources, ceremonial obligations and defined routes of trade" (Yarra Healing, n.d., cited in Peters & Higgins-Desbiolles, 2012:80). There was also trade, inter-marriage and cross-cultural exchanges with external peoples, most notably the Macassans arguably before the arrival of Europeans; this had lasting impacts and the cultural exchanges have survived until today (Museums Victoria, 2010).

More recently, concerted efforts were made at all levels of government to develop, train and support an Indigenous Australian tourism sector in the run-up to the Sydney Olympic Games of 2000. The results of these efforts were the development of a variety of Indigenous Australian tourism ventures all across the country that offered outstanding cultural, ecological and adventure tourism experiences that gained a high profile. Tourism academics have written about these enterprises and have illuminated a great variety of models, approaches and motivations (e.g. Bennett, 2005; Dyer et al., 2003; James, 1994; Higgins-Desbiolles et al., 2014; Nielsen, 2010). Such cases made it clear that some businesses were addressing the tensions between Indigenous Australian cultural values and the demands of modern tourism business practices. Debates ensued about the role of culture in tourism businesses (Miller, 2000) and whether stereotypes of traditionality used in marketing were putting Indigenous Australian tourism products in a straightjacket, depicting Indigenous Australians as primitive and failing to show the great diversity of these nations (Ahoy, 2000). However one key feature of most Indigenous Australian tourism ventures at that time was an effort to impart an understanding of the Dreaming, ranging from brief and entertaining story-telling experiences to much deeper educational efforts to explain the Dreaming as an engagement with the land and its laws.

Desert Tracks

An example of the latter is that of Desert Tracks. This was a tour company that offered tours to Pitjantjatara country in Central Australia. It focused on deep education of tourists and was founded by Elders Nganyinytja and Ilyatjari in collaboration with non-Indigenous business partners Diana James and Greg Snowdon. Nganyinytja offered an invitation: "Come and see my country. This land is sacred! This has been my grandmother's and grandfather's country from a long time ago. Come with open ears, open eyes and an open heart." (James, 1994:330) A key feature of this tourism experience was learning the law of the land, the *Tjukurpa*, which is shared through the Dreaming stories which tell of creation and the laws of living. As James (1994:332 & 334) reported, the Tjukurpa:

> "...*imbues all their activities with spiritual significance. There is Tjurkurpa related to daily hunting and gathering; their dance, song and stories; their painting, carving and making of utensils and weapons... visitors are taken and shown some of the sacred places so that they will,*

kulira wanantjaka tjukurpa – following the Dreaming and learn. They
are taught verses of the song cycle and the dances that correspond to
Ngintaka's [a Creation Being of the Dreaming] actions at these places."

In another work, James (2010: 110) has explained how such story-telling and ceremonial performances can shape an ontology of place:

"The rhythms of deep time of this land are the rhythms of the songs
and dances of its original people ... Listening to their voices tunes the
ear to hear the composed ontology of place, the songs and stories that tell
the nature of its being. Place is performed by storytelling, singing and
dancing at each site along the creation ancestors' travels ... "

That tourists can be affected by this exposure to the stories and laws of the Tjukurpa to the point of also feeling this ontology of place is surprising but it seems indeed they were. This is illustrated in a documentary film that was made about Desert Tracks (1991). This film shows a small tour group comprised mostly of domestic Australian tourists who camp on country and learn from Anangu Elders. During the tour they are taught about Tjukurpa and invited to participate in caring for country through custodial practices including ritual and ceremonies. Tourists are interviewed on film and some explain how experiencing these tours change their feelings of belonging in Australia and understanding country. Some of these visitors are repeat visitors who come back again to learn more deeply. In fact it is clear that the Desert Tracks leaders saw their tours as something different than conventional understandings of tourism; Greg Snowdon states in this film that the Anangu Elders see the tourists as students and the tour as education (Desert Tracks, 1991).

While Desert Tracks unfortunately no longer operates, we find that Tjukurpa also informs ongoing collaborations at the UNESCO World Heritage site of Uluru – Kata Tjuta, which is under a joint management strategy between National Parks Australia and the Aboriginal traditional owners of Uluru–Kata Tjuta National Park (Nguraritja) (Uluru-Kata Tjuta National Park Management Plan 2010-2020, 2010). Tjukurpa is the underpinning value system to the joint management of this important site and like Desert Tracks, learning is a key feature promoted by the Anangu custodians; in the foreward to the Plan, it states the aim of promoting "...Uluru–Kata Tjuta National Park to become known as a place of learning, knowledge, and understanding about culture, country and custom" (Uluru-Kata Tjuta Board of Management, 2010:ii).

The plan explains:

Tjukurpa is the foundation of Anangu life. It encompasses:

- *Anangu religion, law and moral systems*
- *the past, the present and the future*
- *the creation period when ancestral beings, Tjukaritja/Waparitja, created the world as it is now*
- *the relationship between people, plants, animals and the physical features of the land*
- *the knowledge of how these relationships came to be, what they mean, and how they must be maintained in daily life and in ceremony.*

> *Tjukurpa is also the foundation of joint management for the park. Anangu consider that, to care properly for the park, Tjukurpa must come first.* (Uluru-Kata Tjuta Board of Management, 2010: 2-11)

While controversies remain with the joint management arrangement and its failure to address such difficulties as the ongoing climbing of Uluru despite Anangu's opposition to this and the relationship of the site with Mutitjulu community (Brooks, 2015), the steady assertion of Anangu cultural values and Tjukurpa shows that many Indigenous Australians remain steadfast in their approach to maintaining cultural values while they engage with modern tourism and related endeavours.

Lirrwi Tourism

The final example we would like to explore is that of Lirrwi Tourism. This:

> "...was established in 2010 to develop, support and promote Yolŋu tourism in Arnhem Land ... Lirrwi's main objective is to create a new economy for Yolŋu people in Arnhem Land through tourism. It does this by bringing people together to share Yolŋu culture, connecting Aboriginal and non-Aboriginal people." (About Lirrwi Tourism, n.d.)

The various clans of the Yolngu peoples have shown extraordinary leadership in Australia and are known for initiatives such as the 1963 Bark Petition (considered a turning point in recognition of Indigenous rights in Australia) and more recently the Garma Festival which is "recognised as the nation's premier forum for discussion of Indigenous affairs" (ABC News, 2015). Now the Yolngu are showing leadership with this Lirrwi Tourism venture and its supporting Yolngu Tourism Masterplan. Key Australian tourism industry leaders, including John Morse and Geoff Dixon, have supported this work and it could set a powerful example of community initiated and community-controlled tourism if it proves successful in the long-term.

The Lirrwi Yolngu Tourism Aboriginal Corporation's Tourism Masterplan features Yolngu values at the centre of the plan. It states:

> *Lirrwi is a powerful Yolngu word which means 'charcoal' (Ŋurrŋgitj). Lirrwi defines the layers of charcoal, which go deep into the earth and deep into the past. It is the place where Yolngu people always return to, in life and beyond life. A single piece of charcoal cannot burn brightly on its own. It takes many pieces. So too with the people and the culture. In the Yolngu world everything is connected, the country, the people, the plants and the animals, even the sky and the world above*

(Lirrwi Yolngu Tourism Aboriginal Corporation, 2014: 10).

In fact country, people and people's responsibilities for country are placed front and centre in the planning. The guiding principles put forward for Lirrwi Tourism are organised under headings: the country, tourism business, people, culture and respect. These are worth providing in full:

The country:

- Arnhem Land has been the home of Yolngu people since the beginning of time; they have always been there, and this must be acknowledged and respected.
- Yolngu have a responsibility to care for country.
- Tourism should never control what happens on country.

Tourism business

- Yolngu must have the right to say who can and who cannot visit the country.
- Yolngu wish to share knowledge with people from other places.
- The marketing and promotion of Arnhem Land must embrace all these values.
- The tourism calendar must synchronise with the Yolngu calendar.
- Yolngu should partner with Balanda, but not depend on Balanda.
- Tourism must be flexible and fit in with Yolngu culture, not control it.
- Infrastructure must be not overdone and kept in harmony with the country.

- Finances are only an instrumental means for achieving success and will never be considered an end in themselves: maximising profit will never be the number one business objective.

People

- Recognition that Yolngu are 'farmers and custodians', not nomads.
- Visitors must recognise that Arnhem Land is a place to be slow and steady.
- Yolngu wish to be inclusive for all Australians.
- Tourism should be a positive influence on Yolngu to provide value.
- Tourism should be a source of pride for Yolngu.
- Yolngu will be open to mentoring.
- Tourism must recognise 'Mulwat' — value.

Culture

- Yolngu will have the right to decide how much and what information to share.
- Surface information is enough for sharing.
- Ceremony takes precedence over tourism.
- External stakeholders must learn Yolngu culture and system.

Respect

- The land and all it contains, needs to be recognised for its significance to Yolngu people.
- Sacred sites must be respected by everyone.
- History must be revised through tourism to recognise the Yolngu people as the first people of Arnhem Land.
- The environment will be respected at all times.
- Respect is a key requirement for all visitors.

(Lirrwi Yolngu Tourism Aboriginal Corporation, 2014: 6).

These guiding principles illustrate two important points for this chapter: the assertion of Yolngu values as the terms under which tourists are welcomed, and strong assertions of what form of tourism Lirrwi tourism wishes to engage. In terms of the former, the key demands are respect and entering this different cultural land on the terms of the local people by not demanding what is not offered and slowing down to listen and learn while with

Yolngu. These guiding principles also present a challenge to the tourism industry to transform the way it does 'business' with the Yolngu and Lirrwi Tourism. These challenges in fact are an attempt to disrupt the assimilationist efforts of industrial tourism. Perhaps most important is the assertion that "external stakeholders must learn Yolngu culture and system" which is a foundation stone for many of the other terms. Additionally the assertion that economic values will not dominate the business objectives of Lirrwi Tourism demonstrates resistance to the narrow focus of profits that feature in mainstream tourism business and suggests that culture and well-being are the main priorities. The final points on tourism business assert Yolngu authority over Yolngu engagement with tourism, including the right to say no to tourism and tourists.

Final reflections

This chapter has presented some explorations of the roles Indigenous values play in the Indigenous engagement with tourism following a proposition that these values may shape a form of tourism quite different from the current western paradigm that predominates. We have done this through an exploration of brief case studies of Aotearoa/New Zealand and the Australian contexts. From this brief exploration, we conclude that an Indigenous-led business practice is essential for Indigenous peoples such as the Māori and Indigenous Australians to be able to engage with tourism on their terms and be successful in this. As we have demonstrated here, Māori tourism businesses and Indigenous Australian tourism businesses are already operationalising this by building businesses that reflect authentic values and culture. Love and Love (2005) identified five common features of Māori tourism businesses:

- They have management control (control of their lives)
- Responsibility and accountability are due to a broader range of beneficiaries and stakeholders
- *Tikanga* (cultural practices) are applied in the business environment
- There are obligations to an extended family group as opposed to focusing solely on individual advancement
- The organisation has an ethos that mirrors the broad goals, values and aspirations of the Māori world.

These features are reflected in the daily business practices of many Māori enterprises, which are not evident in most traditional non-Indigenous tourism businesses. These principles are adaptable to the contexts of other Indigenous peoples and assert a self-determining approach to tourism. The key requirement is to allow for Indigenous peoples to traverse modern day business practices whilst still maintaining the values and traditions that are essential to their culture.

We have illustrated two significant outcomes that may be gained from the assertion of Indigenous values in tourism: a meaningful cross-cultural engagement and learning experience for the tourists, and a different model of tourism that accentuates the social and human values of the phenomenon above the economic ones. In this era where humanism is under challenge, we need this diversity of practice more than ever. We advocate coalitions of proponents to ensure support for Indigenous led spaces of tourism that can thrive and lead the way in a values driven form of tourism.

References

About Lirrwi Tourism (n.d.) http://www.lirrwitourism.com.au/about-us/. Accessed 05/12/2016.

ABC News (2015). Garma Festival 2015: What is it, where is it, who goes, and what should we expect this year? from http://www.abc.net.au/news/2015-07-31/garma-festival-2015-premier-forum-for-indigenous-affairs/6659372. Accessed 05/12/2016.

Ahoy, L. (2000). *Promotion vs product. Tourism – the Indigenous Opportunity: National Indigenous Tourism Forum Proceedings Report*. Sydney, 3-4 June, p.59-65.

Amoamo, M. & Thompson, A. (2010). (Re)imaging Māori tourism: Representation and cultural hybridity in postcolonial New Zealand. *Tourist Studies*, **10**(1), 35–55. http://dx.doi.org/10.1177/1468797610390989

Bangs, R. (2008). *The Quest for Kaitiakitanga: The ancient Māori secret from New Zealand that could save the Earth*. Birmingham, AL: Menasha Ridge Press.

Barnett, S. (2001). Manaakitanga: Māori hospitality – a case study of Māori accommodation providers. *Tourism Management*, **22**, 83-92.

Bennett, J. (2005). *Indigenous entrepreneurship, social capital and tourism enterprise development: Lessons from Cape York*. Unpublished PhD thesis submitted to LaTrobe University.

Boulten, A. & Brannelly, T. (2015). Care ethics and indigenous values: political, tribal and personal. In M. Barnes, T. Brannelly, L. Ward, & N. Ward (eds), *Ethics of care: Critical advances in international perspective*, Bristol, UK: Policy Press.

Brooks, S. (2015, 26 October). Uluru: joint management model 'not too good'. ABC AM radio program, http://www.abc.net.au/am/content/2015/s4338679.htm. Accessed 03/12/2016.

Butler, S. (2010). *New Zealand - Culture Smart: The essential guide to customs and culture.* London: Bravo Limited.

Carr, A. (2007). Māori nature tourism businesses: Connecting with the land. In R. Butler & T. Hinch (eds) *Tourism and Indigenous peoples: Issues and implications.* Amsterdam: Elsevier, 113-127.

Desert Tracks (1991). *Desert Tracks*, True Stories series, ABC TV.

Dyer, P., Aberdeen, L. & Schuler, S. (2003). Tourism impacts on an Australian Indigenous community: a Djabugay case study. *Tourism Management*, **24**, 83-95.

Gagné, N. (2013). *Being Māori in the City: Indigenous everyday life in Auckland, Toronto, Canada*: University of Toronto Press.

Gifford, H. & Boulton, A. (2015). Is sharing tobacco within the home really good manaakitanga? In M. Kepa, M. McPherson & L. Manu'atu (eds.), *Home: Here to stay.* Wellington, New Zealand: Huia Publishers.

Higgins-Desbiolles, F. (2006). More than an industry: Tourism as a social force. *Tourism Management,* **27**(6), 1192-1208.

Higgins-Desbiolles, F. (2007). Taming tourism: Indigenous rights as a check to unbridled tourism. In P. Burns & M. Novelli (eds) *Tourism and Politics: Global frameworks and local realities, Amsterdam*: Elsevier, 83-107.

Higgins-Desbiolles, F., Trevorrow, G. & Sparrow, S. (2014). The Coorong Wilderness Lodge: A case study of planning failures in Indigenous tourism. *Tourism Management,* **44**, 46-57.

Huia, A and Liu, J. (2012). Maori culture as a psychological asset for New Zealanders: Acculturation experiences abroad. *International Journal of Intercultural Relations* **36**, 140-150.

International Forum on Indigenous Tourism (2002). *Oaxaca Declaration.* Oaxaca, Mexico.

James, D. (1994). Desert Tracks – Pitjantjatjara Tours. In S. Hawthorne & R. Klein (eds), *Australia for Women.* North Melbourne: Spinifex Press, 330-335.

James, D. (2008). An Anangu ontology of place. In F. Vanclay, M. Higgins & A. Blackshaw (eds), *Making Sense of Place*. Canberra: National Museum of Australia.

Johnston, A. M. (2003). Self-determination: Exercising Indigenous rights in tourism. In S. Singh, D. J. Timothy & R. K. Dowling (eds), *Tourism in Destination Communities*. Oxon: CABI, 115-134.

Lirrwi Yolngu Tourism Aboriginal Corporation (2014). *Yolngu Tourism Masterplan Arnhem Land 2014–2032*, http://www.lirrwitourism.com.au/tourism-masterplan/. Accessed 05/12/2016.

Love, M. & Love, T. (2005) Māori and self-employment, in C. Massey (ed) *Entrepreneurship and small business management in New Zealand*, Auckland: Pearson Education New Zealand.

Love, M. & Love, T. (2010) 'Ngā umanga – Māori business enterprise - Opportunities for Māori enterprise', *Te Ara - the Encyclopedia of New Zealand*, http://www.TeAra.govt.nz/en/nga-umanga-Māori-business-enterprise/3. Accessed 05/12/2016.

McGrinnis, M (2016) *Science and Sensibility: Negotiating an ecology of place*. Berkley, CA: University of California Press.

McIntosh, A. J., Zygardio, F. K. & Matunga, H. (2004) 'Rethinking Māori tourism', *Asia Pacific Journal of Tourism Research*, **9**(4), 331–352.

Mcintosh, N., Maly, K. & Kittinger, J. (2014) Integrating traditional ecological knowledge and community engagement in marine mammal protected areas, in J. Higham, L. Bejder, & R. Williams (eds), *Whale-watching: Sustainable tourism and ecological management*, Cambridge, UK: Cambridge University Press, 163-176.

McKean, P. F. (1989) Towards a theoretical analysis of tourism: Economic dualism and cultural involution in Bali, in V. L. Smith (ed), *Hosts and Guests: The anthropology of tourism*, Philadelphia: University of Pennsylvania Press, 119-138.

McLaren, D. R. (2003) Indigenous peoples and ecotourism, in M. Honey & S. Thullen (eds), *Rights and Responsibilities: A compilation of codes of conduct for tourism and Indigenous and local communities*, Centre for Ecotourism and Sustainable Development and International Ecotourism Society, http://ecotourism.org/rights_responsibilities.html. Accessed 11/11/2003.

Miller, G. (2000) Is it culture or is it business?, *Tourism –the Indigenous Opportunity: National Indigenous Tourism Forum Proceedings Report*, Sydney, 3-4 June, p.92-94.

Ministry of Tourism (2007) New Zealand tourism strategy 2015, retrieved 3 August 2016, from https://www.tianz.org.nz/content/library/ FINAL_NZTS2015_HR.pdf. Accessed 03/08/2016.

Mitchell, H., & Mitchell, M. (2007). *History of Māori of Nelson and Marlborough*,Wellington, New Zealand: Huia Publishers.

NZ Māori Tourism (n.d.) About us, http://www.Māoritourism.co.nz/about/ our-values. Accessed 03/04/2016.

Nielsen, N.R. (2010) Strengths, support and self-determination: Indigenous tourism planning and the Biamie Dreaming Cooperative, unpublished PhD thesis Southern Cross University.

Mowforth, M. & Munt, I. (2003) *Tourism and Sustainability: Development and new tourism in the Third World* , 2nd ed., London: Routledge.

Museums Victoria (2010) Aboriginal people and trade, https:// museumvictoria.com.au/discoverycentre/discovery-centre-news/2010-archive/aboriginal-trade/ Accessed 03/12/2016.

O' Carroll, A. (2013) Virtual whanaungatanga: Māori utilizing social networking sites to attain and maintain relationships, *Alternative: An International Journal of Indigenous Peoples*, **9**(3), 230-245.

Pacific Asia Indigenous Tourism Conference (2012) The Larrakia Declaration on the Development of Indigenous Tourism, www.winta. org/the-larrakia-declaration/ Accessed 12/08/2016.

Peters, A. & Higgins-Desbiolles, F. (2012) 'De-marginalising tourism research: Indigenous Australians as tourists', *Journal of Hospitality and Tourism Management*, **19**, 1-9.

Rhodda, S. (2012) Accessible tourism in New Zealand in D. Buhalis, S. Darcy & I. Ambrose (eds), *Best Practice in Accessible Tourism: Inclusion, disability, ageing population and tourism*, Bristol, UK: Channel View Publications, 114-124.

Richards, G. (2003) What is cultural tourism?, in van Maaren, A. (ed) *Erfgoed voor Toerisme*, Nationaal Contact Monumenten, https:// www.academia.edu/1869136/What_is_Cultural_Tourism. Accessed 03/06/2017

Ritzer, G. (2016) *Essentials of Sociology*, Thousand Oaks: Sage Publications.

Ryan, C. (2002), Tourism and cultural proximity: Examples from New Zealand, *Annals of Tourism Research*, **29**(4), 952–997.

Smith, C., Burke, H., & Ward, G. (2010) Globalisation and Indigenous peoples: Threat or empowerment?, in C. Smith & G. Ward (eds), *Indigenous Cultures in an Interconnected World*, London: Allen & Unwin.

Spiller, C. (2012) Wayfinding in strategy research, in C. Wang, D. Ketchen & D. Bergh (eds), *West Meets East: Building theoretical bridges*, Bingley, UK: Emerald Group Publishing Ltd, 61-90.

Te Ahukaramu, C. (2009) 'Kaitiakitanga - guardianship and conservation', *Te Ara - the Encyclopaedia of New Zealand*, http://www.teara.govt.nz/en/kaitiakitanga-guardianship-&-conservation. Accessed 20/03/2016.

Tribe, J. (2002) The philosophic practitioner, *Annals of Tourism Research*, **29**(2), 338-357.

Uluru-Kata Tjuta Board of Management (2010) Uluru-Kata Tjuta National Park Management Plan 2010-2020, Tjukurpa Katutja Ngarantja, Canberra: Director of National Parks, https://www.legislation.gov.au/Details/F2010L00057. Accessed 03/03/2016.

Welch, C. (2011).Savagery on show: The popular visual representation of Native American peoples and their lifeways at the World's Fairs (1851–1904) and in Buffalo Bill's Wild West (1884–1904), *Early Popular Visual Culture*, **9**(4), 337-352.

Whitford, M., Bell, B. & Watkins, M. (2001) Indigenous tourism policy in Australia: 25 years of rhetoric and economic rationalism, *Current Issues in Tourism*, **4**(2-4) 151-181.

Yarra Healing (n.d.) Essential learnings and understandings, http://www.yarrahealing.catholic.edu.au/teaching-learning/index.cfm?loadref=47. Accessed 20/10/2010.

9 Māori Tourism in New Zealand

Anna Carr

Introduction

Māori cultural experiences have been commercialized and marketed for over 120 years by New Zealand tourism agencies and providers. Since the mid-1980s there has been increasing engagement and leadership by Māori people in the management, development and promotion of cultural and non-cultural tourism experiences. Māori are involved as owner/operators, managers, employers, employees and as residents in communities where tourism activities manifest. From the perspective of the country's primary tourism marketing organization, Tourism New Zealand (TNZ), Māori cultural experiences are presented as a 'must see' component of the New Zealand experience; subsequently international marketing informs international travelers' expectations of the culture (TNZ, 2014; 2017).

Māori tourism ventures have proven they can be developed sustainably and endure over time, with many employing successive generations and incorporating long term planning principles focused on intergenerational wealth and wellbeing. The diversification of Māori owned tourism businesses to include those that might not necessarily have a cultural theme or focus (i.e. in the hotel and transport sectors) have been observed to, nevertheless, be grounded in or informed by Māori values such as *kaitiakitanga* (guardianship) or collective *iwi* (Māori tribe) decision making influencing business plans and management styles. The 1980s to 1990s saw organizational foundations laid for the professionalization of Māori tourism, especially since the Māori Tourism Development Board was established in 1994. In 1996 a report to Te Puni Kōkiri, (TPK) the Ministry for Māori Development, identified Māori tourism experiences including:

> "Unique, indigenous, cultural experiences, such as: hangi and concert performances, Māori arts and crafts. Māori owned tourism activities that are not culturally Māori but are special because they give the visitor a unique Māori perspective and interpretation, e.g. ecotourism products or Māori owned accommodation" (Ingram, 1996:2).

Since Ingram's report, TPK have continued with research and support for Māori tourism, for instance the Māori Tourism Capability Assessment Report (TPK, 2014). Māori tourism ventures have diversified, whilst increasing in the number of operations, visitor capacity and geographical distribution. Māori with cultural values and identities grounded in iwi, hapu (subtribal) and whanau (family) histories have become employed or otherwise engaged in the provision and management of such ventures, motivated by a mix of economic, socio-cultural and environmental factors. This chapter draws upon both academic and industry research to overview the history of Māori tourism development and consider the future of Māori tourism.

Early development

The Tuhourangi and Ngāti Whakaue hapu (subtribes) of the Te Arawa tribal community were early leaders of commercial tourism, providing guiding and accommodation services in the Rotorua region since the 1850s (Te Awekotuku, 1981; Barnett, 1997; McClure, 2004; Bremner, 2013). In the early 1870s there were four accommodation houses in the Rotorua district, whilst the natural resources of the geothermal region, particularly the Pink and White Terraces, provided tourism employment opportunities for Māori. Guide Sophia (Te Paea Hinerangi) of Ngāti Ruanui had shifted to Wairoa village from Te Tai Tokerau (Northland) to remarry and pursued a livelihood guiding tourists until the Mt Tarawera eruption in June 1886. After the eruption, which devastated the Terraces, tourism activities relocated to neighboring Rotorua and by the late 1890s the town was renowned as a tourism spa destination and geothermal region, whilst Whakarewarewa Village became the focus for Māori cultural tourism experiences in New Zealand (Te Awekotuku, 1981; Barnett, 1997; Wikitera, 2006; Bremner, 2013).

The early decades of cultural tourism were not without tensions. Whilst financial returns were a positive aspect of engaging in tourism, Maori were also conscious of compromising their cultural identity through tourism activities. From the 1890s to 1970s the national tourism promotion was *pakeha* (non-Māori New Zealander) controlled through various national agencies. Whilst some artists produced photographic and artistic representations of Māori that were authentic and realistic, many postcards, posters and related marketing perpetuated stereotypes such as the Māori maiden and *haka* performing warrior (Alsop et al., 2012). Government involvement in the sector saw legislation aimed at encouraging tourism to revitalize culture, particularly the *Rotorua Insititute for Arts and Crafts Act (1963)* establishing the Māori Arts and Craft Institute, which today operates as Te Puia. According to McClure (2004) by the 1970s there were concerns that tourists were having a 'plastic' experience of Māori culture with the mass-production of cheap souvenirs that presented traditional artistic symbolism inappropriately. Rotorua hotels provided packaged tourism experiences of Māori culture that were criticized for being non-Māori controlled, yet Ngahuia Te Awekotuku's PhD research, notable for its analysis of the intergenerational impact of tourism on Te Arawa, concluded that, despite some negative impacts, tourism provided benefits beyond employment, including the retention of *te reo* (language), *waiata* (songs) and other artistic traditions within the local community.

During the 1980s Māori tourism experiences began to be managed in a more strategic manner. This was partly due to the influence of the museum cultural interpretation and consultation processes associated with the Te Māori exhibition of 1984 – a turning point for the international recognition of Māori arts and culture on the world stage. The curated collection of *taonga* (treasured objects, art works or resources) travelled to Chicago, Illinois, San Francisco and New York before returning to a final exhibition in Auckland. Traditional *powhiri* (welcoming ceremonies) preceded the opening of the exhibition in each city. The valuing of Māori taonga by the museum-going public had a flow-on effect fueling international visitors' demand for experiences of Māori culture at tourism attractions, museums and art gallery exhibitions, whilst also increasing involvement by Māori museum and gallery staff in curatorial and exhibition development roles. Until the Te Māori exhibition many Māori cultural performances in hotel settings, or museum exhibitions, had been under the management or direction of non-Māori (Barnett, 1997; Tahana & Opperman, 1998; McClure, 2004).

Professionalism and cultural identity

Two conferences, the *Māori Economic Development Summit Conference Hui Taumata* in Wellington (1984) and the *Manaakitanga Hospitality Conference* in Rotorua (1985) were pivotal events that further explored ways of collaborating for the sustainable development of the cultural tourism product. More inclusive, culturally appropriate management approaches, such as consulting with *kaumatua* (elders) as to the authenticity of what was conveyed to visitors in museum and tourism contexts, were advocated in the post-conference report (Māori Tourism Task Force, 1987). Researchers observed that increased Māori ownership meant the staging of Māori performances had to meet the needs of the performers and not just those of visitors. By the mid-1990s the uniqueness of Māori culture was regarded as a significant economic asset that needed to be respectfully managed. The Aotearoa Māori Tourism Federation became proactive in identifying marketing opportunities and addressing issues around cultural authenticity (Aotearoa Māori Tourism Federation, 1994; 1995a; 1995b). Barnett (1997) reported 159 Māori tourism enterprises throughout the country and the Māori Tourism Development Board had the vision to "develop policy and strategies for sustainable Māori tourism to enable Māori to gain maximum value and profit and increase potential benefits from participation in a sustainable tourism industry while maintaining cultural integrity" (Māori Tourism Development Board, 1997:2). In 1998 the first national Māori tourism directory provided an overview of Māori businesses throughout the country (TPK, 1998). The need to ensure social and cultural sustainability within commercial Māori tourism attractions became an increasing focus for research in numerous academic publications and government reports (for example Mahuta, 1987; Aotearoa Māori Tourism Federation, 1994; 1995a; 1995b; Ryan 1997; Tahana & Opperman, 1998; Cloher, 1998; McIntosh et al., 1999; Cloher & Johnston, 1999; McIntosh & Johnson, 2000; Stafford Group, 2001).

The report by the Stafford Group, *Closing the Gaps in Tourism: He matai tapoi Māori*, identified barriers to Māori participation in the industry which included under-capitalized businesses, lack of representation at a government level, a lack of data about Māori tourism businesses and inadequate government support. The report's researchers interviewed Māori tourism operators who identified the need for practical assistance in the form of legal advice, access to marketing networks and finance as key concerns (Stafford Group, 2001:16). One of the report's controversial recommendations was the Qualmark certification of Māori tourism attractions which, whilst now widely adopted as a benchmark for many Maori businesses, initially met with some resistance because of what was perceived to be the external assessment of the cultural identity of the people. Furthermore, inbound tour operators surveyed for the report still identified the traditional *hangi* and Māori concert party as the most marketable Māori tourism product – tourism demand preferred the convenience of a traditional, commodified, experience (Stafford Group, 2001:37).

Staged performances (*hangi* and Māori performances or concerts) have endured over the years as an economically feasible option for some Māori tourism operators, however there has been increased attention to the authenticity of the language and presentation of *waiata*, stories and dance by Māori performers themselves. Not compromising cultural integrity and recognising key Māori values underpinning such enterprises was urged for by Māori development agencies. Researchers in the 2000s continued to explore issues surrounding entrepreneurship, cultural identity, opportunities for cultural or language revitalization, sustainable marketing, community development, networks and business clusters (e.g. Broughton et al., 2006; Carr, 2007a; 2007b; 2008; Horn & Tahi, 2009; Amoamo & Thompson, 2010; Ringham et al., 2016; Whitney-Squire, 2016).

Research has also probed the varying levels of domestic and international visitor demand for Māori cultural experiences (e.g. McIntosh & Johnson, 2004; Horn & Tahi, 2009; Statistics New Zealand, 2016). Consistent low demand amongst the domestic visitor market for such experiences was attributed to 'cultural proximity' – the notion that Māori culture was not exotic enough for New Zealander visitors (Ryan, 2002). Ryan and Pike (2003) suggested more contemporary Māori cultural opportunities (for instance contemporary music or theatre performances) may have greater appeal to the domestic market. Researchers such as McIntosh and Johnson (2004) have also investigated the incorporation of Māori cultural values within tourism businesses through 'Māori-centred' approaches. Whether cultural themes are absent from or present as the core of the tourism product, it has been acknowledged that Māori staff within Māori owned tourism businesses do explore and reaffirm their cultural identity, "integrating Māori values into their lived geographies...to create diverse tourism economies based on Te Ao Māori" (Ringham et al., 2016:110).

Te Tiriti and empowerment

A notable development in the past few decades has been the increase of Māori concessionaires as providers of ecotourism and nature tourism activities in national parks and other protected areas. This can be attributed to Treaty of Waitangi (*Te Tiriti*) settlements. The Treaty of Waitangi, signed and in 1840, is the founding document by which the British Crown and New Zealand Māori agreed to the settlement of New Zealand by British subjects. Under the Treaty the traditional rights of Māori were to be protected, however, throughout the mid to late nineteenth century a combination of colonisation, government legislation, land wars and land confiscations disenfranchised Māori society, with many individuals and *iwi* losing their lands (Sinclair, 1992). Article Two of the Treaty of Waitangi had intended to guarantee Māori their exclusive rights and interests to collective land, resources and *taonga* (Sinclair, 1992). From the mid-1970s an intense revival of pride in Māori culture resulted in increased Māori pressure on government for recognition of Māori to exercise these traditional rights, including the *kaitiaki* of natural resources (Keelan, 1996). In 1975 the Waitangi Tribunal was established to settle Māori land and resource claims surrounding Treaty grievances. This was a commitment to meeting Treaty obligations by the New Zealand government and Treaty Settlement processes in New Zealand have improved the ability of Māori *iwi* to engage in tourism.

Settlements have recognised cultural values through a variety of resource management techniques including the designation of a *Tōpuni* or statutory cloak of *iwi* (Māori tribes) values on a significant area(s) to enhance the *mana* (pride) of iwi. The *Ngāi Tahu Claims Settlement Act 1998* legally recognised the traditional relationships between the Ngāi Tahu iwi and the natural world, returning not only land but legal ownership and management of natural resources such as *pounamu* (greenstone) which is prized for jewelry and carvings within tourism and non-tourism spaces. Treaty settlements mean Māori have benefited from the ability to invest in developing tourism infrastructure, thus leading to cultural revival and employment through becoming owners of accommodation, transportation, ecocultural tourism and recreational guiding concessions. The Tourism New Zealand (TNZ) strategies include a commitment to upholding the principles of the Treaty of Waitangi, with emphasis on partnership with *tangata whenua* for product development and protection of the 'integrity' and 'authenticity' of the culture and the environment (TNZ, 2003:8). Visitor interpretation of cultural landscapes and the human history of national parks are now provided through place-based, eco-cultural tourism with Māori nature tourism guides or businesses throughout the country (Carr, 2004; 2008). Iwi consultation and partnerships, Māori representation as Department of Conservation staff, and Māori appointments on conservation boards nowadays inform policy and planning around the delivery and content of interpretation about cultural values for landscapes to both domestic and international visitors.

Whale Watch Kaikoura

No chapter about Māori tourism in New Zealand can ignore the significance of one particular ecotourism business that elevated Māori as tourism entrepreneurs internationally. The establishment of Whale Watch Kaikoura in 1987 was an innovative enterprise at the time. Taking tourists out on boats to view whales and other marine mammals has since benefited the destination of Kaikoura both economically and socially. The business arose from the efforts of Ngāti Kuri people (a subtribe of the Kai Tahu iwi), led by Bill Solomon who became "worried when unemployment among Māori reached 90%" (McClure, 2004:274). The local families mortgaged their homes to commence their ecotourism business, motivated by the immediate need to provide employment and economic well-being. Initially the business had one boat and ten staff and was known as Kaikoura Tours, however within several years the whale watching had extended from being a seasonal business to a year-round operation, the name was changed to Whale Watch Kaikoura Ltd and funds were loaned from the Ngāi Tahu Trust Board to further invest in the business's infrastructure. From the first year with 1,000 whale watchers, the business grew rapidly and by the late 1990s Whale Watch Kaikoura accepted approximately 100,000 reservations per year. The benefits to the community were economic, in the number of jobs created, and social, in the *mana* (self-esteem) for the Māori population. Whale Watch Kaikoura did experience controversy, for instance the monopoly marine mammal viewing concession granted through the Department of Conservation (DoC) negated competition from other local whale watching ventures. The company countered such controversy through employing local staff and innovative efforts, including instigating research to monitor the effects of tourism on marine mammals through partnerships with universities, DoC and international organizations including National Geographic. By 1994, conservative estimates suggested that multiplier effects from whale watching totalled over eight times the gross sales from whale watching (Lewis et al., 1996). Whale Watch Kaikoura received a British Airways Tourism for Tomorrow Award, a World Travel and Tourism Council Tourism for Tomorrow Community Benefit Award (2010) and a 2011 Pacific Asia Travel Association (PATA) Gold Award in the Environment and Ecotourism Category.

The success of Kaikoura Whale Watch may have contributed to a confident atmosphere enabling other Māori ecocultural operations to emerge from the late 1990s onward. Ulva Goodwillie started Ulva Tours on Rakiura (Stewart Island) in 2000; sister and brother Amo and John Barrett (Ngāti Toa, Te Ati Awa, Ngāti Raukawa) established their family ecotourism and ecolodge venture Kapiti Island Nature Tours in 2000-2001. In Kaikoura itself, former Whale Watch employees Heather and Maurice Manawatu (Ngāti Kuri) established Māori Tours Kaikoura in 2002. In Northland Koro Carman helped the Copthorne Omapere hotel, owned by Shayne and Pip Lloyd of Ngapuhi, to develop Footprints Waipoua guiding tours to the *kauri* trees of Waipoua Forest. Footprints Waipoua featured in Lonely Planet's 2006 publication *Code Green Experiences of a Lifetime* and each ecocultural tourism operation continues to flourish with international recognition through visiting media programs, awards and international partnerships furthering conservation and cultural tourism initiatives.

Expansion and international influence

By 2011 the Māori commercial asset base was estimated to be worth NZD$36.5 billion (Business Economic Research Limited, 2011). Māori tourism managers and operators have been active in policy and decision-making roles at national and international levels, for instance Wally Stone (formerly of Whale Watch Kaikoura) was Chairperson of Tourism New Zealand in the early 2000s. John Barrett of Kapiti Island Nature Tours has been Chair of the New Zealand Māori Tourism Council, a Board member with Tourism New Zealand, a Board member with Birding New Zealand and a founding member of the World Indigenous Tourism Alliance (WINTA) Leadership Council, mentoring Indigenous tourism operators overseas. The advocacy of Maori tourism operators also influenced the New Zealand National Tourism Strategies (TNZ, 2003; Tourism Strategy Group, 2007) with the incorporation of key Māori cultural values of *manaakitanga* (hospitality) and *kaitiakitanga* (environmental stewardship) underpinning the sustainable direction of how the entire New Zealand tourism industry interacts with and cares for visitors and the environment. The Tourism New Zealand Three Year Marketing Strategy for 2014-16 specified the need to continue working alongside Māori tourism providers for branding and marketing including "opportunities to build differentiation for New Zealand in the international marketplace through deeper integration of Māori culture will be sought" (TNZ, 2015). This has led to the organisation educating staff and increasing awareness of issues within the Māori tourism space by strengthening ties with New Zealand Māori Tourism thus "building the organisation's own internal capacity and understanding of Māori culture; helping build the capability of Māori tourism businesses; working with international travel sellers to raise awareness of Māori tourism products" (TNZ, 2017).

Some national support initiatives have been short-lived, for instance the government funding of staff for 13 Māori Regional Tourism Organisations in 2001 was discontinued after several years. Te Puni Kokiri continued to provide a range of services and advice to mentor and guide start-up and growing SMTE businesses. In 2011, a Māori Tourism Action Plan was developed by New Zealand Māori Tourism (founded in 2004 and based in Wellington) to strategically guide a NZD$4.5 million government investment in Māori tourism ventures over three years (MBIE, 2017). The initial funding was extended in 2014 with a commitment of NZD$1.5 million per annum, enabling initiatives such as the increased participation of Māori businesses within the International Visitor Survey by Statistics New Zealand. New Zealand Māori Tourism and Poutama Trust ("a pan tribal business development organisation", https://poutama.co.nz/about), collaborated to provide advisory services alongside volunteer-led networks such as Tai Tokerau Māori Tourism (Northland) and KUMA (Te Kupeka Umaka Māori Ki Ariateuru, Southern Māori Business Network) to support Māori tourism operators. In another collaboration, New Zealand Maori Tourism, TPK and Poutama Trust undertook research to examine Māori businesses capability with meeting future market needs. 309 Māori tourism businesses were invited to participate in the research and the 105 respondents identified that 55% were seasonal and 48% part time only (TPK, 2014: Foreword). New Zealand Māori Tourism strategically planned to improve the quality of Māori tourism enterprises through branding, promotions and trade relationships (TPK, 2014).

By 2015 Māori tourism businesses provided 2,230 EFT jobs according to the March 2015 quarter of the Statistics New Zealand (SNZ) Tourism Satellite Account (SNZ, 2016: 40). Statistics New Zealand noted that 31% of the Māori owned businesses provided arts or recreation services (including cultural performances and tour guiding) and the next largest proportion was accommodation (19%), whilst two thirds of employees were based in the Bay of Plenty/Rotorua region or the South Island. There was an increase in domestic and international guest nights hosted by Māori tourism accommodation providers (SNZ, 2016:9). Industry and government support for New Zealand Māori Tourism, ongoing government funding for Tourism New Zealand's offshore marketing and online marketing by Māori tourism operations contributed to growing the international profile for the Māori tourism sector. The International Visitor Survey year ended December 2015 noted a 33.7% increase of visitors to "activities related to, or associated with, Māori" (an increase from 4,065, 197 to 5,434,463 visitors (MBIE, 2015). 53% of international visitors participated in a Māori cultural activity with visitors from the United Kingdom (72%) and Germany (68%) having the highest participation rates (TNZ, 2015). Data from a Statistics New Zealand Business Operations Survey also noted that the highest proportion of Māori tourism businesses was still located in the Bay of Plenty/Rotorua region. Operators reported 100% engagement in online marketing by Māori tourism businesses with 100% engagement in Australian and European markets, "while 75% reported engaging with the US, the UK, China, Japan, India and other markets" (SNZ, 2016: 41).

By 2017 the Māori tourism sector was benefitting from record visitor numbers with the inbound tourism boom for New Zealand, and tourism had become the country's prime export industry and foreign exchange earner (Statistics New Zealand, 2017). Echoing Tourism New Zealand's earlier strategies, the Ministry of Business, Innovation and Employment (MBIE) states on its website that "Māori tourism adds a rich dimension to New Zealand's visitor experience, and helps set New Zealand apart from the rest of the world. Engaging with Māori culture and concepts can add depth to visitors' interaction with New Zealand's landscapes and communities" (MBIE, 2017). Increased air links with the emerging visitor market growth from India, Indonesia, South America and China have had a positive flow-on effect of confidence for many Māori operations, but such cross-cultural opportunities are accompanied with new challenges for Māori and non-Māori tourism operators, as they balance the differing expectations of such diverse visitors. As Māori businesses have diversified and invested in the transportation and accommodation sectors of the industry they have accessed economic benefits including an increase in patronage from the domestic market. Statistics New Zealand observed that some Māori tourism businesses were struggling to generate income that exceeded expenditure despite growing international visitor numbers, but on a positive note, domestic visitors were found to be increasingly underpinning the economic viability of Māori-owned tourism services and attractions.

Future prospects

Looking forward, new opportunities exist with continuing Treaty settlements recognising Māori relationships with traditional landscapes, for instance the *Te Urewera Act 2014* resulted in Urewera National Park being delisted as a national park and Te Urewera recognized as a legal entity in its own right under the *kaitiaki* (care) of the Tūhoe people, with assistance from the Department of Conservation. Similarly the *Te Awa Tupua (Whanganui River Settlement) Act 2017* has extended rights as a human entity to the Whanganui River. Existing operations such as Te Urewera Treks have opportunities to extend ecocultural tourism development by employing or mentoring local Māori in the Urewera. As a result, the ecocultural tourism possibilities of the Whanganui region could be realized. Whilst a sociocultural opportunity, such ventures must also be economically sustainable and face challenges of isolation, seasonality, being located away from traditional tourism hubs and attracting staff to what are low wage regional economies (compared to the average wages in the main cities). The responsibilities of tribal entities in such new land governance settings will also be accompanied by costs for iwi, such as those associated with providing access, infrastructure, visitor management, pest and predator control. But long-term prosperity is possible when such opportunities arise. For Ngāi Tahu Tourism (NTT) the tribe's Treaty settlement has helped it become one of the most prominent Māori entities in the sector, acting as an umbrella organsiation for twelve tourism businesses throughout the country and hosting one million plus visitors a year (https://www.ngāitahutourism.co.nz/).

NTT have positioned themselves as leaders within the adventure and nature tourism sectors through acquiring existing businesses. For instance, in 2016 NTT entered into a joint venture with Earth and Sky providing dark sky, star gazing tourism experiences at Lake Tekapo. Not all businesses run by members of the Ngāi Tahu iwi are managed under NTT's portfolio. Kaikoura Whale Watch continues to operate independently, whilst further south Pukekura Penguins (Otago Peninsula) is a joint venture between Korako Karetai Trust and the Otago Peninsula Trust. Pukekura Penguins is operated by the Pukekura Trust to provide an ecocultural experience of a kororā blue penguin colony. Te Ana Whakairo (Ngāi Tahu Māori Rock Art Centre, Timaru) is another ecocultural tourism venture outside the NTT portfolio which was partially funded by three local runanga (Moeraki, Waihao and Arowhenua) of the Ngāi Tahu iwi. Elsewhere Treaty financial settlements have enabled Waikato's Tainui iwi to jointly invest, through partnerships with Accor, Hamilton City Council and Auckland International Airport Ltd, in a portfolio of hotels, including Novotel Tainui, 1999, Ibis Tainui, 2007 and Novotel Auckland Airport Tainui, 2011. These, whilst not providing Māori experiences, are underpinned by management styles incorporating (as per the national strategies) the Māori values of *manaakitanga* and *kaitiakitanga* (http://www.tgh.co.nz/en/about-tgh/).

The Māori tourism sector is thus well positioned to take advantage of significant growth forecast in global demand for New Zealand experiences. Cultural events based around arts or creative industries are emerging opportunities whilst contemporary innovations including the adaptation of social media, apps and virtual reality can develop or improve products and processes. Online and physical networking is a modern day reality of the Indigenous tourism market place. Māori tourism operators and managers now travel internationally to attend conferences, trade and marketing events alongside other international Indigenous tourism organisations. Such information sharing and networking opportunities build internal capabilities and also offer access to domestic and international markets through collaborative marketing promotions which reach global audiences via the internet (for example http://www.tikitourmap.co.nz/ and http://www.maoritourism.co.nz/). Tourism New Zealand, MBIE and the former Ministry of Economic Development have supported a number of initiatives to assist businesses, including Māori tourism entrepreneurs (http://www.tourism.govt.nz/funding/find-Māori.html). New Zealand Māori Tourism notes possibilities for business incubators and start-up accommodation provision via engagement in sharing economy experiences such as AirBnB and AirBnB Experiences (www.maoritourism.co.nz/blog/airbnb-experiences-opportunity-m%C4%81ori) whilst internet links improve management efficiencies (e.g. recruitment advertisements).

The internet and transport technologies are improving access between operators and their visitor markets, enabling information-sharing and product marketing to be conveyed to visitors and inbound operators instantaneously. This was demonstrated recently by the 2016 Kaikoura Earthquake as Kaikoura tourism businesses continued updating followers on Facebook, Twitter and internet websites about the operators' efforts to remain open when access to the township was limited by landslides and road damage. Internet posts enabled the operators to inform visitor markets of how businesses were adapting to the altered landscape and coastal environment. Developing an online presence enabled direct business to business and business to customer engagement, enhancing international and national connections despite the earthquake. Kaikoura region's business activities have been reduced and economically challenged by the subsequent downfall in visitor numbers, and decreased employment opportunities, however this is accompanied by a supportive base of online followers.

Conclusion

The continued potential of tourism as an economic and social development for Māori people will invariably be accompanied by the costs and benefits associated with business. The active participation and engagement of Māori in all facets of the tourism industry (policy, planning, marketing, product development and delivery) are integral to the professionalism of Māori tourism.

Ongoing issues around authentic experiences, professional delivery, economic efficiencies, the appropriate care for cultural taonga, intellectual property within tourism spaces will undoubtedly continue to be debated as people seek how best to pre-empt or mitigate any negative impacts. Tourism New Zealand and New Zealand Māori Tourism collaborate to ensure promotional material presents diverse and realistic expectations of Māori tourism experiences to new and emerging markets, for instance from India, China and Indonesia. The core tourism activities of New Zealand Māori Tourism continue with off-shore marketing visits, attendance at international Indigenous tourism symposia and trade conferences, alongside Māori tourism operators who have transcended from being significant players not just within the New Zealand sector but by becoming involved internationally as leaders, planners, innovators, investors and networkers.

The increased mentoring role by Māori tourism business leaders of other Indigenous peoples also strengthens international relationships, for instance the 2017 hosting of Indigenous Chilean tourism operators in New Zealand. Internally, with the country's robust Pasifika population there is potential for further links between Māori tourism and Pacifica tourism providers such as the WINTA and New Zealand Māori Tourism initiative of a Manaaki Tāpoi cultural tourism education program for Māori and Pasifika youth in 2016. Networking and leadership from Tourism New Zealand and New Zealand Māori Tourism alongside the owner-operators, family ventures, co-operative trusts and corporate Māori entities, such as Ngāi Tahu Tourism or Tainui Holdings, will ensure continued cultural revitalisation and opportunities for intergenerational economic and social wellbeing. The diversification of Māori tourism experiences, both geographically and in terms of the broader range of services and products, enhances resilience to economic, political or environmental crises that may affect domestic and international market places. Cultural and economic sustainability in Māori tourism thus balances the lessons from over a century of engagement in the tourism industry with an outward looking future that nurtures professionalism and responsible governance within Māori entities.

References

Alsop, P., Stewart, G. & Bamford, D. (2012). *Selling the dream: The art of early New Zealand tourism*, Nelson: Craig Potton Publishing.

Amoamo, M. & Thompson, A. (2010). (Re) imaging Māori tourism: representation and cultural hybridity in postcolonial New Zealand, *Tourist Studies,* **10**(1), 35-55.

Aotearoa Māori Tourism Federation, (1994). Position paper on the protection of Māori cultural and intellectual property within the tourism Industry. Rotorua: Aotearoa Māori Tourism Federation.

Aotearoa Māori Tourism Federation, (1995a). *Report on the current market position of Māori tourism product*, Rotorua. Aotearoa Māori Tourism Federation.

Aotearoa Māori Tourism Federation, (1995b). *Strategic marketing plan for Māori tourism.* Rotorua: Aotearoa Māori Tourism Federation.

Barnett, S. (1997). Māori tourism. *Tourism Management,* **18**(7), 471-473.

Bremner, H. (2013). Tourism development in the Hot Lakes District, New Zealand c. 1900, *International Journal of Contemporary Hospitality Management,* **25**(2), 282-298.

Broughton, P., Wilson, T. & Ruwhiu, D. (2006). *Hui Taumata project building business partnerships: Closer collaboration between Māori and general business communities*. Wellington: Hui Taumata Action Taskforce.

Business and Economic Research Limited, (2011). *The Māori Economy, Science and Innovation*. Wellington: BERL.

Carr, A. (2004). *Visitor Experiences of Cultural Landscapes*. Unpublished PhD thesis, Dunedin: University of Otago.

Carr, A. (2007a). Strengthening of identity through participation in tourism guiding. In R. Butler & T. Hinch (eds.), *Tourism and Indigenous Peoples*, (2nd Ed.) Oxford: Butterworth-Heinemann, pp. 113-127.

Carr, A. (2007b). Negotiating the obstacles: Owner/operator perspectives on 'nature' tourism. In J. Higham (ed.), *Critical Issues in Ecotourism: Understanding a complex tourism phenomenon*. Oxford: Butterworth-Heinemann, pp. 406-427.

Carr, A. (2008). Cultural landscapes and heritage tourism. In B. Prideaux, D. Timothy & K. Chon (eds.), *Cultural and Heritage Tourism in Asia and the Pacific*. Oxon, UK: Routledge, pp. 35-48.

Cloher, D. (1998). Sustainable Māori tourism in Northland. New Zealand. In J. Kandampully (ed.) *Proceedings of New Zealand Tourism and Hospitality Research Conference*, 3rd Biennial conference, Advances in Research, December 1998: Akaroa.

Cloher, D. & Johnston, C. (1999). Māori sustainability concepts applied to tourism: A North Hokianga study. *New Zealand Geographer*, **55**(1), 46-52.

Horn, C. & Tahi, B. (2009). Some cultural and historical factors influencing rural Māori tourism development in New Zealand. *Journal of Rural and Community Development*, **4**(1) 84-101.

Ingram, T. (1996). *Māori tourism development: A Strategic plan and policy for Ministry of Māori Development*. Wellington: Te Puni Kokiri.

Keelan, N. (1996). Māori heritage: Visitor management and interpretation. In Hall, C. & S. McArthur (eds.) *Heritage Management in New Zealand and Australia*. Melbourne: Oxford University Press, pp. 195-201.

Lewis, G., Morkel, A., Hubbard, G., Stockport, G. & Davenport, S. (1996). *Cases in Strategic Management. Australia and New Zealand*. (2nd ed.) Sydney: Prentice Hall.

Mahuta, R. (1987). *Tourism and culture: The Māori Case*. Hamilton: Centre for Māori Studies and Research, University of Waikato.

Māori Tourism Development Board, (1997). *Hikoi: The official newsletter of the Māori Tourism Development Board*. Auckland: Māori Tourism Development Board.

Māori Tourism Task Force, (1987). *NZ Māori Tourism Task Force Report.* Wellington: Ministry of Māori Development.

McClure, M. (2004). *The wonder country: Making New Zealand tourism.* Auckland: Auckland University Press.

McIntosh, A., Hinch, T. & Ingram, T. (1999). *Māori attractions in Aotearoa, New Zealand: Setting a context for sustainable tourism.* Dunedin: Centre for Tourism, University of Otago.

McIntosh, A. & Johnson, H. (2004). Exploring the nature of the Māori experience in New Zealand: Views from hosts and tourists. *Tourism: An International Interdiscplinary Journal,* **52**(2), 117-129.

McIntosh, A., Smith, A. & Ingram, T. (2000). *Tourist experiences of Māori culture in Aotearoa, New Zealand.* Dunedin: Centre for Tourism, University of Otago.

McIntosh, A., Zygadlo, F. & Matunga, H. (2004). Rethinking Māori tourism. *Asia Pacific Journal of Tourism Research,* **9**(4), 331-352.

Ministry of Business, Innovation and Employment, (2017). *Supporting Māori tourism,* www.mbie.govt.nz/info-services/sectors-industries/tourism/supporting-maori-tourism. Accessed 08/04/2017.

Ngāi Tahu Tourism, (2017). https://www.ngaitahutourism.co.nz/. Accessed 20/04/2017.

Ringham, S., Simmonds, N. & Johnston, L. (2016). Māori tourism geographies: Values, morals and diverse economies. *MAI Journal,* 5(2), 99-112.

Ryan, C. (1997). Māori and tourism: A relationship of history, constitutions and rites, *Journal of Sustainable Tourism,* **5**(4), 257-278.

Ryan, C. (2002), Tourism and cultural proximity: Examples from New Zealand. *Annals of Tourism Research,* **29**(4), 952-971.

Ryan, C., & Pike, S. (2003). Māori-based tourism in Rotorua: Perceptions of place by domestic visitors. *Journal of Sustainable Tourism,* **11**(4), 307-321.

Sinclair, D. (1992). Land since the Treaty. In M. King (ed.), *Te Ao Hurihuri: Aspects of Māoritanga,* Auckland: Reed Books, pp. 85-105.

Stafford Group, (2001). *He Matai Tapoi Māori: A Study of barriers, impediments and opportunities for Māori in tourism,* Wellington: Ministry of Māori Development and the Office of Tourism and Sport.

Tahana, N. and Opperman, M. (1998). Māori cultural performances and tourism. *Tourism Recreation Research,* **23**(1), 23-30.

Te Awekotuku, N. (1981). *The Sociocultural impact of tourism on the Te Arawa People.* Unpublished Ph.D. Thesis, Hamilton: University of Waikato.

Te Puni Kōkiri. (1998). *Māori tourism directory Aotearoa New Zealand.* Wellington: Ministry of Māori Development.

Te Puni Kōkiri, (2008). *The Māori Asset Base.* Wellington: Ministry of Māori Development.

Te Puni Kōkiri, (2014). *Māori Tourism Capability Assessment Report.* Wellington: Ministry of Māori Development.

Tourism New Zealand, (2003). *Tourism New Zealand 3 Year Strategic Plan 2003-2006.* Wellington: Tourism New Zealand.

Tourism New Zealand, (2014). *Tourism New Zealand Three Year Marketing Strategy 2014-2016: Leveraging a strong foundation to accelerate growth.* http://www.tourismnewzealand.com/media/1543/tourism-new-zealand-3-year-marketing-strategy-fy14-fy16.pdf. Accessed 08/04/2017.

Tourism New Zealand, (2015). *International visitor experience 2015.* http://www.tourismnewzealand.com/markets-stats/research/infographics/visitor-experience/. Accessed 08/04/2017.

Tourism New Zealand, (2017). *About the Industry,* http://www.tourismnewzealand.com/about/about-the-industry/m%C4%81ori-tourism/. Accessed 08/04/2017.

Tourism Strategy Group, (2007). *New Zealand Tourism Strategy 2015,* Wellington: Tourism Strategy Group.

Whitney-Squire, K. (2016) Sustaining local language relationships through indigenous community-based tourism initiatives, *Journal of Sustainable Tourism,* **24**(8-9), 1156-1176

Wikitera, K-A. (2006). *Whakarewarewa Tourism development: A critical analysis of place and space.* Unpublished Master thesis. Auckland: Auckland University of Technology.

WINTA, (2016). *Welcome page.* Retrieved from http://www.winta.org/. Accessed 04/04/2017.

10 The Economic Value of Identity: (re)thinking Maori tourism

Maria Amoamo

Introduction

"*Promoters of a specifically Māori tourist experience need to bear firmly in mind that Māori culture is tribal. This means that it will vary from tribe to tribe and this diversity needs to be positively encouraged*" (Māori Tourism Taskforce, 1987).

Territory-identifications, for the most part, establish differences between Indigenous Māori groups in New Zealand. When asked "who are you?", Māori may answer along individual, *hapu* (sub-tribe), *iwi* (tribal) or collective dimensions. All dimensions are interrelated. This chapter draws from doctorate studies and expands on a research project titled *Increasing investment in Māori Tourism: The economic value of identity*, undertaken between 2010 and 2012 by the author. It examines the economics of identity in relation to (re)thinking Māori tourism in New Zealand. The first part of the paper theoretically challenges tourism academia to move toward more flexible forms of understanding and interpreting identifications and the "new sense/new-register" (Hollinshead, 2010) aspirations of Indigenous populations today – notably those in ambiguous/hybrid postcolonial settings. The second part of the paper examines, in a case study of Māori tourism development in Otepoti[1] Dunedin, the way in which Māori negotiate the economics of identity in a tourism context. The premise here is that tribal (and thus regional)

---

1   Otepoti is the Maori name for Dunedin, and means "the place of the corners".

differences are key elements of the development and sustainability of the Māori tourism product. Case study methodology integrates social theories of identity with Māori epistemology that moves beyond traditional activity-based analyses of tourism to an approach that is space and subject-centred. As a result, Indigenous Māori develop an economics of identity.

Māori culture

Māori are the *tangata whenua* or 'people of the land' and are officially recognised as the Indigenous people of Aotearoa New Zealand. Despite the enormous impacts of colonization, Maori have retained strong and thriving tribal traditions. Tribes were the key social, economic and political units of Māoridom represented in two forms: the *hapu* or sub tribe and *iwi*. Each *iwi* had its own history, myths, proverbs, dialect, customs and practices, and therefore, its own cultural identity (King, 1992; Walker, 2004). Although *iwi* share a degree of common cultural tradition they also chose to accentuate differences through geographical territories and histories by constructing cultural boundaries on a tribal basis. Tribal autonomy took precedence over any view of a unified ethnic collective; the term 'Māori' grew out of contact with European settlers (*Pakeha*) and the current choice of either Māori or *iwi/hapu* is a reflection of the wider social construct that both accommodates and is in tension with more particularistic and traditional lines of affiliation. Furthermore, Māori cultural identity is underpinned by a distinct system of values and knowledge known as *whakapapa*; an ordering principle and spiritual link between generations (Spiller & Stockdale, 2012). As an oral culture, Māori used various techniques to communicate information and knowledge including *waiata* (songs), *whakatauki* (proverbs), and *purakau* (folklore). Visual art forms such as carving and weaving also expressed a form of oral tradition and cultural identity through association with myths and legends. Akin to many Indigenous peoples, Māori had a holistic world view, with a relational epistemology that linked the natural and cultural world, through past, present and future.

For the purposes of this chapter, my discussion focuses on Ngai Tahu, the recognised *iwi* of Te Waipounamu, the South Island of New Zealand. Ngai Tahu hold rights as *tangata whenua* with a *rohe* (tribal homeland), the largest in New Zealand at over 80% of the South Island and constituting 18 *rununga* (governing council/administrative body) representing geographical areas (www.ngaitahu.iwi.nz). Under the Ngai Tahu Claims Settlement Act 1998, economic redress of $170million in Treaty settlement was made, and this included the right and opportunity to buy certain Crown assets, enabling the tribe to fund their social and cultural development. Since then, Ngai Tahu has invested in diverse tourism interests including businesses with non-cultural sectors such as Queenstown based operation, Shotover Jet. By 2016, Ngai Tahu Tourism has broadened its geographical reach to nine nationwide businesses including five visitor attractions throughout the South Island; one of the most notable of these being Whale Watch Kaikoura. The company philosophy is one that promotes strong *iwi* identity with intrinsic connection to the natural landscape and intergenerational wellbeing. This identification is iterated in the *iwi's* mission statement:

"Mō tātou, ā, mō kā uri, ā muri ake nei: for us and our children after us".

Hybridity: (re)thinking Māori tourism

"In tourism, ethnic populations are frequently far from being as distinct and singular as the brochure designers and travel promoters would have it" (Hollinshead, 1998:124-25)

Keeping pace with consumer demand and changing motivations means constructing a vast array of cultural and experiential tourism experiences that more readily admit the heterogeneity and the hybridity of cultural, material and spatial repertoires within which tourism operates. In what follows, I describe Māori culture and tourism development through a postcolonial lens of hybridity. In this respect, I am not using hybridity in its more dominant theoretical and political form (re-inscribing binary thinking) but its more variegated vocabulary of heterogeneity, multiplicity and difference. Accordingly, I apply the concept of hybridity as one transformed into cultural creativity and new configurations of diversity.

Since the late nineteenth century, the tourism industry has focused on two things in selling holidays to New Zealand: the natural landscape and Māori culture. Tourism New Zealand (TNZ) continues to concentrate on the former theme with its successful global campaign 100% PURE. Though Māori have been involved in tourism for more than 160 years, their identity as tourist 'attractions' rather than tourism 'managers' has to some extent marginalized Māori from the control of their own cultural expression (Amoamo & Thompson, 2010). Prior to the 1990s, much of New Zealand's offshore tourism marketing represented Māori as the exotic 'Other', manifest through the discursive and textual production of what Edward Said termed *Orientalism*. Stereotypical images have tended to fix Māori culture in a temporal zone of traditionalised and pre-colonial, akin to Bhabha's (1994: 217) notion of 'non-sense'; a discourse and praxis that is locked within totalized and historic visions of peoplehood. Such images have constructed a homogenous identity of Māori culture without particular individual or tribal identities and has not "captured the true value Māori culture can add to this marketing program and to New Zealand's tourism industry" (Te Puni Kokiri (TPK), 2009:11).

Demand from Māori for more contemporary representation of their tourism image means deciding which symbols and markers of 'traditional' Māori culture (customs, stories, beliefs, and so on) they engage in (McIntosh, 2004). This is a cultural selection process that is the first step of identity construction. The second step involves the adaptation of those systems and practices to the new environment, and therefore a process of reinterpretation and meaning and thus transformation. Take for instance Māori performance of *haka,* which has undergone transformation on the rugby field. The All Blacks traditionally perform this 'dance' before a major international game. The setting is re-inscribed through new styles of costume; re-articulated through new derivations of song and performative style. Rather than being expressive representations of a prior substance, cultural signs instead become *active agents* in themselves, creating new social forms and social realities. This is where new expressive cultural identities open out – the "signs of culture can be appropriated, translated, re-historicized and read anew" (Bhabha, 1994:37). Tradition can thus be reinvented *performatively* in the face of a multiplicity of alternative practices, mores and identities, and the co-existence of the old with the new. Although it may be argued such representation sees Māori culture as belonging to the past rather than the present it also represents the past 'in the present' if we relate this to the concept of *whakapapa* and Māori epistemology. Such mixing aligns with hybridity theory that understands boundaries as fluid and re-inventions of tradition as the creation of new transcultural forms within the contact zone produced by colonization (Ashcroft et al., 2002:118).

In order to re-think Māori tourism, it is important to recognise regional and hence tribal diversity of Māori culture; how this influences and contributes to product development. Since 2000, there has been steady growth and diversification of Maori tourism products ranging from traditional cultural based performances in regions like Rotorua to a wide range of accommodation, adventure experiences, cuisine, and transport and tour operations. But despite increased attention over the past decades to issues of Māori tourism (Barnett, 1997; Ryan, 1999; Ryan & Higgins, 2006), there has been a lack of research examining the economics of tribal identity; how this is valued, managed and represented in the tourism environment. Although tourists are interested in contemporary Māori culture, there is a paradox in that tourists "wish to experience Māori culture in recognisable ways, which often means engaging with the traditional marketed aspects of culture rather than with contemporary culture" (Wilson et al., 2006:5). The representation of this experience is however renegotiated if mandated *by* Māori and *from* a Māori perspective. A reclaimed and hybrid identity is created through the attempt by Māori to constitute and (re)present touristic identity; confirmed by self-representation, ownership and control of development (Butler & Hinch, 2007; McIntosh et al., 2002). Moreover, the host-guest relationality is constructed through a negotiation of difference, of which tribal identities are an integral part. In the sections that follow, I attempt to describe a profile of Māori regional tourism in a case study of Dunedin from which to contend tribal differences create regionally diverse representations of Maori working within a third space of equity, innovation and creativity.

Research design and methodology

The general research agenda aims to stud y the phenomenon of identity as it relates to Māori tourism development. More specifically, research questions ask: (1) what is the sector profile of Māori tourism in Otepoti Dunedin; and (2) in what ways do regional Māori construct an 'economics of identity' through involvement in tourism development. These questions are underpinned by a social valuing approach that recognizes local Indigenous communities hold extensive knowledge about places. Exposure to this knowledge can play a key role in the tourist experience, provided of course that Maori are in control of the interpretation and transmission of this knowledge. Moreover, a social-valuing approach to tourism requires all levels of government and locals working together to achieve sustainable outcomes that focus on the wishes of the community. A mixed method qualitative approach includes interviews with key tourism stakeholders (10 Māori and 6 non-Māori) involved in promoting local and regional tourism, attendance at two (Dunedin and Queenstown) Māori tourism operators workshops, content analysis of promotional literature from Dunedin's i-SITE Office and tourism website, a survey of 24 Dunedin tourism operators, and secondary literature. In addition, two brief case studies contribute to research data.

Māori tourism: The regional context

Increasing investment in Māori tourism has two substantive benefits to local regions and communities: economic and cultural development. The development of tourist services and activities within the regions will create jobs and develop infrastructure of *whanau* (extended family grouping based on *whakapapa* and tribal world view) and communities, while development, documentation and transfer of traditional Maori knowledge to the next generation will serve to increase domestic awareness of New Zealand's rich history and customs (TPK, 2009:5). Between 2001 and 2015, collaborative action between government and various Māori tourism stakeholders has seen the establishment of the New Zealand Māori Tourism Council (2004) and 13 Māori Regional Tourism Organizations, charged with advancing regional initiatives and support to Māori business owners (Whitford & Ruhanen, 2016). By 2008, there were more than 350 Indigenous themed or Māori owned and managed operations across the country. The New Zealand Tourism Strategy (NZTS) 2015 now reiterates the importance of Māori culture to the industry as a unique point of difference that can be further enhanced; adopting Māori values of *kaitiakitanga* (guardianship) and *manaakitanga* (hospitality) as intrinsic elements of the strategy. The strategy further outlines a number of actions and initiatives required from the Māori tourism industry to help build capacity and strengthen relationships between Regional Tourism Organisations, increase branding, and help tourism businesses incorporate a Māori dimension into the products and services they provide (TPK, 2009).

Notwithstanding the above 'progress' for Maori tourism, the current cultural offerings listed on TNZ's main portal (www.newzealand.com) do not promote Māori culture in the regions to the fullest extent possible. Furthermore, Māori culture is under-promoted in the South Island of New Zealand. The following section discusses results from research attendant to the aforementioned research questions.

The study site: Dunedin/Otepoti

Situated on the south-eastern coast of the South Island, Dunedin is geographically New Zealand's largest city by area with a magnificent harbour surrounded by farmland and hills, sandy beaches and rugged rocky outcrops. Dunedin is home to a wide array of wildlife and the surrounding landscape houses a range of visitor experiences both coastal and inland. The former boasts the only mainland breeding colony of the northern royal albatross and viewing of the rare yellow-eyed penguin in their natural habitat. Modelled on Edinburgh, Dunedin is widely regarded as the best preserved Victorian and Edwardian heritage city in the southern hemisphere, with many stunning buildings, including the Dunedin Railway station (promoted as the most photographed building in New Zealand) and Larnach Castle. It is a culturally vibrant city with New Zealand's oldest university, including around 20,000 students per year within in its resident population of nearly 120,000. The city is well known as having a 'lively, edgy feel' because of its student influence, which has contributed to a unique subculture, breeding leading edge fashion design and music. Events such as the annual iD Dunedin Fashion Show draw international interest alongside annual events like 'Festival of the Arts' which attracts visitors from outside the region. In 2014 Dunedin was granted 'city of literature' UNESCO status, adding to the latter's focus on global priorities of culture and development. Although the region was settled as early as 1100 AD by Māori explorers, many of whom inter-married with the Scottish settlers who arrived in the nineteenth century, it is the more colonially based influence of Scottish culture that underpins the region's identity.

Discussion

Research findings reveal little recognition of a Māori tourism profile in Dunedin; a result supported by a local interviewee who said, "We are invisible to our *Pakeha* neighbours...so these opportunities (i.e. tourism development) enable us to re-locate ourselves". Failure to be incorporated in the existing psyche of the local tourism industry is evident in the question posed by a Ngai Tahu spokesperson at a Māori Tourism Workshop in Dunedin, "Who are we?" His question was in response to lack of awareness and promotion of anything Māori upon his arrival in Dunedin; originating from the airport and use of transportation and hospitality services.

In response to his comments about lack of imagery or recognition of Maori culture in the region, I undertook a content analysis of local tourism promotional material. My analysis looked for both Māori images and descriptions of Māori cultural heritage depicted in Dunedin tourism brochures. The recorded unit of analysis was either the word "Māori" (singular or within a sentence), and/or visual images of Māori culture. Data collection was based on the hypothesis *there would be a significant lack of representation of Māori culture in local tourism brochures*. A total of 31 brochures from the local i-SITE were examined. Specific icons depicted on brochure covers were grouped under six main themes: nature (17), built heritage (3), activities (4), gardens (2), Māori (0), and other (5). The selection focused only on brochures promoting tourism experiences of Dunedin (i.e. attractions, activities, tours, heritage), and did not include brochures advertising accommodation, transport and restaurants/dining (although these were sometimes a component of the former).

Analysis of images on Dunedin's visitor information website (www.dunedinnz.com) also supported Dunedin's established reputation as a 'nature, wildlife and heritage' destination, emphasizing popular resources such as Otago Peninsula and marine wildlife. An initial search of 'Māori culture' on the portal elicited 12 hits but was not a true indication of any Māori content as several of the links had no mention or imagery of anything such as 'Māori', 'Māori culture', or 'Māori heritage'. Moreover, an examination of 153 images available on the 'Trade and Media' section of the website reinforced the strong influence of Dunedin's nature and wildlife, historic buildings, student culture, and local attractions such as museums, art galleries and services such as restaurants. Under the heading 'What to see and do' a single introductory sentence stated: "Dunedin's dramatic hills surround a long, natural harbour, which attracted Māori settlers to the site over four centuries ago". Māori names were attached to the 'Surrounding Areas' section identifying Port Chalmers as 'Koputai' (the local Ngai Tahu name) but further afield areas like Waitaki – featuring the famous Moeraki Boulders – made no mention of the local Māori story attached to this popular visitor attraction, a site culturally significant to Ngai Tahu history and identity. Not unexpectedly, the only visual image (Māori carving) was shown under the sub-heading 'Museums and Libraries' (part of Arts and Culture) as part of the description of the Otago Museum while the 'Events and Festivals' section of the website mainly directed viewers to the Dunedin City Council website for more information and calendar of events.

In 2009, a tourism-related research report titled *The Potentials of Māori Cultural Tourism Products in Otepoti Dunedin* (Gnoth et al., 2009) sought to establish the needs, barriers and opportunities for Māori cultural tourism products in Dunedin. It examined the current use of Māori culture in existing tourism services and sought to establish the demand from overseas tourists for Māori culture in Dunedin. Funded by Ngai Tahu, Otago University and the Dunedin City Council (DCC), the project indicates local community and government commitment to furthering Māori economic development in the region. The report identified the potential of Māori cultural tourism product development in Otepoti Dunedin as residing in the following offerings:

- Landscape interpretation
- Nature-based ventures
- Contemporary Māori art
- Māori cuisine
- Boutique personalized tours

The report indicated that 36% of international visitors to Dunedin are interested in experiencing Māori culture while 33% were identified as a 'potential market'. Of the interviewed sample (n=319) of tourism characteristic businesses, over 80 indicated that they believe incorporating Māori culture into their operations would add value to their business. However, the report also identified that historical and stereotypical forms of mass Māori tourism would not be sustainable in Otepoti. This point was reiterated by one of my research interviewees who stated, "Ngai Tahu identity is diverse here – and southern – that is different from the north". Although members of the Māori community showed a desire to grow Māori centred tourism in Dunedin, there were some concerns voiced around issues of controlling intellectual property, disruption of *tikanga* (culture and custom), and misrepresentation of the local community. But while the report highlighted the potential for Māori tourism development, it also identified a number of obstacles, incl uding the embryonic stage of Maori tourism in Dunedin, the need for collaboration amongst tourism stakeholders, and a need to change the perception of what Maori tourism is about. Albeit a third of businesses had a "concrete to very strong intention to expand on the Māori component in their business" (Gnoth et al., 2009:47) interviews identified several barriers, including uncertainty where to gain information about Maori culture in the area, lack of funding and skills to develop product, and perceived resistance from the community.

In response to findings from the 2009 research report, I decided to survey interest in the production of a Māori tourism resource (e.g. guidebook or operator's manual) as a tool for existing (and potential) tourism stakeholders. The manager of the local i-SITE agreed such a resource "would be very beneficial from an i-SITE perspective". She also agreed that Māori cultural product in Dunedin "would need to be different" as visitors usually arrive via gateways such as Queenstown or Christchurch, and have often already been to the North Island. Hence, the 'Māori experience' has already been undertaken in more traditional ways.

> *"For Dunedin, there needs to be a different 'characterisation' of Māori culture. This can still rely on traditional strengths – but needs to be presented in different ways."* (Interviewee comment)

I surveyed 24 local tourism businesses to ask the question "How beneficial would an information resource about Māori culture/heritage be to their business?". My selection focused on businesses that were well established, with some being recognized as Dunedin's leading tourism attractions. Responses to the question indicated a very strong interest and desire from some business owners, with 19 answering 'yes', two 'no', and three 'probably'. Table 10.1 provides a sample of interviewee comments:

These comments highlight a need for such resources and show potential for stakeholder collaboration to strengthen Māori tourism product development. Of note, there were then two Māori guidebooks in the New Zealand market – one being *The Rough Guide to Māori New Zealand* (released in 2006) which aimed to provide a snapshot of key regions, a brief history and some local attractions. However, according to TPK (2009) the "Guide lacks the authenticity required to become an important reference guide", with phrases like "Maui[2] hauls up a whopper" lacking the cultural respect to be endorsed by Māori, thus underselling the uniqueness of Māori culture and its importance to attract a greater number of new tourists. Emphasis on the quality, diversity, and *difference* of Māori culture within the regions could be capitalized on more fully to strengthen Māori tourism offering whilst also providing Māori communities self-determining avenues with economic benefit. Comments from Maori tourism interviewees like "we have diversity in our thinking, we have diversity in our being...we are not plastic Māori" reinforce regional *differences* that exist within Māori culture.

---

2   Maui is a famous character in Maori mythology – often referred to as the "trickster" for his adventurous spirit and entrepreneurial traits.

Table 10.1: Comments from survey interviewees

Descriptor of Attraction / Transport Operator (N=24)	Comments
Adventure	"Definitely – yes. We have done our own research but don't know much or where/how to get information" "Yes I am sure it would, definitely. We include some Māori history about the river on the tours already.
Food/cuisine	"I think it would be great – we really need that. Place names, what foods, where Māori settled, moved, etc. is of great interest. Well – step on it!"
Nature/wildlife/ ecotourism	"Yes, definitely. This would help staff/guides – the more information they have the more they can tell visitors. There is a 'big gap'; in the market for something like this" "Yes it would be useful to us. We do a full commentary on the tour including history, culture, and heritage of the peninsula with special mention of Otakau marae". "Yes it would. We already work closely with local marae for information and interpretation material they provide. I see value in having this as a broader resource with input from local Māori.
Transport	"Yes it would. We have a rich Māori heritage here in Dunedin. Absolutely it would. There is a lot of cultural ignorance here in Dunedin (by locals) to this heritage. In particular the North American and European market ask questions about this here. Several sites of interest en route feature Māori significance to the landscape – we have been working with Heritage New Zealand on some of this interpretation. There needs to be more respect and collaboration amongst local stakeholders. I also think this could lead to commercial reality here in Dunedin". "Absolutely – I've scoured the local bookshops looking for information. We would be very interested in this resource and keen to see something produced. Have also struggled to find dvds with Māori culture relevant to our region for our bus tours – this would be very useful"

In concluding this discussion, two brief case studies illustrate the economic value of identity in creating any profile of Maori tourism in the Dunedin region.

Case studies

1. Tiki Tour – Māori Guide to the Lower South Island (www.tikitourmap.co.nz)

Figure 10.1: Tiki Tour Map Guide. Source. http://www.tikitourmap.co.nz

Tiki Tour Map Guide provides visitors with an interactive web-based Māori-oriented roadmap of local Māori businesses and tourism experiences in the southern region of Te Waipounamu. The concept was developed by Te Kupeka Umaka Māori Ki Ariateuru (KUMA) – the Southern Māori Business Network in Dunedin, to support and strengthen Māori owned businesses in the region who are members of the network. The map guide has three main components showing the geographic location of each tourist attraction, Māori artist, or site of local Māori stories and histories. Each component is designated by a colour coded symbol with attractions further depicted by an associated icon such as 'hiker/walker', 'water-based', 'food/restaurant' 'wildlife'. When clicked, each symbol opens an information panel including description, photo and link to 'view more information'. There are currently eight attractions, eight artists and nine stories included on the map. Stories are divided into specific region areas such as Fiordland, Central Otago, Queenstown/Wakatipu, Stewart Island/Rakiura, The Catlins, Coastal Otago, Waitaki, etc.

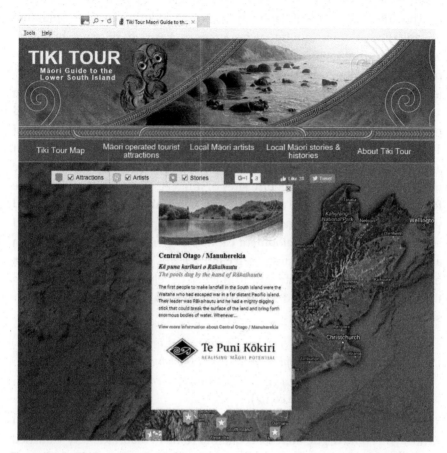

Figure 10.1: Tiki Tour Map Guide, showing an information panel. Source. http://www. tikitourmap.co.nz

Māori have long been telling histories in which, for example, they have created a sense of landscape, community and place (Attwood & Magowan, 2001). Stories for land have been among the most important element in cross-cultural interaction between Indigenous and settler peoples. For Indigenous people stories have also been a vehicle for colonial processes – contesting rights to land ownership, telling their own histories of their colonial experiences, and explaining their culture to those who have regarded them as 'other'. Importantly for Māori, stories are a vehicle to sustain a genealogy of history for themselves. This is reiterated by an interviewee who stated, "Stories are the key and the foundation" of the guide. He said:

> *"Ngai Tahu culture was 'lost' for over 100 years due to colonialism...*
> *but the stories were never lost. If you travel around the region you still*
> *hear a rich cohort of stories that go back."*

The internalization of land and cultural identity enables operators to capitalize on their individual resources in a variety of ways; however, issues of cultural integrity and misappropriation can be problematic if not presented with the correct *kawa* (protocol). In this, ownership and authenticity remains uncompromised. The stories were developed with permission and in partnership with people in the regions. *Mana* (authority, control and power) was secured by the oversight and writing of stories by local Ngai Tahu *kaumatua* (elders) and included more unknown and unique sites that are often overlooked by mainstream promotional material. As such, the motive to include more in-depth 'sites of interest' was a point of difference for the tourism product. The identity of Ngai Tahu and the South Island were viewed as both distinctive and diverse – opportunities that provided scope for growth and development capitalizing on Ngai Tahu's reputation as an entrepreneurial and progressive iwi. KUMA's aim is to expand media marketing from the website and to further develop tangible benefit from their work. This is reflected in the aspect of 'social value' depicted in their statement:

> KUMA *continually searches for new ways to showcase and promote Māori culture and people. Our core goal is whanaungatanga; being there for one another, encouraging, supporting and learning.*
> (www.tikitourmap.co.nz).

Importantly, KUMA want people who use the product to see **value** in it – thus, you could argue there is 'economic value in Māori identity' attached to the Tiki Tour Guide tourism product.

2. Puaka Matariki – the Māori New Year (www.matarikidunedin.co.nz/)

There has been increasing interest in New Zealand in the Māori New Year, usually referred to as '*Matariki*'[3]. In traditional times different iwi observed the rising of Puaka (Rigel) or the Matariki cluster of stars to denote the beginning of the Māori New Year. The New Year starts at the first new moon following the rising of Puaka – usually in late May or early June – the nature of which was a portent of weather to come and was closely associated with the coming season's crop. Puaka is the principal star of the *iwi* Ngai Tahu and is seen as an important time for family to gather and reflect on the past

---

3   Matariki is the Maori name for the group of stars also known as the Pleiades star cluster. This is also recognized the world over as the Winter Solstice period.

and the future. Over the period of three weeks a number of regional events are held throughout the country, including Dunedin, to celebrate Matariki.

"This festival is unique to Dunedin, it's one of the significant ways the Council celebrates their partnership with iwi and engages with te ao Māori" (www.matarikidunedin.co.nz)

For over 20 years, Māori in Dunedin have celebrated *Puaka Matariki* (PM) with a diverse program of activities such as: cultural performances, exhibitions of art and craft, weaving and carving classes, musical shows, parades, story-telling based on legends of stars, waka races, astronomy viewings, planting and conservation/environment educational days, food and dinner gatherings, and sports events. There is strong emphasis on *whanau* involvement and education; transferred to public shows and events in institutions such as the Otago Museum and Dunedin Art Gallery. The profile of PM within the Dunedin community has consistently grown – due largely to stakeholder collaboration. In 2008/09 the Dunedin City Council agreed to fund a coordinator role and established a contestable funding pool which has grown from \$6,000 to \$35,000 in 2016. At this time, a Steering Roopu (SR)[4] group came together with the purpose to liaise with event organisers and the wider Māori community, DCC and other interested Dunedin collectives. In addition the SR is charged with the coordination and promotion of the overall PM program and gives feedback to the DCC as to how the event as a whole is being managed. The number of events have grown from 15 in 2009 to over 50 in 2016.

In terms of cultural identity, PM provides Māori a *performative* space of cultural construction (Coleman & Crang, 2002) that mixes with outside influences. It is here that elements of hybridity become more evident. Māori identity, in this sense, relates to the capacity to ascribe both similarity and difference through cultural (re)presentation. Together, similarity and difference are the dynamic principles of identification. In this, identity is understood as a process of 'being' and 'becoming' – singular and plural, always multi-dimensional (Jenkins, 2008). An example being a local Māori band that closed the 2010 opening event with traditional *waiata* mixed with reggae style music; thus adapting other forms of music within their repertoire. Another example was the marae event 'Puketeraki Wearable Arts Show', drawing on and (re)presenting from a Māori perspective, the internationally recognized New Zealand annual event 'World of Wearable

---

4 The SR is a voluntary grouping keen to support PM events across the Dunedin area.

Arts'. Likewise the event 'Marae Idol' imitated media shows like 'USA Idol' to showcase Māori talent. Another event - 'Puaka Matariki Pecha Kucha Night' was a visual display of Māori oratory and imagery in which speakers project 20 images in 20 seconds while telling their stories. Initiated in Japan and inspired by similar events in over 300 cities around the world, the inaugural 2010 Pecha Kucha marked a new partnership between the Dunedin Fringe Arts Trust, the DCC and the SR. One further example is Oi! The Māorified One! The concept of *oi* means to be in continuous motion or to stir constantly. This creative space revolved around a 20-foot shipping container being dropped into the 'Octagon' – the central hub of Dunedin city. The container was then transformed into Oi! Pods – that were *Māorified* into the smallest picture theatre in Dunedin and one of experimental video installation space. Producers of Oi! teamed up with a graffiti art troupe who decorated the exterior of the container with their own unique artwork. Over six days a continuous display of Māori flavoured documentaries, short films and video installations played from morning to evening.

Notwithstanding, some problems have been encountered since PM became a more formally integrated event in Dunedin. Consistent funding and clarity around application, coupled with growing demand and events, means the SR has had to seek other opportunities to raise funds and increase the pool of potential funds available. To some extent this hinders enhancement of future PM programs. The SR would like to see PM elevated to major event status so that a range of high quality activities and events can be sustained in the future. Demand from other local organisations for support plus constraints on DCC funding for the city's 'large projects' (such as the new Dunedin Stadium) mean PM, as a marker of identification for Māori, competes with the wider populace. Media coverage and support in liaising with the media has also been a contentious issue. Here, the 2010 coordinator interviewee stated "many news reporters in Dunedin find it 'challenging' to cover stories with a Māori theme". In a similar vein, the coordinator highlighted the need to encourage DCC staff to attend PM events as they will "gain a greater understanding of the significance of this cultural event to local Māori". The latter links DCC to their responsibilities and obligations as partners in the Treaty of Waitangi and the Ngai Tahu Memorandum of Understanding enshrined in the Local Government Act 2002.

Conclusion

The accelerated pace of tourism studies in the past few years has shifted the broader context of Indigenous tourism to a more complex and fractured domain when describing cultural tourism experiences. In both the process and discourse of tourism development, problematic issues of representation and identity have become de-contextualized, post-colonized, and re-spatialized. It is precisely the scope and speed of such change that prompt this paper's aim to re-think Maori tourism in the broader context of Indigenous tourism. The aim of this chapter has been to examine the economics of Māori identity upon which to create a sector profile for Māori tourism in Otepoti Dunedin. My discussion contends the relationship between identity and product development is intrinsic to increasing investment in Māori tourism beyond the current status of the Māori tourism sector.

Although Māori tourism in Otepoti Dunedin is embryonic, results from this research show a desire by both local Māori and tourism stakeholders to develop opportunities in which a Māori 'dimension' offers a unique point of difference to tourism experiences. The involvement of local communities in the marketing of their cultures also allows for a greater range of diversity of images, messages and symbols to be communicated. Thus, locals determine the identity of their place. In so doing they also adopt a social value approach through effective use of local community and tribal resources in ways that reflect regional and thus tribal difference to visitors. In answer to the question "What is the profile of Māori tourism in Dunedin?" I would argue it is one that extends beyond the *rohe* of Otepoti Dunedin to encompass a wider regional identity of people and place that differentiate the South from the rest of New Zealand. It incorporates the historical associations which have, over time, been given to a place by the diversity of people who have inhabited it. The production of cultural identity, in a self-determined sense in events like Matariki and the website Tiki Tours, offers Maori a discursive space in which they re-articulate and embrace the diversity of cultural difference. Multi-layered narratives underpin both traditional and contemporary approaches to re-interpreting and re-presenting Māori culture and thus intersect with the concept of hybridity. Hybridity exposes the layers of cultural identity and provides a window on diversity of Māori tourism.

References

Amoamo, M. & Thompson, A. (2010). (Re)imaging Māori tourism: Representation and cultural hybridity in postcolonial New Zealand. *Tourist Studies,* **10**(1), 35-55.

Ashcroft, B., Griffiths, G. & Tiffin, H. (2002). *The Empire Writes Back.* London: Routledge.

Attwood, B. & Magowan, F. (2001). *Telling Stories: Indigenous history and memory in Australia and Aotearoa New Zealand.* Wellington: Bridget Williams Books Ltd.

Barnett, S. (1997). Māori Tourism. *Tourism Management,* **18**(7), 471-473.

Bhabha, H. (1994). *The Location of Culture.* London: Routledge.

Butler, R. & Hinch, T. (Eds.). (2007). *Tourism and Indigenous Peoples: issues and implications.* Oxford, UK: Butterworth-Heinemann.

Coleman, S. & Crang, M. (2002). *Tourism Between Place and Performance,* New York: Berghahn Books.

Gnoth, J., Boyes, S. & Gnoth, D. (2009). *The Potentials of Māori Cultural Tourism Products in Otepoti Dunedin Research Report.* Dunedin: University of Otago.

Hollinshead, K. (1998). Tourism, hybridity and ambiguity: The relevance of Bhabha's 'third space' cultures. *Journal of Leisure Research,* **30**(1), 121-156.

Hollinshead, K. (2010). Tourism studies and confined understanding: The call for a 'new sense' postdisciplinary imaginary. *Tourism Analysis,* **15**, 499-512.

Jenkins, R. (2008). *Social Identity,* Third ed. Oxon, UK: Routledge.

King, M. (1992). *Te Ao Hurihuri: Aspects of Māori tanga.* Auckland: Reed Books.

Māori Tourism Taskforce. (1987). *Māori Tourism Task Force Report.* Wellington: The Task Force.

McIntosh, A. (2004). Tourists' Appreciation of Māori Culture in New Zealand. *Tourism Management,* **25**, 1-15.

McIntosh, A., Hinch, T. & Ingram, T. D. (2002). Cultural identity and tourism. *International Journal of Arts Management,* **4**(2), 39-49.

Ryan, C. (1999). Some dimensions of Māori involvement in tourism. In M. Robinson & P. Boniface (Eds.), *Tourism and Culture Studies* (pp. 229-245). Oxon, UK: CABI Publishing.

Ryan, C. & Higgins, O. (2006). Experiencing CulturalTourism: Visitors at the Māori Arts and Crafts Institute New Zealand. *Journal of Travel Research,* **44**, 308-317.

Spiller, C. & Stockdale, M. (2012). Managing and leading from a Māori perspective: Bringing new life and energy to organizations. In J. Neal (Ed.), *Handbook for Faith and Spirtuality in the Workplace.* New York: Springer Publishing Company.

Te Puni Kokiri, (2009). *There is value to be found beyond the cliché: Increasing investment in Māori tourism.* Report prepared by Deloitte New Zealand for TPK, Wellington New Zealand.

Walker, R. (2004). *Ka Whawhai Tonu Matou - Struggle without End.* Auckland: Penguin.

Whitford, M. & Ruhanen, L. (2016). Indigenous tourism research, past and present: where to from here? *Journal of Sustainable Tourism,* **24**(8-9), 1080-1099.

Wilson, J., Horn, K., Sampson, K., Doherty, J., Becken, S. & Hart, P. (2006). Demand for Māori Eco-Cultural Tourism *Landcare Research Science Series (no 31).* Canterbury, NZ: Lincoln University.

11 Tourism and Ethno-development:
Inclusion, empowerment and self-determination – a case study of the Chatham Islands

Andrew Cardow and Peter Wiltshire

Introduction

A visit to the Chathams was undertaken in early 2015. The aim of the research was to provide a follow up to previous consultant reports and assess how successful tourism has been on the Islands in building both community cohesiveness and economic success. In this chapter, recent tourism developments on the Chatham Islands of New Zealand are reviewed in line with the concept of relational wellbeing (Spiller et al., 2011). In doing so, the voices of Chatham Island tourism operators both inbound and outbound will be made explicit. We have also included impressions from visitors we encountered while on the Islands and we demonstrate how by owning and operating the tourism product, the Indigenous people are in some places starting to build a 'sense of belonging' (Spiller et al., 2011) rather than as Spiller et al. suggest, a 'sense of existence'. However, we also demonstrate how, although there are changes in terms of ownership of 'place', there is a disconnect between the commercial reality of the tourism product and the identity that the Chatham Islanders hold. By reporting upon conversations we had on the Islands we use the operators' own voices to explain the impacts of tourism on their values. We found developments are largely driven by the community's contemporary needs, the socio-cultural expectations of the people and their concomitant values, beliefs and identified goals. It is illustrated that these needs and expectations are largely explored through a cultural and political identity. This identity and contemporary practices in Māori and Moriori contexts have been conceptually explored (for examples see Foley, 2008; Frederick & Henry, 2003). Using stakeholder theory (Getz & Jamal, 1994; Jamal & Getz, 1995) the authors visited the Islands and subsequently conducted a literature review encompassing the contemporary political structure and policy implications impacting tourism development. It is worth pointing out at this stage that those elements that comprise the major tourism infrastructure are owned separately by both Indigenous Morori and Māori descendants. We also identify responses from the sector that identify collaboration, networks, skills, aspirations and shared values. At the same time the research explores the extent to which local identity is reinforced by new tourism strategies, which explore Indigenous options and signify change; practices informed by policy and research are now in place on the Islands.

Background

The Chatham Islands are the most remote continuously inhabited islands of New Zealand. Since 2001, they have had a declining population. The group lies in the Southern Pacific Ocean some 800 kilometres to the east of New Zealand. This remoteness has led to the development of both a homogenous identity among the inhabitants, in that they identify as 'Chatham Islanders' and a more heterogeneous identity based on at times competing Indigenous backgrounds. On the Chathams, two large groups vie for the position of being the indigenous people. They are the Morori, and New Zealand Māori , and it is the former group, the Morori that are the original inhabitants of the Islands. King and Morrison (1990) record that this group was then followed by European sealers and whalers, and finally in 1840, by a Māori invasion which decimated the Morori. However, the Māori group on the Islands claim to be the people of the land (Aotearoa/New Zealand) as the Māori are recognised as the original settlers of New Zealand – of which the Chatham group are a part (King & Morrison, 1990). This has in the past created much tension and confusion between the two groups.

The isolation of the Islands has also led to the development of a unique system of governance which in some respects has not always been to the Islands' benefit. Since 1991, there has been an almost complete separation of operations and policy in terms of the local government; local government is represented on the Islands by the Chathams Islands District Council (CIDC) and there is also a private trust, The Chatham Islands Enterprise Trust (CIET). The latter body owns and operates the majority of the infrastructure including the wharves, airport, electricity generation and reticulation. In addition, CIET owns fishing quota and forestry, and until 2005 also owned the electronic tourism portal for the Islands. In comparison, the CIDC has responsibility for roads and rates but it undertakes this with minimal income from residents' property taxes.

It is the very physical separation from the rest of the world, the isolation, and the desire to experience something considered to be authentic that has attracted visitors to the Islands (Bellingham & Cardow, 2005). Indeed, it is a desire to experience a wilderness that is an attraction for a great number of visitors to New Zealand generally. On the Chathams, tourism as a tool for sustainable economic development, has been very slow to be recognised. Despite a self-image of entrepreneurism from the Islanders, inertia has been an outcome of the inherent lack of an entrepreneurial tourism orientation by the Islanders and a poor systemic tourism competence on the Chathams in that, on the Islands at least, fishing, not tourism has historically been seen as the tool for sustainable economic development. CIET has in the past decade also been slow to recognise the benefits of tourism. The growing awareness that fishing is declining has led some on the Islands to shift their focus towards the emergent tourism industry (Bellingham & Cardow, 2005; Wiltshier & Cardow, 2001; 2006).

Tourism for Indigenous peoples and for New Zealand was given a much needed boost in 1999 with the first of two millennial celebrations. The Chatham Islands were the first inhabited location to see the dawn of the third millennium owing to their location at the International Dateline. The CIDC were awarded NZ$500,000 from New Zealand public funds to celebrate the Millennium with specific cultural activities including arts and events on the two main Islands, Chatham and Pitt, and the events received coverage in the media. The celebrations were parochial, entertaining and the subject of mirth and some derision mostly in mainland New Zealand as contemporaneous newspaper articles will attest. For example, the New Zealand Herald reporting on an unsuccessful complaint made about their coverage to the press council, in which the *Herald* reported that the conch blower was "alleged to be so inebriated by the time the sun rose that it was unclear whether he was going to blow the giant shell or vomit into it" (New Zealand Herald, 14 Nov 2000), was typical of the reporting at the time. This derision was resented by Islanders and reinforced the need for an indigenous and endogenous policy refocus by the CIDC in 2001 (personal communication, P. Smith, February 2000).

From small beginnings in 2001 to an acceptance that by 2005 tourism was important, through to a more emergent view of tourism in 2015, various tourism operators on the Chathams have grouped together to form a visitor industry stakeholder group (VISG). This industry group comprises the operators of accommodation and tourist activity providers. Since 2005, the VISG has branded the experience a visitor receives on the Islands as – *'life on the edge'*. It was clear that by 2015, the VISG had a brand, although it was divided as to what that brand actually means, and in the past the VISG has not worked cooperatively to provide a tourism product (Bellingham & Cardow, 2005). In addition, there has in the past been reluctance within the Chatham Islands tourism community to cooperatively offer their products by way of joint marketing opportunities. Cai (2002) suggests that one way in which a remote location can begin to utilise tourism as a tool for economic development is to cooperatively brand the destination. For this to happen, Cai suggests that all actors involved in the tourism industry have both bought into the brand as opposed to a destination name, and act cooperatively in order to secure the economic advantages that spring from such a collective image (Cai, 2002). However for the tourism operators on the Chathams, despite having a brand, it would appear that there has been a failure of the collective.

Past commentary

It is fair to say that prior to the turn of the 20th Century, the Chatham Islands, due to their isolation, have not had much in the way of academic attention. It would of course be a mistake to reason that there were no attempts at providing an academic viewpoint of the Islands. There have been throughout the 20th century, attempts to explain the social and economic conditions of the Islands and Seymour (1924) in his Masters thesis titled *A History of the Chatham Islands*, was possibly one of the first to consolidate the extant literature on the Chathams into one volume. However the sources are mainly

19th Century anthropologists and biologists. It was not until 66 years later that another more comprehensive account of the Chathams was produced. *A Land Apart: The Chatham Islands of New Zealand* (King & Morrison, 1990) is an accessible history co-written by one of the country's foremost historians (King). This study was intended for general consumption and was at once, a critical success inspiring both tourism and further academic study. Contemporaneous with the King and Morrison book was the emergence of a more academic interest in the economic and social development of the Chatham Islands in the late 20th Century. Such interest took the form of consultant reports and academic research articles.

The origin of these more academic studies and the impetus for future academic investigations was the first Taylor Baines report of 1989. Taylor Baines are a private social research group, headed by an ex-academic, that specialises in providing economic and social development advice. Their first report, referred to above, was undertaken on behalf of the Ministry of Internal Affairs. Taylor Baines subsequently provided a follow-up report in 2002; this time on behalf of the Chatham Islands Enterprise Trust. Within the first decade of the 21st Century there has been a great deal of effort expended in attempts to gauge the viability of the Chatham Islands as both a tourism destination and in terms of economic sustainability (Bellingham & Cardow, 2005; Morrison & Rennie, 2009; Taylor Baines, 2002; Wiltshier & Cardow, 2001). These first few exercises were interested in finding out from the Chatham Islanders in particular, what their vision for economic development looked like and what new areas they believed could be encouraged. As a result, in the early years of the 21st Century, a number of articles have been written including Cardow and Wiltshier (2007; 2010) and three separate consultants' reports (Bellingham & Cardow, 2005; Taylor Baines, 2002; Wiltshier & Cardow, 2001; 2008). In each of the studies, recommendations have been made to the Chatham Islanders. A common theme within all of the works cited was that the information provided as a part of the feedback, was drawn from the words of the Chatham Islanders themselves. Each subsequent work used the experience of the Islanders to suggest ways in which collectively they envisaged how and in what way they could enhance the economic viability of the Islands. It is also fair to say that agriculture and tourism played a large part in such future visions.

From the outset, taking into account the Taylor Baines and Lincoln International (1989) report and recognising that this is now over 26 years ago, tourism is mentioned in each of the above reports as being one way in which an isolated rural community may achieve economic development. The more interesting aspect of the above is that since 1989, it has been recognised by both the visiting investigators and the community as a whole that tourism may be the key to future wealth. However it is also clear that upon each subsequent visit little had been done in relation to the advice that was being provided. Further, subsequent visits by researchers from the University of Otago also highlighted the need to have a cohesive and community owned approach to the tourism product (Aitken & Campelo, 2011; Campelo et al., 2011). As we, the authors of this chapter, were looking to gauge the impact of various consultant and academic interventions on the Islands, we chose 2005 as a starting point. We chose this date as it had been 10 years since the Bellingham and Cardow (2005) report and this timeframe also included recent studies by the University of Otago researchers (Aitken & Campelo, 2011; Aitken et al., 2014).

Moving beyond the concepts of 'de-colonising' and empowerment of local communities to develop, manage and monitor their own destiny (Bhandari, 2007), somehow tourism development within isolated communities depends in part on the support and advocacy of local government and empowerment of local hosts. This is particularly evident when examining the experience of the Chatham Islands. Such a theme was made explicit in the first Taylor Baines report and reiterated in subsequent visits (Taylor Baines and Lincoln International, 1989; Taylor Baines 1989; 2002). The challenge facing both policy makers and operators on the ground is how to provide a model of development that befits a very small but enterprising community operating at a geographic distance from New Zealand. See for example the work to empower people by Fontana (2014) in Bolivia and Larson (2007) in Guatemala.

When assessing isolated local communities for possible tourism expansion, it is important to remember, in the words of Valdivia (2012) that:

> *"Indigenous communities generally show cultural and anthropological features that can be considered as enabling factors for the establishment of social enterprises. Social enterprises, intended as community-based economic initiatives with a social aim, appear to be able to support the involvement of indigenous peoples at the community level and tackle specific economic and social concerns affecting these communities. This capacity is mainly ascribable to the alleged capacity of social enterprises in exploiting cultural and identity factors that are embedded in the indigenous community and re-direct them towards development objectives."* (p. 285)

In both speaking with the operators on the Islands and reviewing literature on isolated and Indigenous tourism product we were very conscious
that the tourism offering on the Chathams rests on the community's ability to capitalise on their unique selling position and realise their inherent
competitive advantage. Tourism is seen as a vehicle and opportunity for
self-determination as part of a broader socio-political outcome. Tourism
does not leverage the development but is one tool to use in an increasingly
connected, sophisticated and globally transformed market economy (Berkes
& Davidson-Hunt, 2010; Copeland, 2015; Giovannini, 2015; Pickerill, 2008;
Schellhorn, 2010). In effect, tourism is seen as being the vanguard of agreed
and mutually sustainable development for all hosts.

There is evidence that on the Chathams, there is an attitude built around
evaluation of beliefs and identity that underpins the offer to visitors, which
is commensurate with local values, beliefs and expectations built around
the defined community of the Chatham Islands. For example in a study
by Aitken and Campelo (2011), one of their respondents mentions that "[I]
believe there is a Chatham Island way of doing things. I guess it's a bit of a
hybrid of all those different cultures that have come together and merged.
You can't really tell what's Māori , what's Morori, what's European influence. It's all come in together" (p. 922). In this sense the issue of Indigeneity
is defined as being a 'Chatham Islander'. In some respects, the Chathams
have the same underlying issues that have been identified in an Australian
study by Pickerill (2009) concerning Indigenous tourism. Like the studies
undertaken in the Chathams, Pickerill uncovered similar concerns regarding the practice of tourism. For example:

> "Four issues were identified that have proved particularly contentious in
> negotiations to build collaborative campaigns: language; power and owner-
> ship; scale and timeframes; and economics. There are examples of both suc-
> cesses and ongoing problematic practices across these tensions. However
> there is also a growing mutual ownership of the issues. Moving beyond a
> colonial paternal sense of responsibility, to a dynamic and engaged mutual-
> ity of concern for both processes and outcomes has resulted in gradual,
> small, and progressive steps forward in Indigenous/ non-Indigenous col-
> laborative environmental campaigning." (Pickerill, 2009:1)

The language used by the Islanders expressed their preference to use
the designation 'visitors' rather than 'tourists' were a factor in tourism
development. Major aspects that helped and continue to hinder tourism
development are based around power, ownership, economics and distance;

particularly the impression of distance from New Zealand. These aspects were clearly highlighted in the data that was uncovered during our discussions with tourism operators, tourists and business travellers that follows.

Gathering the responses

This research is based upon a series of encounters that academic (Aitken & Campelo, 2011; Campello et al., 2014; Cardow & Wiltshier, 2007, 2010; Wiltshier & Cardow, 2001, 2008) and consultant observers (Bellingham & Cardow, 2005; Morrison & Rennie, 2009; Taylor Baines, 2002) have had with the Chatham Islanders since 2000. We wished in particular to revisit observations that were last made in 2005 by the authors with the aim of assessing what, if anything, in relation to the tourism product had changed. To that end our methods are based upon that of extant previous studies. As such it is worth outlining the methods originally utilised and then how and why we altered our approach.

The aim of the earlier studies was to research the ways in which Indigenous owners of the tourism offerings on the Chatham Islands were embracing tourism as a means to economic growth. Previous studies, although attempting a sustainability argument, were not so much concentrating on the sustainability aspect or the Indigenous aspect of tourism so much as the ownership and branding aspects of the Chathams. This was demonstrated through reporting on how the participants viewed themselves and their businesses in relation to the continued success of the Chatham Island community (see Table 11.1 for a summary).

On the whole the publications are qualitative investigations with a heavy reliance upon interviews and subsequent interpretation. In this study, as we are attempting to follow a similar method and in order to have like with like comparisons, we have adopted a similar approach. Originally we considered following a very loose adapted grounded approach based upon the ideas of Strauss and Corbin (1990). This approach was not completely adopted as it was considered that as we had undertaken an extensive literature review and had prior knowledge of the Chatham Islands tourism product, a grounded theory approach could not be sustained. Instead we adopted an approach suggested by several authors based on discourse and stakeholder analysis (Jamal & Getz, 1995; Soper, 2007; Yang & Wall, 2009).

Table 11.1: A summary of relevant tourism publications

Taylor Baines & Associates	1989	An economic development survey concentrating on existing conditions, notes the need to establish a long term sustainable tourism product
Taylor Baines & Associates	1989	A follow-up on the above visit reiterates previous findings and urges cooperation within the tourism market
Wiltshier & Cardow	2001	A specific tourism focused report. An attempt to consolidate the VISG. Recommends centralisation, end to duplication and cooperation in the market. Recommends greater brand awareness.
Taylor Baines & Associates	2002	Economic development report, not specifically tourism oriented, however which recommends consolidation and cooperation in terms of the tourism product
Bellingham & Cardow	2005	Commissioned report advocating a strong cooperative tourism sector aided by a clear brand that could be applied to locally produced goods and services on the Islands
Wiltshier & Cardow	2006	Reiterates that differentiation, consolidation and cooperation within tourism product can build sustainable economic development.
Wiltshier & Cardow	2006	Emphasis on guardians of the land, the residents holding a mandate to offer visitors an experience and required to protect the same experience
Wiltshier & Cardow	2007	Political will is defeating rational decisions to develop some offer for visitors. The problem is authority and power base decision making and support. The suppliers are not the brokers of the offer.
Wiltshier & Cardow	2008	Suggested that sustainable economic development be achieved through tourism, operated and owned by the Chatham Islanders
Lovelock, Lovelock & Normann	2010	A case study of commercial fishers whom have turned tourism operators. Also suggests that cooperation on the wider tourism market and some 'awareness' would be useful
Cardow and Wiltshier	2010	Tension between community cohesion and economic development. Highlights Indigenous and endogenous components of community capacity development through a focus on enterprise. A model of Indigenous tourism development and its endogenous antecedents is considered at the conclusion.
Aitken & Campelo	2011	The need to have an identified and accepted brand for geographic location.
Campelo, Aitken, Thyne & Gnoth	2014	The need for communities to be cooperative, differentiated and branded in order to achieve sustainable development through tourism.

The essential difference between the two approaches is that the premise of grounded theory is to uncover or develop theory from gathered data; whilst the premise of discourse is to establish an interpretation of meaning based on these uncovered social facts (Charmaz, 2014; Fram, 2013). Our epistemology is based around the voices of the tourism operators and their customers, and so we considered that discourse, being a more critical tool and based essentially upon construction of stories, would suit our purposes more than the previously adopted grounded approaches. Our approach therefore, follows the ideas of Czarniawska (1998:6-7) being "a mode of association, of putting different things together". This method fits both our epistemology and the ontological processes adopted in interpretation of the interviews. As we are utilising the tourists' and the Indigenous tourist operators' voices in order to construct stories, it was necessary that both the context, personal motivations and possible subtle assumptions of those being interviewed was taken into account (Phillips & Hardy, 2002). It is for that reason that we personally visited the Chathams in early 2015.

The information that forms the discussion below was gathered during interviews with tourism operators and two sets of tourists on the Islands in February 2015. We listened to and recorded each interview and then interpreted the stories through the isolation of common phrases and words, and the identification of patterns (Czarniawska, 1998; Tyson, 1999). The data was gathered by personal interviews undertaken at the informants' place of business and, in the case of the tourists, in the hotel in which they were staying. This was done to mitigate as much as possible, the influence that we as researchers would have upon those being interviewed, while at the same time allowing us to understand the influence context may have upon those being interviewed (Horkheimer & Adorno, 1944; Stewart, 1998). The interviews all followed an approach that involved asking the same set of questions, except for the tourists. For the tourists, we eliminated the questions regarding business operations. Following Dey (1999), the data interpretation stopped when no more conceptual variations were evident. Given the numbers of 'engaged' tourism operators this was not a large sample, yet included the major accommodation providers and four of the larger service operators on the Islands.

One aspect of qualitative methodology is the need to provide a basis for others to validate, internally and externally, both the results discovered and the underlying theory or interpretations that emerge from the recorded interviews (Gummeson, 1991). This is generally achieved through triangulation. In our case triangulation relies on extant research, combined with personal interviews, situational analysis and reference to recent similar investigations that have taken place within the Chatham Islands tourism sector (Stewart, 1998).

In the remainder of this chapter we will construct an image of how, if and to what extent, the Chatham Island tourism operators have changed their method of business and interactions with both their peers and the customers over the last 10 years. We answer the question regarding if and how the descendants of Indigenous Chatham Islanders have diversified, not necessarily their economy but certainly their tourism business in an attempt to gain economic development. It is worth mentioning that our interpretation is just one view of the social and economic environment in which the Chatham Islands tourism product exists. In doing so, we are aware that the reader will apply his or her ideological lens to the situation presented by our interpretation of the interviewees' words. To summarise, we aimed to achieve, through application of the existing spoken word, plausible suggestions of observable action. As such we are providing, in essence, a 10 year discussion of how of Indigenous tourism development has appeared on the Islands.

What we found

We were interested in the changes in the tourism environment, specifically in relation to the perceived experiences and expectations of the descendants of Indigenous operators that have taken place over the last ten years. We also wished to ascertain what, if any, changes had been undertaken as a result of the academic and practitioner interventions over the last ten years.

At first glance, there was the impression that nothing much had changed. This is despite tourism being highlighted as a potential source of economic development since the first Taylor Baines report (1989). Subsequent investigations, mentioned above, (Bellingham & Cardow, 2005; Campelo et al., 2011, 2014; Cardow & Wiltshier, 2011) only reinforced the need to seriously consider tourism as a source of future community and economic wealth. Although community involvement is strongly indicated as way for isolated communities leverage their talents (Aitken et al., 2014, Jamal & Getz, 1994), there is a reluctance for those on the Chathams to band together in order to achieve commercial synergy. For example, one of our Indigenous informants, an owner of an accommodation provider told us "No one is wishing to put money into the sector" while another suggested the Visitor Industry Group "is not getting enough people involved". Further, the fishing charters, which are a major player in the activity sector, encourage " [an] all you can catch" approach with their customers. Finally, it was suggested to us that the hotel, again owned by people with an Indigenous background encourages "package tours" and concentrates on their traditional market of those over 50 years of age. As 90% of the tourism sights on the Islands are in private hands, the 'sights' need to be negotiated and "only the hotel has access". As the operator of the hotel told us, "the week for them [the tourists] is fantastic".

Table 11.2: Themes from the data

Major theme	Explanation	Indicative quote
Nothing changed in last 10 years	Sentiment that fundamentally nothing has changed in terms of demand for the tourism offering	"Mainly older groups" "Reluctance to pay for collective branding" "Fishing pretty much rules here" "Trust wants to review viability of tourism"
Some changes in the last 10 years	Despite fundamentals some subtle changes in the Indigenous offering have taken place	"Henga Lodge closed" "CI Enterprise Trust conducts trade shows" "Hotel is working well with all"
Current business models	Essentially relies on the unchanging and traditional type of customers	"Mostly working people" "Package tours best for the experience" "We know the Chathams and we know how to sell it"
Barriers to change	Despite opportunities there are barriers to growth	"airfares" "the hotel and two others [heavily involved] the rest appear happy to trade on their shirt tails" "local Indigenous operators need to be associated with larger operators in order to be successful" "90% of people don't know where we are"
Future	Ideas for future development Empowering Indigenous stakeholders Sustaining endogenous development processes	"tourism and visitors play a big part in sharing our history" "Increase numbers from 1.5K to 3.5K" "Branding, we could do the same as King Islanders" "development of Indigenous tourism"

The viewpoint that the Chathams is only attractive to the traditional customer pool of over 55 years of age and on package tours, is reinforced by one of the major suppliers based in Auckland. This particular travel agency has been a long term operator within the market and provides a great deal of seasonal traffic to the hotel. They only target the over 55+ package tour as they believe that there is no interest in any other market for the Chathams. Such an attitude is reinforced by the Hotel Chathams who suggested that of the 17,000 people on their database, "90% are over 55 [years of age]".

The feedback from the operators of the hotel and the major inbound tourism provider is not that encouraging. Like many isolated islands, the attractions are closely held, there is a lack of collaboration and concentrated accommodation options. These are all aspects which have been highlighted in previous reports referenced above, and have only recently started to be addressed on the Islands.

It is however not all gloom and doom on the Chathams with regard to the tourism offering and collaboration. Such is the nature of the product on the Islands that the Indigenous operators find they must collaborate to a certain extent. For example, the Enterprise Trust conducts trade shows on the New Zealand mainland and the Air Chatham's airline is active in attempting to generate new customers. The business models adopted on the Islands have positive and negative factors but again, despite some positive comments from studies undertaken by the University of Otago in 2015 (Campelo et al., 2015), the business landscape has only recently started to change.

The two largest accommodation providers in the main town are the Hotel and the Black Robin, a competing accommodation provider. A recent newcomer (2013) which is building both leisure and business traffic is the Flower Pot Lodge on Pitt Island. Changes in the last ten years have been the closure of the Chatham Lodge, a large hotel, and the opening of the Hokiti Trust Marae, which caters mainly for school and cultural conference groups. However the package tour is the mainstay of the tourism market on the Islands and one informant told us that he was "a great believer in the package deal". That may be as a result of affinity but for the local café owner, another Indigenous tourism operator, things are a little different as the owner "does not see a lot of tourists, mainly local people, the farmers, the fishermen – I don't have anything against the tourist; they just don't come in here". Such comments point to a closed tourism market, where the customers are encouraged to patronise only certain establishments. When the largest operator is a full service hotel, there is of course a vested interest in encouraging tourists to spend their time and money within the orbit of the hotel. The dominance of one large player has the tendency to shape the commercial environment. This dominance creates some barriers for development of the tourism product on the Chathams, but also provides opportunity for alternative Indigenous ventures on the Islands.

Governance, barriers and opportunities

The barriers to change on the Chathams fall mainly into two distinct categories; infrastructure and external perception. Local people are largely descendants of the Morori/Māori and their beliefs and values are hugely entrenched in the market-forces model espoused by stakeholders, both suppliers and consumers. As stated, the most obvious infrastructural issue is that 90% of the Islands are privately owned, and such ownership is substantively in the hands of the descendants of the Morori/Māori .

The larger questions developed from the governance partner (CIET) and private hoteliers relate to sustaining the endogenous development processes; who will provide the skills, training programs, marketing and research and development necessary to build a long term sustainable tourism product? Due to the isolation and limited resources of the Islands these necessarily must be an amalgam of New Zealand-based providers and a substantial contribution from the existing on-site suppliers (see examples from Atiken & Campello, 2015; Moran & Corpus, 2013). Key amongst these enablers are local employability and empowerment (reiterating perspectives from other indigenous cases in South America and Australia). Such factors also need to address the continuing capacity for some form of self-determination (themes emerging from the work of the researchers for over 10 years), re-distribution of wealth according to job opportunities, and new services and products emerging from that self-determination (also recorded over the past decade), as well as catalysts for collaboration through formal and informal partnerships (Moran & Corpus, 2013). It is relatively clear that there has been some improvement over the last ten years, however there is still inertia within the sector on the Islands. There is an unwillingness to build a unified brand – despite clear indications that such would be beneficial (Bellingham & Cardow, 2005).

In the 1980s New Zealand was subject to some of the most aggressive neo-liberal reforms in the OECD. The Chathams were no exception to this. The most visible artefact of such reform was the establishment of the Chatham Island Enterprise Trust (CIET). Essentially this organisation took over a great deal of the revenue-generating assets of the local government. This included electricity generation and reticulation. A reliable and consistent source of power is one of the necessities to build and maintain an effective business environment. One of the respondents suggested to us that "there is a need for self-sufficiently in power. The problem is the [existing] windmills provide more power than we need yet the Cats [industrial generators powered by imported diesel] need to keep going to provide a base level of power". This makes the provision of electricity on the Islands very expensive when compared to that on the mainland. One of the infrastructural issues that came up often in our discussions, and is a long term barrier, was the airline and the monopoly that it enjoys. This aspect is not necessarily a barrier as it depends upon how the product is sold to the market. However for some involved in tourism on the Islands, the airline and the price is a barrier, especially when the trip radius and price opportunity are taken into account.

As part of its role, the CIET was made responsible for economic development. Tourism naturally fits into the purview of the CIET. The downside of this, as noted by one respondent, is that the CIET is supported in their tourism efforts "by one or two key players with the others tending to be happy to trade on their shirt tales". This sentiment was also brought up by another respondent who told us that "local businesses need to be associated with the large operator [the hotel] in order to see benefit". A further enhancement to this impression was given by two businessmen in the hotel bar who told us that "people are not happy with the hotel, people in the bar are saying that the hotel is not good, they have little respect, [for the operators] they own everything". This is one of the major impediments to tourism diversity on the Islands. It is understandable; the largest operator has tapped into a proven model - group tours for the over 55s, for which they have developed a very good product. It is notable that the smaller operators, basically homestay type operators, rely on fishing trips which are another big earner on the Islands. This dominance by large players in a very small market is a disincentive to act collectively. There is reluctance on the Islands to act in an inclusive, cooperative manner. However the CIET does represent all activities on the Island in their trade shows. The barriers outlined above are not necessarily there for the long term. There are a number of people on the Islands who have expressed a future for tourism. On our last visit we met a couple of FIT travellers and two drillers who were very forthcoming in their critique and suggestions for the future of tourism on the Islands.

Probably the largest thing in favour of the Chathams is the desirability of the destination. "This was on my bucket list; I always wanted to come here" said to us by the drillers we spoke to. There are those on the Islands, like the CIET, who are working to encourage tourism. The owner of the lodge on Pitt Island, while not Indigenous, sees a future in which cooperation is the way forward for future development. For him, the future lies in the development of Indigenous tourism, something that, despite its history and the efforts of individual operators, is not yet well developed on the Chathams. This under-development exists despite obvious efforts to move a public-sector dominated economic development zone to the hands of the private sector, of which, as we have noted is 90% owned by Indigenous operators.

The people we spoke to also saw the need for the development of a universal brand and encouragement of a "different type of tourist" – visitors invited by the local hosts. For example, we spoke with two FIT travellers who were very impressed with their stay; however they were utilising the offices of the hotel to ensure and arrange permission for access to the sights. The future of tourism on the Islands is seen as Indigenous, cooperative and having an emphasis on hospitality rather than tourism. However such expressions have been noted in the past and as yet have not been acted upon.

Conclusion

The Chatham Islands is a small community perched on the edge of the Southern Ocean. It is this remoteness that has made it a desirable place for people to visit. It is also its remoteness that has given rise to the fiercely independent nature of the Indigenous citizens. There are a number of positive aspects to tourism on the Islands such as the identity, a sense of place, warm invitation to guests and ownership. There are also a number of barriers that are limiting the construction of tourism products on the Islands. For example, poor infrastructure, concentration of the industry and, to a certain extent, myopia.

In such a small community, cooperation is one of the keys that may possibly unlock future tourism growth. On the Chathams, despite previous attempts, this is a difficult task. Branding (Aitken & Campelo, 2011;

Bellingham & Cardow, 2005) is also seen as a possible way for the Chathams to develop a tourism product. It is clear however that much more work needs to be done to ensure that parties are effectively dealing with barriers to innovation and aspiration in service delivery and Indigenous development. A major issue is that the tourism industry on the Islands needs to ensure that they are using Indigenous and inimitable resources to map visitor needs against expected demand. There is also a need to ensure that marketing and promotion is designed to capture desirable visitor experiences, which may lead to expansion of new business opportunities. Moreover, there is a need to ensure that opportunities for this community are community-owned and that there is a shared understanding of the nature of both the product and the market.

To accomplish all of the above, we propose the need for an Indigenous local governance structure that incorporates human development indicators alongside commercial targets and conservation priorities:

> "to employ a more nuanced and subtle understanding of common ground that takes greater stock of the importance of examining practices, that more clearly considers the construction of values used in discussions of commonality, and acknowledges the potential of a pluralistic and adversarial politics" (Pickerill, 2009:2).

In order to do this, there is a need to incorporate sustainable energy and transport policies into practice for new visitor demand by relinquishing imported fossil fuel resources and identifying options through wind, wave and water power. This could mean that the central government in New Zealand needs to lead on designing such low-carbon options in conjunction with experiences from best-practice case studies sourced globally (Australian example in Craig, 1995; Zeppel, 2006).

The voices noted in this study, particularly from the accommodation providers, have indicated that there is a willingness on the Chathams to expand the offering. However in the last ten years, despite many public and private investigations into tourism on the Islands, there is still some way to go. We would like to end this chapter with the following quote as it both sums up and gives hope to the Indigenous tourism market, particularly on the Chathams.

> "The local community may be an important source of Indigenous identity; and most Indigenous peoples, whatever their economic role and position or geographical location, do tend to maintain close links

with their communities of origin. But they are increasingly earning their livelihood outside their own communities, and it is unlikely that such a trend can be comprehensively reversed." (Plant, 1998:10)

Acknowledgements

This chapter draws upon, and includes work previously undertaken by the authors over the last ten years.The authors wish to thank the editors and two unknown reviewers for their constructive critique and subsequent recommendations for this chapter.

References

Aitken, R. & Campelo, A. (2011). The four Rs of place branding. *Journal of Marketing Management, 27*(9-10), 913-933.

Aitken, R., Campelo, A., Thyne, M. & Gnoth, J., (2014). Sense of place: The importance for destination Branding. *Journal of Travel Research* **53**(2),154-166

Bellingham, M. & Cardow, A. (2005). *Report to the Chatham Island Enterprise Trust on Tourism Opportunities on The Chatham Islands,* Massey University Albany and Aristos Consultants, Auckland.

Berkes, F. & Davidson-Hunt, I. J. (2010). Innovating through commons use: community-based enterprises, *International Journal of the Commons,* **4**(1), 1-7

Bhandari, U. (2007). Socio-economic issues of development plan from Indigenous peoples' point of view. *Socio-Economic Development Panorama,* **1**(2), 101-110.

Cai, L. A. (2002). Cooperative branding for rural destinations. *Annals of tourism research,* **29**(3), 720-742.

Campelo, A., Aitken, R. & Gnoth, J. (2011). Visual rhetoric and ethics in marketing of destinations. *Journal of Travel Research,* **50**(1), 3-14.

Cardow, A. & Wiltshire, P. (2010). Indigenous tourism operators: The vanguard of economic recovery on the Chatham Islands, *International Journal of Entrepreneurship and Small Business.* **10**(4), 484-498.

Charmaz, K. (2014). *Constructing Grounded Theory.* Sage.

Copeland, N. (2015). Regarding development: Governing Indian advancement in revolutionary Guatemala. *Economy and Society,* **44**(3), 418-444.

Craig, D. (1995). Aboriginal and Torres Strait Islander involvement in bioregional planning: requirements and opportunities under international and national law and policy, Consultancy Report prepared for *The Melbourne*, **30**, 121.

Czarniawska, B. (1998). *A Narrative Approach to Organization Studies.* Thousand Oaks, Sage.

Dey, I. (1999). *Grounding Grounded Theory: Guidelines for qualitative inquiry.* Academic Press.

Fram, S. M. (2013). The constant comparative analysis method outside of grounded theory. *The Qualitative Report*, **18**(1), 1

Foley, D. (2008). Does social capital impact on networking for Indigenous entrepreneurs? Swinburne University of Technology, Faculty of Business & Enterprise, Australian Graduate School of Entrepreneurship Conference Paper.

Fontana, L. B. (2014). Indigenous peoples vs peasant unions: land conflicts and rural movements in plurinational Bolivia. *Journal of Peasant Studies*, **41**(3), 297-319.

Frederick, H. & Henry, E. (2003). *Innovation and entrepreneurship amongst Pakeha and Māori in New Zealand. International Research in the Business Disciplines.* Emerald Group Publishing

Getz, D. & Jamal, T.B. (1994). The environment-community symbiosis: A case for collaborative tourism planning. *Journal of Sustainable Tourism*, **2**(3),152-173.

Giovannini, M. (2015). Indigenous community enterprises in Chiapas: A vehicle for buen vivir? *Community Development Journal*, **50**(1), 71-87.

Gummesson, E. (1991). *Qualitative Methods in Management Research.* Newbury Park: Sage Publications.

Horkheimer, M. & Adorno, T.W. (1944, 1947) *Dialectic of Enlightenment.* Amsterdam: Querido Verlag N.V.

Jamal, T.B. & Getz, D. (1995). Collaboration theory and community tourism planning. *Annals of Tourism Research*, **22**(1), 186-204.

King M, & Morrison R. (1990). *A Land Apart: The Chatham Islands of New Zealand.* Glenfield, Random House.

Larson, A. M. (2007). *Representation, Equity and Environment.* Working Paper 27 Indigenous Peoples, Representation and Citizenship in Guatemalan Forestry.

Lovelock, B., Lovelock. K & Normann, Ø., (2010). The big catch: Negotiating the transition from commercial fisher to tourism entrepreneur in Island environments. *Asia Pacific Journal of Toursim Research,* **15**(3), 267-283

Moran, M. & Corpus, G. (2013). Adapting development practice to indigenous contexts. *Developement Bulletin,* **76,** 79-83.

Morrison, B., & Rennie, H., (2009). *Report on Review of Chatham Island Enterprise Trust and Chatham Islands Council.*

Phillips, N., and Hardy, C. (2002) *Discourse Analysis: Investigating processes of social construction.* Thousand Oaks: Sage Publishers

Pickerill, J. (2009). Finding common ground? Spaces of dialogue and the negotiation of Indigenous interests in environmental campaigns in Australia. *Geoforum,* **40**(1), 66-79.

Plant, R. (1998). *Issues in Indigenous Poverty and Development.* Inter-American Development Bank, Sustainable Development Department, Indigenous Peoples and Community Development Unit.

Seymour, M. E. (1924). *A History of the Chatham Islands.* Unpublished Masters thesis. University of Canterbury, New Zealand.

Schellhorn, M. (2010). Development for whom? Social justice and the business of ecotourism. *Journal of Sustainable Tourism,* **18**(1), 115- 135.

Soper, K. (2007). Re-thinking the Good Life: The citizenship dimension of consumer disaffection with consumerism. *Journal of Consumer Culture,* **7**(2), 205-229.

Spiller, C., Erakovic, L., Henare, M. & Pio, E. (2011). Relational well-being and wealth: Māori businesses and an ethic of care. *Journal of Business Ethics,* **98**(1), 153-169.

Stewart, A. (1998). *The Ethnographers Method.* Thousand Oaks, Sage

Strauss, A. & Corbin, J. (1990). *Basics of Qualitative Research* (15). Newbury Park, CA: Sage.

Taylor Baines & Associates, and Lincoln International, (1989), *Review of the Chatham Islands Economy, Commissioned by the Department of Internal Affairs on Behalf of the Ministerial Committee on the Chatham Islands,* Christchurch: Taylor Baines and Associates.

Taylor Baines & Associates, (1989). *Report on the Follow up visit to the Chatham Islands by the review team 12-16 October.* Wellington, Dept of Internal Affairs

Taylor Baines & Associates, (2002). *Cooperation and commitment. The Chatham Islands economic review, 2002.* Christchurch, New Zealand: Taylor Baines and Associates

Valdivia, G. (2005). On indigeneity, change, and representation in the north eastern Ecuadorian Amazon. *Environment and Planning A*, **37**(2), 285-303.

Tyson, L. (1999) *Critical Theory Today*. New York, Garland Publishing

Wiltshier, P. & Cardow, A. (2001). Public Meeting of Chatham Islands visitor industries stakeholders group feedback report.

Wiltshier, P. & Cardow, A. (2006). Chatham Islands, New Zealand. In Baldacchino, G. (ed.) *Extreme Tourism: Lessons from the world's cold water islands*. Amsterdam: Elsevier, Ch. 16.

Wiltshire, P. & Cardow A. (2008). Tourism, Indigenous peoples and endogenity in the Chatham Islands. *Journal of Enterprising Communities*, **2**(3), 265-274.

Yang, L. & Wall, G. (2009). Ethnic tourism: A framework and an application. *Tourism Management*, **30**(4), 559-570.

Zeppel, H. (2006). *Indigenous Ecotourism: Sustainable development and management*. Wallingford, UK: CABI Pub.

12 Mana versus Money: An Indigenous perspective on the tribal tourism destination of Whakarewarewa

Keri-Anne Wikitera and Hamish Bremner

Introduction

Tourism is the largest export industry in Aotearoa New Zealand and has the potential to promote economic prosperity for many communities in the nation (Tourism New Zealand, 2016). Research shows that Māori tourism is one of the main reasons international visitors come to New Zealand, second only to the natural landscapes (Tourism New Zealand, 2015). There has been a dramatic increase in Māori tourism start-up businesses in the past two decades and these businesses are capitalising on their cultural landscapes, that incorporate both the culture and landscape in the visitor experience/ product. The significance of Māori tourism to the national economy also elevates the political position of Māori tourism communities. Issues related to environmental pollution, intellectual property protection and the repre-sentation of Māori in governance positions are taken seriously when there is a threat to tourism development.

Māori tourism businesses do not necessarily follow the mainstream business models that focus on profit maximisation. Indigenous tourism, or in this case Māori tourism, has been and is, a way forward for small com-munities to share their culture while at the same time promoting economic, social and cultural sustainability. Furthermore, due to the importance of the nation's clean green image, primarily marketed through Tourism New Zealand's *100% Pure* campaign, the national tourism industry has a keen commitment to environmental sustainability. This provides the opportunity for Māori to incorporate traditional Māori philosophies of environmental protection and stewardship into their tourism business operations, both in the business organisational functions as well as what is delivered to the visitors.

This case critically reflects upon key concepts identified as important in the success of a tribal tourism collective. The necessity to consider what is authentic related to cultural identity and intellectual property; business control, management and governance; cultural, social and environmental imperatives and the challenges of working within tribal frameworks of knowledge that do not always respond favourably to the many stakeholder groups involved. Māori tourism businesses are now promoting sustainable business models that incorporate a "quadruple bottom line of economic, environmental, social and cultural wealth creation" (Spiller & Erakovic, 2005:219). For example, Whale Watch Kaikoura provides visitors with an experience, while synchronously supporting local, tribal economic imperatives as well as encouraging environmental and cultural sustainability. Another example is Taiamai Tours, where visitors are taken out on traditional *waka* (canoe) and told ancestral stories of the region, the political history and the methods by which the Indigenous operators maintain and protect the environment (Puriri & McIntosh, 2013). Considerations for Māori businesses are not necessarily based primarily on economic imperatives but rather on sustaining ancestral legacies involved in Indigenous people's narratives.

While the increase in Māori tourism offerings is supporting Māori community economic development, this notion of offering visitors 'new' experiences that showcase cultural landscapes has been happening for generations at Whakarewarewa. The case study provides evidence of critical tourism development undertaken by the people of the *hapū* (local sub-tribe) from the mid-19th century. Therefore 'new' tourism development paradigms are not necessarily new but rather are being rediscovered. Accordingly, articulation of development has been largely influenced by what has been considered significant in Western terms – that of a singular and pragmatic economic imperative. This case draws upon tribal perspectives, the history and the current experience of Whakarewarewa Village Tours which is located in the geothermal landscape of Rotorua.

Case study: Whakarewarewa – The Thermal Village

The case study examines a Māori tourism destination that began in the late 1800s. At that time visitors were offered Māori cultural representations in the form of Māori guides, cultural concerts and traditional stories connected to the natural landscape features of the Rotorua region. These are still core products today and are now created for two key reasons:

- To continue the legacy of our ancestors and our heritage, to keep it alive for future generations
- For the tourists who are increasingly becoming interested in heritage imaginations and representation

It is this dialectic between production and consumption of cultural heritage, or the tensions between 'us' as producers and tourists as consumers that has initiated further examination.

The Whakarewarewa Thermal Village is a tribal Māori tourism enterprise that delivers an authentic experience by taking visitors on a tour of a living Māori village in the heart of the geothermal area of Rotorua. The organisation is part of the hapū of Tūhourangi/Ngāti Wahiao and provides employment and residence to those who live in the tribal territory. It is a vital component of tribal cultural identity, even for those members who live away and who may not be directly involved in the business operation. It is a central part of the Māori cultural identity of the hapū, and aspects such as 'guiding' are now part of an ancestral legacy that is considered vitally important to sustain. This organisation contributes to the hapū economy providing financial benefits and is inextricably linked to the strengthening of the hapū culture, traditions and identity of its members.

This generative learning environment is important as it is an environment that promotes diversity and encourages *whānau* (family/tribal) members to participate in hapū development and tourist activities. The Whakarewarewa village is therefore considered more than just a case study of a tourism destination, but more as a reflection of how tribal members continue to have input into the organisation regardless of from whence and in what capacity that entails.

Three hours south of Auckland is Rotorua, promoted by many New Zealand marketing sites as the cultural tourist capital of the country. The steaming hot pools and the Māori concerts are well known to most in New Zealand and famous overseas due to its longevity as a tourist destination.

The region and its people are recognised as leaders in tourism participation in Aotearoa (Te Awekotuku, 1981). Whakarewarewa Valley is situated two kilometres south of the Rotorua township. The people of Tūhourangi/ Ngāti Wahiao have lived in and around Whakarewarewa for over 300 years (Waaka, 1982).

Tourism in Whakarewarewa and its operations started in the mid-19th century, becoming more prominent in the period after the Tarawera eruption of 1886 when the famed Pink and White Terraces were destroyed along with the homes and tourism economy of the people of Tūhourangi. Approximately 300 Tūhourangi escaped Te Wairoa from the eruption of Mount Tarawera, and moved to Whakarewarewa at the invitation of Ngāti Wahiao. Both hapū together developed a tourism trade that is still operating there today.

The people of the Whakarewarewa Thermal Village, while providing tourism related services since the mid 19th century, have only operated this actual enterprise since 1998. It is located in Rotorua amongst a landscape of geothermal activity and a living Māori village. This organisation's shareholders have been left this legacy from their ancestors, all originating from the eponymous chief named Wahiao. Wahiao was a great chief of Tūhourangi who had settled in Whakarewarewa in about 1710. A reflective narrative of how the transference of Tūhourangi/Ngāti Wahiao intellectual property further contextualises the case showing the links between this generational learning and the tourism enterprise that exists today.

The Whakarewarewa Thermal Village is a subsidiary of the Whakarewarewa Village Charitable Trust. This charitable trust leases rights to operate the tourism venture off the Rahui Trust Board who represent the village shareholders. The enterprise was set up in 1998:

> "to foster and promote our Village/Tour Package as par excellence of tourism, to enable the growth and development of economic, health, social and cultural issues of the people of Tūhourangi/Ngāti Wahiao"

(Mission Statement).

A trust board facilitates and administers on behalf of the 3,107 shareholders. The Trust Board structure is a legacy of government policy and is regulated by the Government's Ministry of Māori Development, Te Puni Kōkiri. At first, these structures were implemented to facilitate management of newly formed land tenure laws and this Trust structure has continued as a way to manage the communally owned Rahui area. The Whakarewarewa

Thermal Village enterprise leases rights from the Rahui Trust at a nominal rate to take tourists through the village (Rahui Trust AGM minutes, 2008).

Adjacent and physically connected to the village area is Te Puia, the New Zealand Māori Arts and Crafts Institute (NZMACI). The government plan in 1907, while developing the NZMACI, was to give the villagers a source of financial profit and as such early government intervention sought to change the communal nature of tourism in the Whakarewarewa village to one of a commercial nature. In their proposed plans the recommendation was that "the villagers could make carvings and mats for sale, thereby earning sustenance" (AJHR, 1902:H2). This notion was reiterated in 1967 as part of the New Zealand Māori Arts and Crafts Act (1967) which maintained the practice was:

> "to encourage, foster, and promote all types of Māori culture and the practice and appreciation of Māori arts and crafts: To train Māoris in the practice of Māori arts and crafts: To provide demonstrations or exhibitions of Māori arts and crafts: To foster and maintain public interest in Māori culture and Māori arts and crafts" (The New Zealand Māori Arts and Crafts Institute Amendment Act, 1967: Subsection 14).

This to some degree was achieved. The Arts and Crafts Institute has built and maintained a very good reputation amongst the industry and is a focal point of the NZMACI tourist product. Tūhourangi/Ngāti Wahiao has worked and developed the cultural product in the government-run organisation, supplying their cultural capital into the enterprise and selling the arts and crafts made as souvenirs for the tourists. However these activities and support provided to the NZMACI development did not translate into economic success for the hapū. The NZMACI management positions are government appointments and while the cultural capital of Tūhourangi/Ngāti Wahiao presents in most of the organisation's promotional material (see Te Puia, Rotorua website) and presentation, senior positions are predominantly non-tribal.

The NZMACI is a national centre for both the training of Māori in Māori arts and crafts, and another tourist destination. This tourist venture includes much of the geothermal sites in the Whakarewarewa valley, such as the Pohutu Geyser, a museum, a model Māori village, Kiwi house, carving school and restaurant. The people of Tūhourangi/Ngāti Wahiao were part of the NZMACI package, having developed the cultural capital in the organisation and holding *mana whenua* (power associated with possession and occupation of tribal land) over the land there.

In 1998, Whakarewarewa Thermal Village was created largely in response to the actions of the government owned and managed tourist complex. The Rahui Trust and villagers were unhappy about the NZMACI's non-recognition of an informal agreement made between the parties on 21 October 1965. This agreement referred to charging rights of the institute and village of tourists going through the Whakarewarewa valley. This gentleman's agreement, as determined by the New Zealand High Court (1998), provided the parties a charging scheme whereby:

> "...a single fee [was] to be charged and collected by the institute and for an agreed amount to be paid to the incorporation/trust"
> (CP16/97, High Court Rotorua. 22 April 1998).

The Rahui Trust, in 1998, took the NZMACI to the High Court seeking enforcement of this agreement and the judgement from this hearing stated that:

> "Overall, it was at least arguable that each of the agreements was no more than an agreement binding in honour, and a summary judgment should not therefore issue" (High Court Rotorua, 1998).

Following this High Court judgment and the disharmony between the Rahui Trust and government, a fence was erected on the hapū/NZMACI boundary in 1998. Thus, tourists entering the gates at the western part of the valley (the government owned region) would no longer have open access to the village. This High Court decision and the dishonouring of the gentlemen's agreement by the NZMACI was the catalyst for the hapū to create an autonomous enterprise. Subsequently, a tourism enterprise was consolidated in the form of the Whakarewarewa Thermal Village, owned and operated by the tribe.

The fence represents the many tensions found in the Whakarewarewa valley that have resulted from tourism and the reality of commercial enterprise in an Indigenous community. The NZMACI, for example, utilises much of the cultural capital of the tribe, employs tribal members and adapts the heritage stories to tourist wants. Sometimes the economic imperative ignores the reality and cultural capital rights of the actual people the stories are about. This reflects the tensions that arise when external agency demands that heritage tourism be adapted to what they determine are tourist perceptions of authentic, or an example of the production-consumption dialectic.

The Whakarewarewa business responds to tourist behaviours. It is now marketed heavily as the 'living Māori village' targeting the traveller with a desire for unique destinations and authentic experiences (aligned to Tourism New Zealand's 2016/17 Premium Sector strategy). The whole enterprise, including the government-run part, has responded to tourist wants since tourism began in the valley. It is now so much a part of the place that there sometimes is no difference between tourism and everyday living, traditions, culture and heritage. Our stories of our heritage inspire imaginations of past times which re-inforces the ideal of an authentic experience.

In the early 20th century, government development policies regarding tourism increased as tourism became a key economic factor for the nation. The government's role in 'improving' the region relegated the tribe to a passive role, whereby tourist needs and perceived wants became paramount. This is reflected in several development projects by the government. For example, the formation of the Department of Tourist and Health Resorts that was set up to develop the region into a tourist resort and spa. This was to the detriment of the social, economic and cultural issues embedded in the Indigenous hosts. The concept of staged authenticity too is highlighted during this time, as tourists increasing interest in Māori culture, lead to government proposals to build the model Māori *pā* (village) at Whakarewarewa, with little regard to the Māori of Whakarewarewa. As Ngahuia Te Awekotuku (1981:108) reflected, "that the minister had even anticipated [people living in the village] and that a selection process was required, reveals how insensitive the *pākeha* (non-Māori) sector was to the Māori reality of the period". This type of staged authenticity, is a major theme of state controlled tourism development (MacCannell, 1976) and thus this form of staging has continued with much legislation and control of the region by the government.

The guided tour of Whakarewarewa Thermal Village

The village is open to tourists from 8.30am to 5.00pm every day of the year except for Christmas day. Standard admission to the village, which includes a guided tour and cultural performance, is NZD $35.00 per adult and $15.00 per child. There are various package deals and family discounts (Whakarewarewa Thermal Village, nd). Tourists enter the village at the eastern end of the Whakarewarewa Valley. Prior to entering the village gates, on the left, is the *wharekai* or dining room. This dining room, named Te Rau Aroha, has facilities to cater for 300 people and is used for hapū meetings and other gatherings at the *marae*. It is not used for tour groups, however it is hired out as a conference facility or meeting venue occasionally. In front of the *wharekai* are bays for tour buses and cars to park. Just in front of the archway or entrance to the village are the offices for ticketing, a small café, a gallery and a souvenir shop. Large boards provide imagery of famous past guides of the village. The guides usually meet their visitors at the entrance and give a brief commentary of the area. The following is the path of the guided tours tourists take and a brief insight into Whakarewarewa, 'the village'.

The entrance to the village is an archway and a memorial to those hapū members that served in the world wars. Soldiers' names are engraved into the stone and all that pass see and read the names of our forefathers. This archway is the southern boundary of the village and main gate for tourists and locals to enter and is both the physical and spiritual gateway to the village. This is the *hapū tūrangawaewae* (place where one has rights of residence and belonging through kinship and *whakapapa*), the base of which Tūhourangi/Ngāti Wahiao still gather in times of joy and sadness. *Tangi* (Māori funeral rituals) are held here, weddings, family reunions, 21st birthdays and family day to day living all occur in the village.

The community, according to Peter Waaka are:

> "... both physically and symbolically set apart from the 'rest of the world' by the bridge and memorial archway at the village entrance. The village is the last remaining foothold of the tribe in the thermal area and of strong spiritual significance to the tribe as a whole" (Waaka, 1982:7).

Through the archway is the bridge which traverses the Puarenga River. To the children of Whakarewarewa the bridge has been, and still is, a place to earn pocket money. Tourists throw money into the river and the children dive and enjoy swimming in the river below. They are popularly known as the Whakarewarewa penny divers. This activity forms the beginnings of the interactive experience of the tourist with the people of the village. The name, 'penny divers', is a legacy from when pound sterling was still the national currency and despite the change to decimal currency, the name 'penny diver' has remained. A change in currency in 1989 saw the elimination of one and two cent coins and in 1991 the introduction of one and two dollar coins enabled the penny divers' income to increase dramatically. Strict rules apply when penny diving which have been determined by previous divers, elders and village tourism management since the beginning of tourist activity in the village. Rules such as age restrictions (no older than fifteen), hapū membership (must be of Tūhourangi/Ngāti Wahiao descent) and behaviour are monitored by the villagers and Wahiao Thermal Village staff. There is also a 'pecking' order in the river with prime spots allocated to those children that live in the village so they tend to earn more than visiting children.

During one *noho marae* (marae stay) held at Whakarewarewa in June, 2004, with a non-Māori community from Auckland a cousin stood up and explained the joy of penny-diving. In jest, he stated that perhaps some people would consider it begging but for the children of the village, he said, 'at least we were rich beggars!' Children can make a sizable amount in the river, which contributes to the village economy as well as the tourist product on offer to visitors. This money goes towards school uniforms, school fees, and holiday entertainment, amongst other things.

Tourists cross the bridge by foot, although it is a roadway for villagers and family to drive across. Alongside that is the pathway that leads to the geothermal bathing and cooking facilities which are shared by the villagers. The guides take tour groups into this area first and explain how the landscape has changed over time with the hapū still controlling the geothermal supply enabling bathing and cooking to continue. This area is called the *rahui* and is a shared area for the villagers to utilise.

The central building in the village is the elaborately carved *wharenui* or meeting house of the hapū. The wharenui is named after one of the eponymous leaders of the hapū, Wahiao. The guides take tourists to the front of the wharenui and share ancestral stories using the carved figures as reference points. Visitors are not allowed inside as this is for use by tribal members only. This highlights the controls in place to differentiate between tribal cultural practices and tourist activity. Over time tribal elders have made decisions on what information is utilised for tourism. This has been integral to the procurement of the tourist product provided at the village. An example is the story of Hinemoa and Tutanekai, a well-known love story of two of our ancestors. While tourists receive this story in guide books and commentaries, the story has a much deeper meaning and significance to their descendants and this meaning is communicated in traditional practices such as *waiata* (tribal song), *whaikorero* (speechmaking) and naming of descendents. This alludes to what Te Awekotuku (1981) asserted that there is a need for a control mechanism whereby the hapū have power over what is presented, maintaining the *mana* of the people that procreated the hapū, the village and its tourism operations. Not all tribal practices, beliefs and knowledge systems are shared with tourists, and much of the tourist information is moderated by tribal elders. In practical daily tourist activity, for example, tourists are not allowed to enter the meeting house. The wharenui is now solely for tribal members' usage.

As the tour progresses, tourists are taken to the cooking pools and can purchase food cooked in the pools (currently only corn cobs). Along the roadway just outside the Rahui area is the village Kohanga Reo. Te Kohanga Reo is a national total immersion Māori language preschool movement, translated as 'language nests'. The village and whānau preschoolers attend this Kohanga and tourists often have the opportunity to meet and see these children sing and play. The children are exposed at a very young age to touristic activity and can be seen participating in the tourist activities in the village.

Further along the path are viewing platforms to the famous Pohutu and Prince of Wales geysers. Prior to the fence being erected, tourists were able to walk right up to the geysers which now are only accessible through the government-run operation. Throughout the tour, residential homes are observed, some of which are traditionally carved and the guides tell stories of who lived in these 'whare' and how they were built.

Souvenir shops are also prominent in the village. Many of the houses in the village have set up to share culture through the sale of souvenirs – often crafted on site; also in operation is a *taa moko* studio (Māori tattoo). All of these operations are independently owned. Throughout the village is geothermal activity, steaming vents, mud pools, hot pools and geysers. Behind the wharenui is a nature walk where there is a hot lake and where native fauna and flora are predominant. This is not part of the guided tour, however tourists are able to walk through at their own leisure. All are signposted and paths are clearly demarcated. To the left of the whare is Lake Roto-a-Tamaheke, which is actually part of the government-owned reserve. The lake continues to feed a major bathing complex named 'the *Hirere*' in the village. This bathing facility is important to *whānaungatanga*, a central concept of hapū identity, where *whānau* gather, discuss whānau news, politics, and arrange meetings; and this practice provides an excellent opportunity to regularly come together. Over the past twenty years, due to the variations in the lake, the bath has been closed which was a major upset for the hapū. It is currently in use and is looked after and opened in the morning and evenings. It is locked during tourist hours and overnight.

The guides take tourists up through the residential area and at the northern end of the village is a Catholic church, where services are still conducted although, now only once per month. Surrounding the church is a graveyard and it seems a place of intrigue to the tourists as the graves are built up above ground due to the geothermal activity below. Also there are memorials of famous guides such as Guide Maggie Papakura and Guide Rangi, who became well-known through their professional association with a number of celebrity tourists including the Duke and Duchess of Cornwall (Stafford, 1967).

Tourism and tribal effect

Currently there are approximately 50 families residing at Whakarewarewa, most of whom live in the village. The majority of the 15,000 hapū members live outside the village with approximately 80% in urban areas outside of Rotorua. This is a result of social changes of the 1950s in New Zealand, whereby many Māori relocated to the city centres for work. Whakarewarewa is considered home by tribal members, who often return to enjoy the thermal bathing and food cooked in the steam and hot pools. Many become involved in the tourism activity in the village when visiting (as tour guides, cooks, cleaners, weavers, concert party members etc). Most can quite naturally participate in tourism activities as it is our heritage and our cultural stories that are told to paying visitors. It also provides a place where city children can learn about their heritage and be part of the tribe. Therefore the Village Tour benefits the many hapū members living away and extends past the financial profit generated from the business. Whānau can return to their *tūrangawaewae*, meet whānau and learn about their tribal connections. Visiting tribal members can engage with their ancestral stories, narratives, histories, identities through being part of the legacy of tourism that is presented as an authentic experience to tourists.

Despite claims that the enterprise is a successful Māori tourism destination, it is evident that this does not necessarily translate to economic and social development for the community in which it's positioned. Whakarewarewa Thermal Village is a small enterprise and has limited capacity for individual career opportunities. Capacity development is therefore a priority for progressing individual staff development. Therefore, the enterprise has been attempting to address these issues by promoting capacity through education initiatives for its staff. Guides in particular, have external training offered through the local tertiary polytechnic and industry training organisations. While different initiatives have seen guides and administration staff gain national certificates in tourism and business management, the capacity within the village, or Māori tourism in general, to progress into broader career development is limited. Formal qualifications are government controlled through the New Zealand Qualification Authority Framework, which also determines funding criteria of the training establishments that provide the courses. This is not dissimilar to the guiding certificates process of 1909 when the government passed a by-law regulating guiding at Whakarewarewa through guide licensing. This essentially affected how the guides in the region were controlled, transferring more control from the hapū operation in the valley to the Rotorua Tourist Board. This law regulated the tourist guides, specifying requirements of guides in the hope of improving tourist experiences in this thermal wonderland. The transfer of control from the hapū to the Rotorua Tourist Board in 1909 initiated not only guiding standards but essentially gave the government power to stipulate how the tourist product in Whakarewarewa was produced.

There are two distinct rationales for regulating and educating the guiding staff of Whakarewarewa Thermal Village. First, training with regard to regulatory requirements reflects government interest in tourists' experiences and influences core training programs. Second, the enterprise is attempting to up-skill their staff to meet its mission, "to enable the growth and development of economic, health, social and cultural issues of the people of Tūhourangi/Ngāti Wahiao" (Mission Statement). The dialectical nature of tourism in Whakarewarewa is illustrated whereby both production and consumption factors influence tourism operations and social areas such as education.

In the village there is a mixture of full-time and part-time roles with the jobs ranging from grounds maintenance, guiding, performing, catering personnel, retail store and administration workers. Most staff are members of the hapū or are married to members. Professional development for most of these roles is limited and specific to development within Whakarewarewa because knowledge systems and stories are not easily transferable. The existing capacity for staff professional development appears to be limited to guiding or management as a career. This then poses a potential issue of tourism in the village stifling growth.

While many of the hapū who live in and around Whakarewarewa work in the tourism industry in different capacities, high level permanent positions are few and far between, and therefore they tend to move into non-tourism careers. This provides evidence of what Brien (2004) asserts is the perception that employment in the tourism or hospitality industry are not considered as 'real' jobs. Thus for Whakarewarewa, tourism development is about promoting other tourism industry opportunities to those ready to leave their performing, guiding roles and/or creating capacity for individuals to develop in the tourism industry. More important, is the need to identify and create future capacity for the hapū to develop its own educational processes and professional development for the hapū. While tourism is sometimes perceived as having negative impacts on destination communities, Te Awekotuku (1981) found that there are definite benefits and opportunities for the Māori of Rotorua to progress and increase participation in this industry.

The Treaty of Waitangi settlements, over the past two decades, have been re-energising the Māori economy which is promoting economic development opportunities and capacity development where business, land and other assets are being returned to *iwi*. The reconfiguration of ownership, management and social organisation in the Whakarewarewa Valley with the return to iwi of Te Puia is creating opportunities and presenting new challenges. Issues related to how the hapū re-configures the existing profit driven business models to fit cultural models such as those framed within Māori concepts of wealth have been a major part of Crown negotiations and are currently in process. Spiller et al. (2011) recognise an 'economy of care' and utilise a relational '5 well-beings' approach that demonstrates how business can create spiritual, cultural, social, environmental, and economic well-being. Bringing values and practice together, they say, creates multi-dimensional wealth that far surpasses traditional business models that are triple bottom line focussed. Particularly in businesses where there are multiple key stakeholders, the 'ethic of care' approach is an intrinsic stakeholder view of business.

The metaphor or significance of 'the fence' built in 1998 to separate the two valley enterprises is presented here to illustrate the dialectic nature of Whakarewarewa as a tourist destination and *tūrangawaewae* for the hapū of Tūhourangi/Ngāti Wahiao. The production and consumption of tourism has influenced hapū systems over several generations and the context of the Whakarewarewa Thermal Village provides an example of the circuits that exist between local, regional, national and global tourism imperatives. The enterprise spans eight generations and the importance of *te wa* (time, place and space) to the people of the tribe offers a further perspective of what Oakes (1993) called intentional place creation.

Massey (1994) suggested that tourism development progresses relative to environmental influences and has been influenced by circuits running through the global-local nexus. For example, the global influence of the international tourist's expectations, national influence of governmental regulatory by-laws and local influence of Tūhourangi/Ngāti Wahiao and their mission to enable hapū growth and development. Furthermore, Hall and Tucker (2004:146) asserted that government funded education determines the direction of the tourism industry:

> *In cases where university places are Government funded, the growth in university-level courses in tourism is itself related to broader Government and industry perceptions of where jobs may be created or where human capital needs to be focused.*

Consistent with this are the findings and recommendations by the Ministry of Tourism (2001:42) that policy development should focus on "improving involvement and commercial performance. The options cover the gamut of education, ensuring representation and ensuring good planning". Furthermore in their considerations of future policy development they recommended the need for "...improving access to suitable education (courses that adopt a Māori learning style, that are of high quality and that are relevant to the industry)". Achieved through for example, the growth of Māori economic development programs at the Indigenous-focussed *wānanga* throughout the country. These national economic imperatives consistently stimulate the community level development plans. However, simultaneously the tourism industry is constantly influenced by global issues such as war or increasing oil prices. Specific education requirements of small enterprises such as Whakarewarewa where quite unique geographical and cultural factors add to the 'tourist experience', ensures the issues of education remains a key factor on the local through to national stage.

To the Māori of Whakarewarewa, the Whakarewarewa Thermal Village experience is not owned by any particular organisation or individual, but rather it is a way of life, a legacy passed down through the generations which continue today. The land upon which the tours are guided belong to numerous family groups who generously allow visitors to participate in their communal lifestyle incorporating Māori culture and traditions.

This case study demonstrates the construction of the culture of a tourism organisation through the lens of indigenous tribal members. It shows the importance of locally driven tourism development from an alternative tourism studies approach that looks at aspects of the producers as well as the consumers' wants and needs. Cultural diversity is an important feature of the global tourism industry whereby nations seek to identify differentiating factors from other nations. Small tribal operations such as the Whakarewarewa Thermal Village provide an example of how individuals and communities can create the context where self-determination is based on power and knowledge and social and cultural capital is protected within the global economic development environment.

Whakarewarewa Thermal Village Tours contributes to the tribal economy providing financial benefits and is inextricably linked to the strengthening of the heritage, narratives, culture, traditions and identity of its members. This generative learning environment is important as it is an environment that promotes diversity and encourages tribal members to participate in tribal development and tourism activities. The production and consumption of tourism has largely influenced tribal systems over several generations and the context of the Whakarewarewa Thermal Village provides an example of the circuits that exist between local, regional, national and global tourism imperatives.

Conclusion

In conclusion, the national strategic importance (see Tourism New Zealand corporate website) placed on providing an authentic experience for tourists must address the question of: "What is an authentic Māori experience?" particularly when more than 80% of Māori do not live in Māori communities or contexts. A cultural tourist experience is often not easily found in urban centres such as in Auckland. Rotorua enjoys a long legacy of Māori cultural tourism and most tourists seeking what's presented as an authentic experience attend the numerous tourism destinations in Rotorua.

The hapū of Whakarewarewa have been a leader in this sector and proudly present an authentic experience through the legacy of tourism and existence of an actual Māori village. The tribal peoples of Tūhourangi/Ngāti Wahiao have developed a unique tourism product over several generations through simply sharing their culture and lives with visitors. Traditional philosophies and village practices such as that of environmental protection are maintained within the hapu, controlled by tribal members while synchronously presented as part of the tourist package. The government encourages these cultural practices of environmental protection so as to ensure that the tourism product is sustained as part of the national tourism strategy. This provides the tribal peoples with a level of political leverage as environmental factors directly impact on tourism and thus cultural and social sustainability in the village is maintained.

The 'fence' that divided the village proper from the NZMACI in 1997 presents a dialectic paradigm of tourism in the Whakarewarewa Valley. The *tangata whenua* value *mana*, cultural identity and pride which is maintained through tourism activity. The government value profit-driven development, *money*, also derived through tourism activity. There are holes that run through the fence that blur the boundaries, and through Treaty of Waitangi claims and Crown settlements that are currently being negotiated, the fence quite possibly will be brought down in the future.

MONEY	MANA
TE PUIA NZ MĀORI ARTS AND CRAFTS INSTITUTE	**WHAKAREWAREWA THE LIVING MĀORI VILLAGE**
GOVERNMENT CONTROLLED TOURISM DEVELOPMENT	TUHOURANGI/NGATI WAHIAO CONTROLLED TOURISM
EXISTS FOR NATIONAL TOURISM DEVELOPMENT OF TRADE/COMMERCIAL ECONOMIC	EXISTS AS REAFFIRMATION OF PLACE & TRIBAL IDENTITY AND OBLIGATORY RESPONSE OF MANA WHENUA
NZ Māori Arts & Crafts Institute • Manufactured • Tourist-led • Global • Market research oriented • Government controlled • Illegitimate – e.g. model pā and claim to people of the land • Objective, rational and instrumental • Tourist centred facilities and landscape utilisation • Profit driven - Economic sustainability	**Whakarewarewa the Thermal Village** • Authentic • Tangata Whenua led • Local • Praxis oriented • Tribal controlled • Legitimate – 'our stories, our lives' • Values based – spiritual, cultural and social • Tribal centred facilities and landscape utilisation • Whakapapa-centric – cultural sustainability

References

Appendices to the Journals of House of Representatives (AJHR) (1902). H2 Wellington: Government Printer.

Brien, A. (2004). *Do I want a job in hospitality? Only till I get a real job!* Paper presented at the Tourism Research Advances and Applications, Wellington.

Hall, C. M. & Tucker, H. (Eds). (2004). *Tourism and Postcolonialism: Contested discourses, identities and representations*. New York: Routledge.

MacCannell, D. (1976). Staged authenticity: Arrangements of social space in tourist settings. *American Journal of Sociology*, **79**: 589-603.

Massey, D. (1994). *Space, Place and Gender*. Minneapolis: University of Minnesota Press.

Ministry of Tourism (2001). New Zealand Tourism Strategy 2010. Wellington: Ministry of Tourism.

New Zealand High Court (1998) Tamakore Donald McFarlane & Others v New Zealand Māori Arts and Crafts Institute, *Māori Law Review*, CP16/97 ed. Rotorua: Bennion Law.

New Zealand Māori Arts and Crafts Act (1967) New Zealand Māori Arts and Crafts Institute Amendment Act. http://legislation.govt.nz/act/public/1967/0104/latest/DLM384144.html

Oakes, T. S. (1993). The cultural space of modernity: ethnic tourism and place identity in China. *Environment and Planning D: Society and Space*, **11**: 47-66.

Puriri, A. & McIntosh, A. (2013). Indigenous tourism and heritage: A Māori case study. In A. Fyall & B. Garrod (Eds), *Contemporary Cases in Heritage Tourism* (pp. 79-102). Oxford: Goodfellow Publishers Ltd.

Spiller, C., Erakovic, L., Henare, M. & Pio, E. (2011). Relational well-being and wealth: Maori businesses and an ethic of care. *Journal of Business Ethics* **98**(1), 153–169.

Spiller, M. M. & Erakovic, L. (2005). Flourishing on the edge: Case study of Whale Watch Kaikoura, an Indigenous sustainable business. In M. Wilson (Ed.), *Case in Point: Best cases from the 2005 International Conference on case study teaching and learning* (pp. 219-240). Auckland: GSE Publications.

Stafford, D.M. (1967). *Te Arawa*. Wellington: A. H. & A. W. Reed.

Te Awekotuku, N. (1981). *The socio-cultural impact of tourism on the Te Arawa people of Rotorua, New Zealand*. Unpublished doctoral thesis, University of Waikato, Hamilton.

Tourism New Zealand (2015). http://www.tourismnewzealand.com/about/about-the-industry/m%C4%81ori-tourism/

Tourism New Zealand (2016). http://www.tourismnewzealand.com/about/about-the-industry/

Waaka, P. K. S. (1982). Whakarewarewa - *The growth of a Māori village*. Unpublished Master of Arts thesis, University of Auckland, Auckland.

Whakarewarewa Thermal Village (nd), www.whakarewarewa.com/

13 A Māori Relational Approach to Building Value Chains in Tourism

Chellie Spiller

Introduction

This case examines value chain innovation through the networks of a Māori tourism company, Navigator Tours. The network represents a weaving together of various activities (*flaxes*), pulled together by hub firms, into a value chain (*kete*). The ultimate service experienced by the tourist is woven from a range of individual suppliers that come together to each add more value than they could individually. The chain of activities gives the service more added value than the sum of the added values of all activities. By taking advantage of upstream and downstream inputs, Navigator Tours has created a new business model which maximises value creation while minimising costs. The kete of value, added through the collective value chain, offers unique worth to the customer and the individual suppliers. It constitutes an example of innovation at work in a cultural context.

> *"Life did not take over the globe by combat, but by networking . . . in the end aggressors destroy themselves and those who cooperate survive."*[1]

---

1 Margulis, L. and Sagan, D. (1986). *Microcosmos*. Summit: New York.

Sense connections

Amanda clasped the handles of the flax basket which, as John had explained, was called a *kete* in Māori. Water flowed through the holes, which were large enough to let undersized *pipis* fall through and small enough to hold the larger pipis. The water felt cold. She couldn't believe that just a few minutes ago she had been sitting in a bus wondering what on earth John Panoho was saying to her — something about *pipi* hunting, out there in the chilly ocean, just shorts, T-shirt and this *kete*? It was as far removed from New York as she could imagine. Soon, water was up to Amanda's waist.

'Form a line,' John shouted over the surf. 'Can you see what I am doing?'

Not really thought Amanda, he seemed to be twisting one leg in an Elvis Presley dance move and then reaching down into the water and coming up with a clutch of small white shellfish.

'*Pipis* form feeding chains,' John explained. 'They create clusters, so that where you find one you will often find half a dozen or so.'

The icy-cold chill of the water melted away under the warm pleasure of at last working out how to twist and shuffle her foot to expose the shellfish. Amanda slowly filled her *kete*. She really felt like a *pipi* hunter, and didn't want to let any of the burrowing bivalves escape her efficient footwork. Every now and then one of the others in the group would come over, cradling their bounty in their T-shirt, and pour their *pipis* into her *kete*. Tony, the Tahitian tour leader from Hawaii, seemed to have a natural knack, but Buck, the Midwest American boy hurled himself into the experience and collected more than anyone.

They were still well under the official limit of 50 *pipis* per person by the time they returned to shore and placed the *kete* on the beach. Each person took turns having a photo taken with the haul.

A couple of Kiwis passing by peered into the bags and one offered helpful advice: 'If you chuck them in buckets of water with a bit of flour they will spit all the sand out.'

Afterwards, the group went to a nearby hot pool to warm up and relax before climbing back on board the coach and driving to a seaside apartment where they would have dinner. A Kiwi couple, Gary and Lisa, owned the apartment.

There were twelve of them altogether, seven on the tour and five locals including John, who was their Māori guide and the owner of the tour company taking them around New Zealand's northern region. As far as Amanda could work out, John's company was based in Auckland and handled all the ground arrangements, while the company Tony worked for promoted and sold the tours throughout the US, especially in Hawaii. A number of the group had heard about the tour through their local wine shops in Hawaii, which had been running a special campaign.

Valuing loyalty

John topped up the wine made by Tapata Wines, a South Island-based Māori-owned wine company that often worked with Navigator Tours on offshore promotions.

'This tour is going really well,' Tony reflected. "It's just how I hoped people coming to New Zealand would experience Māori culture. I want them to look back and say, "Wow, I've just been on a tour and enjoyed a Māori meal, I met Māori people, experienced their land . . . touched their land." I want them to understand that they would never have found these special activities unless they were linked with a Māori company that knows the Māori land, and to realise that this experience is priceless. It's packages that we put together like that, John, which make people tell others: "If you want to experience Māori culture tours, you've got to go with these Māori companies because they will take you to the right places to experience Māori culture".'

'It's my bottom line, as you know, people enjoying themselves,' John replied. 'It's important that we give them what they expect, in fact, that we give them more than they expect.'

Tony agreed: 'We're here to please people, to make them smile, make them happy. When that is accomplished, it makes us happy. It was never about the money because if it was all about money, I'd be in a different industry.'

'Along the way, there is no reason why you can't make some money out of these tours,' said John, 'but money doesn't drive me — I don't really care about it, you can't take it with you — what is it? I just want to try and do the best that we can do.'

Tony sat quietly, then chose his words carefully:

'I should tell you that I was approached by UV Tours the other day. Actually it wasn't me they approached, but Philip, the owner of our company. UV have started up an inbound operation, like you, focusing on Māori cultural tourism. Philip feels he has loyalty to these people because they have known and worked together for years, before UV was started.'

John was amazed. Just a few months earlier he had been speaking to UV tours, and they had said there was no future for Māori tourism — they even said so at a national conference. Tony's news seemed quite a U-turn. 'What did you say to Philip?' he asked Tony.

Tony replied: 'For me there was an easy response. I explained to Philip that UV Tours are not doing anything new, and that what they are trying to promote is something with which I'm already familiar. I explained that I've been working with you, and that my loyalty lies with you. John, I don't care if Philip tells me that I have to work with their company. I have addressed my point and my point stands. If he wants me to do this, then he will have to fire me, or . . .'

Tony continued: 'I know you and I agree on the position we are taking to bring these high-end experiences together, connecting people to place and hospitality. I doubt that UV Tours could pull together the network we have. Being able to organise that is difficult unless you have already put the network in place, and have relationships of trust firmly established. We have been building on that for some years now. We have the people with the stories and the knowledge, boys who have been brought up in a Māori world, brought up at their grandfather's knee — where they learnt the flute. It's about culture and heritage. We are finding those people through our networks. Māori are working in every sector of society and they are our net resource.'

Tony agreed on their shared vision: 'In making our product by invitation only, putting our product on the top — premium and that's what we want. We want to portray and take the Māori people to the top. We're just not interested in quantity. I believe that in order to prevail with our project, we need to keep the personal touch, the personal care that we're giving to the people. If you call it simply a "Māori cultural tour", you're basically targeting a very small audience and the only people who will come are people who are already culture-oriented. But that's a very small percentage . . . you need to increase that leverage and how do you make that happen?

By creating the food and wine and incorporating the Māori experience, so that you sort of capture two types of audiences.'

They discussed aspects of the current tour, which could be improved on in the future, until it was time to join the group again for dinner. Tony was in a reflective mood for the rest of the night, however. He knew that if it came down to the wire, he would have to make a decision. Philip, his boss, had the same loyalty to UV Tours that he had toward Navigator Tours. There was no easy answer. Eighteen months of promotion and development were just coming to fruition and the advance bookings were promising. Tony wasn't sure how things were going to go, or, who was going to go.

Sharing connections

Everyone pitched in to cook the food — though by now everyone was calling their food 'kai'. Some were preparing salads, others were cooking on the barbecue, and still others were watching John prepare the food in the kitchen. He was making a paste out of shellfish and baking Māori bread.

'You know,' Amanda observed, 'in New York we just can't do this — gather our own food from the ocean and then eat it. Our waters are too polluted.'

John's cooking lesson incorporated his views on Māori values.

'See it's got that little muscle on there that holds it into the shell, and if you take the other shell and you go like that, that is as sharp as a knife ... Fantastic! If I was thinking about the things that binds this whole experience together, it would have to be these three simple values because eating and food mean celebration really don't they? And I think those values have to do with people — wrong way around Amanda, concentrate — it's around people and around people's connection to the place and around hospitality. And in our way, and I'm talking about a Māori way now, there are three simple values that go to the root of us and that's *He Tangata* or people, *Kaitiakitanga* or connection to place, and *Manaakitanga* or hospitality. Everything we've done today is encapsulated in these values. Bon appetit!'

Before eating, John said a short *karakia*, a prayer to bless the food. Then the group sat around eating the freshest *kai* infused with local herbs such as *kawakawa*, which they had collected themselves during a morning stroll in a local *ngāhere*, native forest. Laughter spilled and wine flowed as they recounted the activities of the day. Everyone collapsed in chortles and whoops when Tony told the story of how one of the party had come back from the changing rooms at the hot pools still fully dressed with a confused look on her face.

'C'mon Sandra,' teased Tony, 'tell them what you said.'

Sandra groaned. 'Okay. There is a sign above the women's changing room saying "No Singlets Allowed", and I thought a singlet was *kiwi* for young single women, which meant we were not allowed in the hot pools. So I came back dejected because I thought I was banned from swimming. I didn't realise that people, even women, would actually wear singlets as bathing suits!'

Buck and Graeme were chatting to Lisa, the host who owned the seaside apartment. She was asking them about their best experiences on the tour.

Buck told her: 'We go to people's houses — it's not like they're just there to serve us or whatever, they're interacting with us which makes us feel more comfortable to be ourselves, instead of trying to be people that we're not. I really like that because you feel as if you are part of their family.. you feel more integrated, it's not that you're a tourist but you're a friend coming over, so that's a good thing.'

Graeme thought his visit to a Māori family living on a farm by the ocean had been a highlight. An old man, a *kaumātua*, especially had moved him. Graeme said: 'He was just being himself, just a simple man and yet a very wise man. Just stunning. So were his wife and family. This whole experience of being invited into people's homes — I think that's really something magical.'

Buck agreed: 'Yeah, and what I like is that we all chipped in, which makes the experience much more memorable. It's not a cater-to-me type of thing ... like you're going to earn what you do. And I don't mean earn it in the sense that it's going to be hard work, but that it's going to be fun to do that stuff you know. It's a lot more fun to actually get out there and do it than watch somebody else do the work.'

Geoff, from Hawaii, wandering past on his way to have his third plate of shellfish, said: 'I don't think I know anybody back in Hawaii who does this ... most people are there for the economic, basic boom-boom — get into the island, get out.'

It was time to leave and John stood up and gave a speech.

'*Ngā mihi nui ki a koutou, ngā mihi mahana.* I just wanted to, firstly, thank Gary and Lisa for their kind hospitality; this is the Kiwi way, just walking into people's houses and making a bloody mess and then buggering off and they'll be sitting there like this, like stunned mullets thinking "What happened here? The Māoris have taken over our place." Thank you to our *manuhiri*, our visitors, for giving us the opportunity to show a little bit of our New Zealand — and I mean that sincerely, it's "our" New Zealand, it's not mine or Gary's or Lisa's or whoever — it belongs to all of us. And I think that there's something that visitors will truly appreciate if they had the opportunity to do these simple things ... just go out and gather some seafood, get a few herbs out of the forest, put them all together in a meal — which hopefully will have some distinctive tastes for you, which you've not had before.'

Graeme stood to respond to John's speech. He had everyone dabbing at the corners of their eyes. He was Japanese Hawaiian, and the company he represented had developed new technology which could be used to snap-freeze fish out at sea. The company worked mainly in Vietnam, its ships going to meet the fishing vessels in the ocean. Graeme had joined the tour to assess how value chains might be built in his own company. He spoke from his heart:

'There was real magic getting together all those who are part of this tour. I mean, it's empowering — it's transforming . . . It gives me a deep appreciation of the respect for the land and for ancestors, which strikes a chord within my own culture and my own beliefs. These are the kind of experiences that promote world peace and understanding. That gives me what we call chicken skin just thinking about it. Something striking a chord, really intrinsic about one's own cultural identity and appreciating that at a deeper level . . . It's almost as if the products were incidental, you know we're building bridges and relationships and finding commonality and inclusion in the whole business model. In the people whom we've met along the way, how passionate they are about what they're doing.'

'This whole tour has seemed so authentic,' Amanda confided to John, 'because it occurs to me that this is how you would spend your time if we weren't here.'

He replied: 'Absolutely, we're not doing anything that's unusual . . . a week is made up of spending time with friends or family and if you're going to do that you just enjoy it. You don't just cook a meal, chuck it in front of somebody, just for the sake of it — you do it so that people enjoy it and they obviously enjoy it because they show that on their faces and by their empty plates.'

The net resource

When John arrived home that night the household was asleep so he let himself in quietly. He stayed up late clearing emails. He had a meeting first thing in the morning with his network, which reminded him to make a mental note to himself to explain to them the new online booking engine tomorrow, and his plans for 'e-famils'. He had just purchased the equipment to create short video clips so that agents abroad could meet the concierge of a hotel, get to know a performer, and be able to meet the people whom their customers in due course would also meet.

Peter, John's partner in the business, had emailed through a financial scenario for the company, which he did every six months or so. They had set up Navigator Tours as a limited liability company in 2002. Peter had another company for which he worked full-time, leaving John to run Navigator Tours. He enjoyed tourism and would often turn up to events. He took an active role in developing the website and looking out for new technology. The third principal was a silent partner. The basic plan was to build the business through John's network, knowing that it would take a good five years before the company would be earning a profit. They were handling around 450 people a year, which was a mix of simple airport meet and greet services, short tours, incentives, independent travel packages and group tours such as the food and wine tour they were currently running. They had one office worker, who did most of the bookings, quotes and itineraries. They were about to employ a Chinese woman with extensive experience in the China tour market. The company was planning a marketing visit to China in a few months to establish relationships there.

One of the company's greatest assets, apart from John's overseas net-work, was the large New Zealand domestic network spanning a number of industries that would come together by *kaupapa*, purpose. This network included storytellers, artists, caterers, winemakers, historians, weavers, cavers, accommodation owners and entertainers. Persuading companies and individuals to be committed to a shared vision, values, and strategic goals had enabled Navigator Tours to present a strong value proposition to the marketplace. Ultimately the value of reciprocity underpinned the enduring success of the network's activities, an equitable process of co-creation between the companies and individuals in the group.

Most of the time John was the hub firm that brought the companies and individuals in the network together. However, Navigator Tours was not always the hub firm. For example, one of the other individuals in the network, an internationally acclaimed performer, had strong ties in Russia. John had recently returned from a trip to Russia organised by this other company, where they had co-created a team-building event for a multinational corporation. Rather than simply doing the usual corporate retreat exercises followed by French champagne and fine food, the top executives, who had flown in from around the world, rolled up their sleeves and learned how to cook a *hangi* and perform a *haka*.

The day after the West Coast barbecue, John met with nine members of the network to debrief about an earlier occasion, something they did after each event. These nine members had already worked together on an event organised by Navigator Tours for an Australian franchise group that had spent a week in New Zealand. John had contacted the other companies in his informal network, and together they had organised two events. One was at a remote cliff-top boutique hotel on Auckland's West Coast. The network had constructed a fortified village wall around the property and flaming torches lit up the scraggy pohutukawa trees, creating an eerie, surreal atmosphere. The performers in the network had re-enacted a dramatic nineteenth century Māori–Pākehā encounter, which had the audience spellbound, particularly the younger men who were fascinated by the Māori warriors.

John always sought to strike a balance between creativity, spontaneity and organisation to make their events better. He started by asking the others: 'Do you think we conveyed all the dimensions that were expected of the cultural experience? What could we have done differently, or better? Think systems, so that if we offered such an event in Invercargill, how would we reproduce it? Let's take the generic out of this West Coast Auckland experience — so that systems can be transferred. While there are variations at different events and the details change, there is a solid core that can be replicated. What didn't work?'

Everyone shared his or her observations from the evening, recalling conversations with customers during the night, comments they had overheard, their own observations, and what had created the general energy. As they had at previous events, the group mingled with the customers, making sure there were no boundaries between 'them' and 'us', thus creating warm, connected spaces. One woman's husband had given his bone carving away to a customer, which was a sign of the heartfelt connection that had been made.

Weaving people together

The meeting ended and John drove to meet the group who were leaving that day. On the way he pondered the situation with UV Tours. He was confident that the value chains he was building would deliver a unique product in the market, which would be difficult for other organisations to replicate. By choosing to work collectively, they could maximise their opportunities and do together what would be a struggle individually. The extended networks operated in a fluid environment, opportunities flowed in every direction, and no one company was forced to occupy a single position in the value chain. Thus each was linked innovatively to global supply chains. Importantly, it was their values that held the relationships together.

Epilogue

Philip, Tony's boss decided to work with UV Tours, Tony left the company and became a partner in another tour company, based in mainland US. He continued to work with John on co-created projects including the food and wine series tour. They grew New Zealand Week and took it successfully around various locations in the US.

Graeme developed the relationships he had forged during the tour. He attended a number of promotional events alongside Tony and John including the Boston International Seafood Show, which he attended with Tapata Wines, whom he had met in New Zealand on tour. At this show, Graeme and Tapata Wines promoted their own wine and seafood products, under the umbrella of tourism. In Graeme's words their stand at the show was a 'major hit' and he was busy after the show answering 'emails and phone calls from the 400-plus entities from all over the world who are interested in doing business with us. Including the Hong Kong importer who wants to buy 10 container loads of greenlipped mussels per month'. Teaming up with New Zealand wine and tourism partners showcased his product in an innovative way. The loosely formed network of companies and individuals with whom John worked continued to meet on an ad hoc basis, some members moving away and new members joining.

Navigator eventually employed the Chinese tourism expert and began a marketing push into China. He entered the Super Yacht sector and built a successful program offering bespoke guiding and cultural consultancy. He also founded Waka Quest with Hoturoa Barclay Kerr which offers sailing trips on double hulled sailing catamaran and teamed up with Hoturoa and Chellie Spiller to offer leadership development and training based on their book Wayfinding leadership: Groundbreaking wisdom for developing leaders.[22.]

This case was written by Associate Professor Chellie Spiller for educational purposes only. This case is not intended to depict effective or ineffective business practice. Other than John Panoho and Navigator Tours, the names of individuals and companies and other identifying information, may have been altered in order to protect subjects' privacy and the confidentiality of information. Reprinted with kind permission of the University of Auckland Press.

2   Spiller, C., Barclay-Kerr, H., & Panoho, J. (2015). *Wayfinding Leadership: Groundbreaking wisdom for developing leaders.* Wellington. Huia Publications.

14 Conclusion

This volume has explored Indigenous tourism in Australia and New Zealand. Both countries have seen tourism grow in importance for their First Peoples. In Australia, Indigenous tourism is an important niche segment of the broader tourism product. However, for the Indigenous people and communities involved in tourism, it is so much more. The same can be seen in New Zealand where tourism continues to be an important socio-economic development tool for Māori people. Some of the chapters have highlighted this importance for a wide spectrum of Indigenous people; from those engaged in family-based businesses to broader joint partnerships and collaboration across multiple stakeholders. The chapters in the book have also shown the innovation and entrepreneurial approaches being led by those engaged in Indigenous tourism in Australia and New Zealand.

The editors are particularly delighted that two of the leaders in Indigenous tourism in Australia and New Zealand respectively accepted our invitation to offer their thoughts on the way forward for Indigenous tourism in the two countries. The insights of Tahn Donovan from Australia, and Johnny Edmond from New Zealand, provide a forward looking platform for us to move ahead with a tourism sector that is appropriate to the needs and wants of the Indigenous people in these two countries.

Indigenous tourism in Western Australia

Tahn Donovan, Chair, Western Australian Indigenous Tourism Operators Council (WAITOC)

Aboriginal tourism in Western Australia is still considered an 'extra' experience and not part of the primary motivation to visit the State. This is in spite of the fact that research shows 78% of visitors to Western Australia would like an Aboriginal experience and only 22% are able to access one. This might be because Aboriginal tourism is often the 'family member' that industry invites after the core (required) 'family' have attended to key policy development issues and/or have initiated significant access strategies to tourism in Western Australia.

Nevertheless, Aboriginal tourism in Western Australia is very much a vehicle for Aboriginal and Torres Strait Islander people to maintain culture and country, while providing non-Indigenous people with insight into Aboriginal culture and society via a range of tourism opportunities, where they can learn about and explore the complexities of the culture. Currently the focus for visitors is around art and dance, however international visitors are seeking more opportunities to explore the deeper intricacies of traditional cultures that are being maintained within a western context on traditional lands.

Over 30 years within the tourism industry, I have seen some changes to the Australian tourism landscape, which continues to undervalue the service industry that is key to successful tourism development. In particular, investment in the skilling of quality service staff who know the products and are skilled in communication to exemplify the visitors' experience continue to be undervalued by the Australian community.

Aboriginal people in Western Australia are well informed about the type of products that could be developed to enhance the visitor experiences. Some products are very much focused on Aboriginal culture while other experiences are based around luxury accommodation and transportation. In Western Australia we have a number of issues impacting on the opportunity for Aboriginal people to develop world class experiences. For instance, land tenure is a major issue impacting on Aboriginal tourism development in Western Australia. Although some areas have received Native Title, the opportunity for investment of major infrastructure is impacted by the very nature of the land tenure and the opportunity to gain capital for development.

WAITOC is a membership driven council of Aboriginal tourism operators that works with State Government departments including Tourism Western Australia, as well as Regional Tourism Organisations and the Tourism Council of Western Australia to further develop authentic Aboriginal tourism experiences in the State. WAITOC is the only Australian organisation to receive the prestigious DRV, German Environmental Tourism Award. The German Association of Tour Operators and Travel Agencies nominated the WAITOC submission from a total of 31 projects from 22 countries. WAITOC was recognised for its objective of recognising and integrating one of the world's oldest living cultures into the tourism industry with conservation and sustainability issues being the core emphasis.

WAITOC is a marketing and advocacy council representing Aboriginal tourism operators across Western Australia. WAITOC is a membership driven council and our focus is marketing the State's Aboriginal tourism products to the intrastate, interstate and international markets. WAITOC continues to work at a State level and at times, engages on a national level in discussions and initiatives for Aboriginal and Torres Strait Islander tourism.

WAITOC's engagement with Indigenous tourism globally has led to WAITOC's membership of the World Indigenous Tourism Alliance and the formation of the Larrakia Declaration. The Larrakia Declaration sets out the principles of Indigenous tourism and recognises that Indigenous people are the ones that own and deliver Indigenous tourism products.

Key to WAITOC's success has been strategic investments in governance processes to ensure that each tourism region in Western Australia has Aboriginal representation on the WAITOC board. There are five tourism regions in Western Australia and the WAITOC board has one Aboriginal tourism operator from each region, three state positions held by Aboriginal tourism operators and the opportunity to secure two experts that may or may not be Aboriginal persons. WAITOC board members are not paid sitting fees however expenses for attending meeting is reimbursed to members but not loss of time within their own business. Board members take significant time away from their businesses to ensure that we collectively continue the growth of authentic Aboriginal tourism in Western Australia.

Indigenous or Māori tourism in New Zealand

Johnny Edmonds, Director, World Indigenous Tourism Alliance

The development of Indigenous or Māori tourism in New Zealand cannot be considered in isolation from the historical context of colonial development in New Zealand. Māori are the original inhabitants of New Zealand (Aotearoa) having arrived on the islands of New Zealand as early as A.D. 800, from East Polynesia. First contact between Māori and European occurred in 1642 with Abel Tasman. Although this initial meeting was peaceful, the misunderstanding and fear aroused by two such different worlds coming together soon led to violence. It would be another 127 years before the next recorded encounter between European and Māori with Captain James Cook's arrival in New Zealand in 1769. He was followed by sealers, whalers, missionaries, the British Crown and ultimately colonisation.

The subsequent impact of colonisation on Māori was severe. The influx of new peoples exposed Māori to introduced diseases, leading to severe epidemics producing a major decline in Māori life expectancy. From 1810 to 1840 there were some 120,000 deaths from illness and other 'normal' causes, an average of 4,000 a year. In the same period, warfare caused perhaps 700 deaths per year, killing less than 1% of the population. The decline in Māori population accelerated after the Treaty of Waitangi was signed in 1840 as settlers began to arrive in greater numbers. In the 1890s the Māori population had fallen to about 40% of its pre-European contact size.

Also, the influx of settlers led to a demand for land, and from the 1840s Māori were under great pressure to sell their ancestral territories. Loss of Māori land – through confiscation following the 1860s land wars, Crown purchase and the Native Land Court – led to the displacement of large numbers of Māori. Deprived of their land, Māori tribes were in many instances reduced to poverty, with no option but to live in overcrowded and unhygienic conditions. Losing land, they also lost access to traditional food sources. Lack of resources, overcrowding and poor diet helped disease to take hold and spread.

The colonization of New Zealand and the subsequent policies adopted by the colonial and New Zealand governments led to the widespread loss and alienation of Māori land, and severely impacted on the social and cultural fabric of Māori communities. This history is still reflected in the disadvantage currently faced by Māori people in comparison to the non-Indigenous population in New Zealand, across a range of indicators. Despite this, Māori continue to possess a strong and vibrant culture, enriching New Zealand society. This is the historical context from which New Zealand Māori tourism has developed and from which Māori and New Zealand government relationships have continued to evolve.

The Treaty of Waitangi

The Treaty of Waitangi, which was signed by the British Crown and Māori Chiefs in 1840, is the founding document of the New Zealand nation. The Treaty enabled the establishment of government by the British Crown, the subsequent colonisation of New Zealand and provided the basis for Māori human rights. The Preamble sets out the purpose of the Treaty: to protect Māori rights and property, keep peace and order, and establish government.

New Zealand's history since the signing of the Treaty has been marked by repeated failures of the Crown and ruling governments to honour these founding promises. Despite this, the Treaty is regarded as an important 'living document', central to New Zealand's present and future, as well as its past, and establishes a relationship 'akin to partnership' between the Crown and Māori, and confers a set of rights and obligations on each Treaty partner. This relationship has been described as 'the promise of two peoples to take the best possible care of each other'.

Internationally, there have been significant recent events regarding the rights of Indigenous peoples which have further underlined the importance of relationships between New Zealand Māori, the government and the tourism sector. These include the promulgation of the *Declaration on the Rights of Indigenous Peoples by the United Nations* in 2007. Together with Australia, Canada and the United States, the New Zealand government initially voted against the declaration in 2007. However, in 2010 the New Zealand government reversed its position and indicated its support for the declaration as "both an affirmation of existing rights and an expression of new and widely supported aspirations". The Declaration provides a clear set of standards that apply to existing human rights treaties specific to all Indigenous peoples and affirms treaties, agreements and partnerships between states and Indigenous peoples. The Treaty of Waitangi is New Zealand's own unique statement of human rights.

Most recently the promulgation of the Larrakia Declaration, during the Pacific Asia Indigenous Tourism Conference in Darwin Australia in 2012, has provided a much more tourism-centric focus on the application of the *Declaration on the Rights of Indigenous Peoples by the United Nations* in 2007.

New Zealand Māori were among the Indigenous peoples to participate with tourism organisations, government representatives, tourism businesses and other non-government organisations in the formulation of the Larrakia Declaration and to articulate the important roles and responsibilities of various stakeholders necessary to give practical effect to the *Declaration on the Rights of Indigenous Peoples by the United Nations* in 2007 in the international development of Indigenous tourism. The Larrakia Declaration also brought to prominence the international importance and role of the World Indigenous Tourism Alliance and especially its role *to facilitate, advocate and network with each affiliated Indigenous tourism body and with industry, governments and multilateral agencies.*

Research into tourism and Māori engagement during the last 25 years

Tourism and Māori have a long history of engagement dating back to the 1800s. The relationship between Māori and the Crown and all New Zealanders has been an evolving one, a roller coast ride, which focused by the Treaty of Waitangi has led to instances of polarisation and to instances of shared celebration. This relationship bound by the Treaty of Waitangi has inevitably impacted on the engagement between tourism and Māori in NZ.

During the last 25 years, a significant number of research papers have been produced, principally by academia, on tourism and Māori engagement. These papers provide the opportunity to see an evolving picture of change in the situation of Māori and tourism following the government responses to resolution of proven grievances under the Treaty of Waitangi. Academic research into Māori and tourism in the early 1990s identified three prevailing issues:

- Māori viewed tourism as a two-edged sword. Māori sought the economic and employment benefits of tourism but also control over access to their physical and cultural environment to control the negative impacts of tourism.

- The potential implications of Māori claims under the Treaty of Waitangi for tourism.

- The conflict between Māori and Pakeha (European) perceptions of the use of the country's conservation estate and the nature of decision-making processes attached to land management for conservation, heritage and tourism purposes.

At that time researchers concluded that:

- To assist in the preservation and promotion of traditional Māori cultural values, tourists and the tourism industry will require greater levels of cultural awareness and sensitivity than currently existed.

- Heritage tourism may be a mechanism for more appropriate tourism development than has existed in the past. However, the pace of development must be controlled by the Tangata Whenua (traditional custodians), in terms of both location and management, if the potential economic and cultural benefits of tourism to Māori people are to be maximized.

Later in the 1990s, academic research examined the effectiveness of government and Māori co-management of New Zealand's conservation estate which under the Conservation Act 1987 required the government to "give effect to the principles of the Treaty of Waitangi". Researchers observed that while government had consulted with Māori and did have Māori advisors in relation to the management of the conservation estate, these did not constitute co-management involving two or more parties who share decision-making in an equitable arrangement, and hence did not meet the constitutional principle of partnership articulated by the Treaty of Waitangi. Researchers further observed that the obstacles to establishing agreements that involve Māori in equitable conservation estate decision-making roles included:

- Divergent philosophies (preservation versus conservation for future use), institutional inertia, a lack of concrete models of co-management to evaluate success or otherwise to promote conservation;

- A lack of resources and opportunities for capacity building and scientific research amongst Māori ;

- Opposition and a lack of trust from euro-centric conservation NGOs; and

- A fundamental reluctance of some to share power with Māori .

Researchers concluded that the New Zealand experience shows that even when legislation signals from the top down that the doorway is open for co-management with Indigenous people, this by itself is unlikely to make it happen and that:

- Active facilitation by innovative middle-level agreements and the creation of new administrative structures was needed to govern co-management of a broad spectrum of resource issues;

- Bottom-up initiatives involving single, or very localized, resource uses could trigger co-management; and

- Models for successful co-management involving Indigenous peoples must focus more strongly on issues of equity or power sharing, and therefore may be very different from models directed at a single conservation outcome.

During the early 2000s, academic research concluded that among other things, more effective Māori participation in the tourism industry in a way that ensures the integrity of their culture required:

- Good working relationships between various Māori organisations and greater clarification of from government on the practical operation of Section 4 under the Conservation Act 1987 requiring implementation of the principles of the Treaty of Waitangi; and

- Strengthened Treaty partnership in the management of the natural environment between Tangata Whenua and local government under the Resource Management legislation to address the lack of effective Māori participation in controlling the effects of tourism on the natural environment.

By the mid 2000s academic research observed that Treaty-specific settlement legislation, passed following negotiations with Māori Tribal claimants, had resulted in the past emphasis on the mountaineering and natural history of the Aoraki/Mount Cook national park now being balanced by the inclusion of traditional Māori cultural values. The interpretation material, produced by government in collaboration with tribal representatives, had assisted government with fulfilling management plan objectives and policy reflecting the spirit of the Treaty of Waitangi.

In more recent times, academic research has observed that the New Zealand Government's policy on the administration of Indigenous people, the settlement of land claims and the negotiation of self-government have ushered in a new era in Indigenous development. This observation follows a review of the progress of two tribal groups with investments in the tourism industry, to have completed negotiation of their modern Treaty settlements with the government in the mid/late 1990s. This research has argued that in an era of globalization, Indigenous development has carried with it normative and neoliberal goals of economic, political and cultural self-reliance and ultimately the continuity of colonialism. The reasoning behind this argument is that capitalism and Western ethnocentrism continues to form the basis for the current tribal development projects of the tribal groups.

Looking forward

In looking forward to the next 10 to 20 years of New Zealand tourism and Māori engagement beyond the Treaty of Waitangi, recent research does beg the question of whether tourism presents Māori with the opportunity to use globalisation and development as a basis for driving the Indigenous agenda, or will it continue to reinforce capitalism and western ethnocentrism.

Index

Printed in the United States
By Bookmasters